THE
SOMERSET
&DORSET
THEN AND NOW

THE
SOMERSET & DORSET
THEN AND NOW

MAC HAWKINS

Grange Books plc
The Grange, Units 1-6, Kingsnorth Industrial Estate
Hoo, Nr Rochester, Kent ME3 9ND

Frontispiece: **Bath Green Park station**
172 ST 744647

A potential usurper comes under close scrutiny from Norman Lockett,
Ivo Peters' friend and fellow photographer: the 10.10 local to Bristol
Temple Meads, hauled by 'Peak' Type 4 diesel No D12, stands at the
northern platform whilst opposite, BR Standard Class 5 4-6-0 No 73164
gets under way with the 09.55 semi-fast for Bournemouth West.
Photo: Ivo Peters. Date: 24 September 1963.

Another busy scene at Bath Green Park: a flurry of activity outside
Sainsbury's supermarket which is about to close for the day; two evening
shoppers try to get to grips with the uncontrollable meanderings of a
heavily-laden supermarket trolley as they propel it
towards the car park opposite.
The train shed roof is all but obscured by the recently-built covered
walkway to and from the supermarket entrance.
Date: 17 March 1995.

Map references

To accompany each pair of photographs, map references are given
for the Ordnance Survey 1:25,000 Pathfinder and 1:50,000
Landranger Series of Great Britain and represent the point from
which they were taken. A grid reference, as in the example below,
quotes sheet No(s) (182/183), 100,000m square identification
letters (ST), eastings (491) and northings (389). The references are
accurate to within 50 metres.

Glastonbury & Street station (1)
182/183 ST 491389

Notes:

1. The maps within this volume are taken from the second and
third editions Ordnance Survey 25in to 1 mile series and their
revision dates between 1902 and 1936.

2. Whilst every endeavour has been made to reproduce the maps
to a high standard, it has not been helped by the age, condition and
poor printing quality of some of the original sheets, which are not
of the high cartographic standards achieved today, but nevertheless
are of great historical interest. To include more area of detail
within these pages, the maps are reproduced at 75 per cent scale.

3. All Somerset & Dorset stations are represented by maps and a
small selection of those on the former LSWR lines have also been
shown, including Broadstone, Poole and Bournemouth West.

4. Although the halts at Bawdrip, Stourpaine & Durweston and
Charlton Marshall were not built until the 1920s, a representation
of them has been superimposed on earlier editions of maps
covering these areas.

Map Scale

The author and publishers have made every effort to ensure that the 'then and now' photographs are
exact equivalents. Due to normal design, production and printing practices, certain details may have
been bled off by the binding or trimming of this book. The differences will be minor and therefore
it is hoped that they do not detract from the accuracy that this publication endeavours to achieve.

This edition published in 1999 by GRANGE BOOKS in association with HAWK EDITIONS
Reprinted 2002
Second edition published in the UK by David & Charles in 1995 under ISBN 0-7153-0384-8
First edition published in the UK by Patrick Stephens in 1986 under ISBN 0-85059-797-8

Grange Books ISBN: 1-84013-321-X
Hawk Editions ISBN: 0-9529081-3-1

Typesetting and reprographics by Character Graphics, Taunton
and printed in Singapore for HAWK EDITIONS, PO Box 184, Cossington, Somerset TA7 8YT

CONTENTS

FOREWORD

My father and Mac Hawkins obviously shared a tremendous amount of common ground, but one particularly strong link was an obsession with detail; a trait which my father recognised and welcomed in Mac when they met in 1985 during the preparation of the first 'then and now' book on the S&D. In the collection of my father's negatives and film, I have endless examples of photographs not printed nor used and film excluded from his programmes because of some minor irritation which rendered them unsatisfactory to his eyes. The problem might have been telephone lines, smoke and steam blowing in the wrong direction, or something in the background appearing to sprout from an engine.

When Mac approached me this year about including a few of these hitherto unseen photographs from the Ivo Peters' Collection, I found it very easy to agree; I think my father would forgive the use of some of his 'unsatisfactory' shots, when so many more aspects of 'then' would otherwise be unrecorded. I found it a great deal more difficult to supply all the correct details required, since my father never wrote up his unprinted negatives. Nevertheless, only one picture has completely defeated me, and I am delighted to have been able to continue the Peters' tradition by contributing to this meticulous book.

My father had stopped taking photographs and film in 1981, but his past struggles for the perfect shot had led to a number of well-known simple solutions to the problems of intrusive branches or long grass, and he always carried an orange box in the boot of his Bentley upon which he could gain those necessary extra inches in height. He was therefore highly entertained by the accounts of Mac's endeavours to take the right photograph from the right position in the teeth of ever more encroaching vegetation, multi-storey car parks, and absent gantries, and was impressed by the scale of his response to these problems.

I understand that for the new version of this book, Mac has done it all over again, and retaken most of his own original photographs besides adding many new archive ones. I can only admire the dedication which has enabled him to bring this edition up to date and expand it as well. I must enter one caveat – that Mac should abstain from all dangerous domestic duties after publication. After the first book was published, given confidence in his head for heights by all the risks he had taken over the past year, he fell off a ladder while cleaning gutters at home and badly injured an arm – not a fitting end to so much effort!

There is no doubt that Mac would have again won the approval of my father. I am equally sure that those whose memory and imagination are stirred by the Somerset & Dorset will find a rich source of pleasure in this new work, as will those whose first love is for the English countryside through which so much of the Somerset & Dorset ran.

Ivo Julian Peters

JULIAN PETERS

PREFACE

Whilst the S&D was being run down and the railway system throughout Britain undergoing dramatic changes, I was blissfully unaware of these events! Despite this, I have always had a strong love of railways and living in Devon from 1949–59 and going to school in Sussex meant that I travelled a fair amount by train. The journeys to school seemed dreadful affairs, catching the 10.00 from Exeter St David's to Paddington and then going across London to Victoria for a train to Horsham. The engine appeared to be working uphill all the way to Paddington and with brakes applied, such was my reluctance to make the journey; however, on the return trip at holiday times my feelings were very different – the mercurial flight west behind a 'King' or a 'Castle' would set my pulse racing.

I left school in 1960 and shortly afterwards joined the Army and trained as a topographical surveyor. Two short tours in the Far East during the Indonesian Confrontation took me through to the mid 1960s. My interest in aviation was an abiding one and therefore the run-down of steam went almost unnoticed, I am ashamed to say. On leaving the Army in 1965 and joining a large tobacco company that year, I was left very little time or opportunity to follow every interest.

My connection with the Somerset & Dorset was tenuous to say the least. I can remember seeing Collett 0-6-0s waiting in the station at Highbridge East whilst I was being hauled towards Nottingham behind a 'Warship'. I did actually travel on the Bridgwater branch as a boy, to my regret my only chance to sample at first hand the line's charm, although I was not old enough to appreciate it.

Over the years my topographical training and interest in old railways has often meant my long-suffering family or a colleague having to endure a broken car journey in order that I could clamber up some embankment to look at an old line formation or peer over a bridge to see derelict platforms of a once-proud station. My amazement as to how so much human endeavour and resource could end this way has never been satisfactorily answered.

One Christmas I was given Robin Atthill's fine book, *The Somerset and Dorset Railway,* and I got the bug, later fed further by Ivo Peters' first book on the S&D, *The Somerset & Dorset – An English Cross Country Railway.* This ensured that my interest in the S&D railway line was well and truly in the blood. I had previously visited Shepton Mallet in 1967 and photographed a diesel-hauled demolition train coming over the Charlton Viaduct on its way down the line. Over the years I was able to pay my respects to the S&D as well as other lines around the country, to see how a scene could change in a relatively short passage of time.

In 1982 I became self-employed and had the chance to utilize cartographic skills acquired some twenty years previously in the Army, together with my interest in photography, which had been directed towards aviation. These two interests happen to combine well and I began to think that they could be put to good use in a way which would add a new dimension to the railway scene. I am the first one to confess that the precise details of running a railway have eluded me to a greater degree! The fact of whether the train was the 13.10 up or the 16.13 down was of no great concern to me. So I bow to the extent of knowledge that experts acquire and to the infinite enjoyment they gain from such. To me the sight and smell of a steam engine passing through gorgeous countryside is reward enough and is something that I will always remember and treasure.

A further four S&D volumes from Ivo Peters convinced me that I should 'go/see'. Over the next year or so and with a lot of planning I was able to produce a synopsis for the publisher. Late in 1984 the green light, or rather the semaphore signal 'off', was given and these plans were put into action. The logistics of collecting suitable material in order to provide such a study were simply horrendous. However, suffice to say that I contacted some of the leading experts on the S&D and it has been my good fortune to have made friends with many charming people in the process, without whose help this book could not have been made possible.

In an attempt to meet publishers' deadlines a planned six months' work was compacted to three in the spring and summer of 1985 spent photographing the line – that was the easy part! I thoroughly enjoyed meeting many more delightful people in the process who were always ready to help in any way they could. I also enjoyed tremendously the company of Mike Arlett and Peter Smith, both of whom accompanied me on forays up and down the line and whose friendly banter kept me going – sometimes in the face of adversity (particularly the weather). I regret to say that welcome visits to a hostelry were seldom made before two o'clock because of my insistence on 'just one more shot to take, then we'll go!'

I have tried to select photographs, both for their content and their quality, and have endeavoured to add as many as possible that have not previously been published. I make no apology for including others that have, particularly those of Ivo Peters, whose photographs are superb and provided me with the content and composition that perfectly summarizes all that I find so interesting in steam; they also provide a tangible link with a once familiar scene. Some superb photographs have been impossible to reproduce because of Mother Nature's insistent restaking of her claim.

I hope the end result is of interest to many, including S&D 'buffs'. I should like to dedicate this volume to all the ex-S&D staff who gave so much of their lives to this wonderful line.

Notes to the 1995 edition:
After it was launched in 1986, I was sufficiently encouraged by the response to this book to produce others, including *The Great Central Then and Now,* and *LSWR West Country Lines Then and Now,* both published by David & Charles in 1990 and 1993 respectively. In the interim, the Somerset &

Dorset title had gone out of print and, with the thirtieth anniversary of the line's closure approaching in March 1996, I felt that it would be appropriate to reprint the book in a new format and update both the photographs and text where necessary, adding some new material, including colour, to give it that extra boost. Little did I realise what lay in store! When I started to survey the line again – albeit only ten years after I had first done so – it immediately became apparent that I had grossly underestimated the task in hand, as the changes had been enormous and it would be necessary to photograph most of the locations again. Partly to fill gaps that were missed in the first addition, I gathered much new material for inclusion in this volume; some of these pictures were from Ivo Peters' unpublished collection, which I had printed for him shortly before he died in June 1989.

In February 1995, with only four weeks set aside for the work, I set about the daunting task of revisiting every location that required a photograph to be taken (over ninety per cent of them had to be re-shot) and this was duly achieved, sometimes in appalling weather and lighting conditions, as many of my comments suggest! I have also tried to add further historical data to the work and in addition have extended the book photographically by some margin, which is the most important element within the publication. However, a compromise has had to be made: there simply was not enough room to include many of the appendices featured in the first edition. With the passage of time some of them have become irrelevant to the main thrust of the book and I trust this will not spoil readers' enjoyment of this edition.

Mac Hawkins COSSINGTON, SOMERSET, *1995*

INTRODUCTION

The 6 March 1966 marked the end of an era, for it was the final day passenger trains ran over the Somerset & Dorset line: it was a remarkable cross-country route which did not survive the Beeching axe and was closed after 104 years of continuous operation. Today, three decades after closure, the remains of this much-loved line are still deeply impressed upon the landscape in many areas. Other parts have totally reverted back to their original use or have been built upon and nothing remains. Ironically, some surviving artefacts are in better condition now than they were in railway days, namely Bath Green Park station and Charlton Viaduct at Shepton Mallet.

Rolling through some of the most beautiful countryside in Britain, the Somerset & Dorset served an essentially rural and isolated population, but the $71^{1}/_{2}$ miles of its penetrating main line from Bath to Bournemouth came into its own as an important holiday route from the Midlands and North to the South Coast.

The main line was notorious for the severity of the gradients, much of it at 1:50, encountered over the Mendip Hills, which tested both engines and their crews to the limit. Many of the heavier trains had to be double-headed, which added considerably to the costs in both locomotive and manpower resources. It was perhaps because of the steep and tortuous nature of the route, thus restricting the speed at which trains could travel over it, that the line acquired the affectionate soubriquet 'The Slow and Dirty'! By contrast to the main line's precipitous traverse of the Mendips, a branch line turned westwards from Evercreech Junction which eventually headed straight across the Somerset Levels to the Bristol Channel at Burnham-on-Sea. Other branches served Bridgwater and Wells, but these were casualties of closures implemented in the early 1950s.

The railway had struggled for financial viability almost since inception in 1862, and from 1875 was jointly leased by the London & South Western and Midland railway companies, becoming the Somerset & Dorset Joint Railway, until the major grouping of 1923, when it became the legal property of the London Midland Scottish and Southern railways, their successors. After nationalisation in 1948, the S&D was assigned to the Southern Region, who supplied many of the locomotives needed to work the line, although the motive power was still largely the responsibility of the London Midland Region. From 1958 the line was transferred to the control of the Western Region, the inheritors of the S&D's old rival, the GWR, although they had been commercially responsible for much of its length since 1950, but not its five motive power depots.

In 1962, the WR announced a decision that was to have catastrophic consequences for the S&D line itself: from the end of summer services, all through trains – including the celebrated 'Pines Express' – would be diverted from the route, which would then offer no more than a local service. The S&D's *raison d'être* was removed at a stroke; in addition much of the goods traffic was also re-routed, particularly from the North Cornwall lines, which had greatly contributed to its revenue over the years, along with coal from the Somerset coalfields and stone from the Mendip quarries.

The need for double-headed operation of heavy trains on the ruling 1:50 gradient over the Mendips played an important factor in diverting passenger traffic from the line, particularly because of the extra manpower required to operate this service. The arrival on the scene of the Standard Class 9F 2-10-0s in the summer of 1960 following a trial in March of that year, was hailed as a saviour by some, but seen as a threat by others: the unions were very chary about the possible reduction in manpower that the introduction of these magnificent engines would bring about. This fear was somewhat unfounded, for although these powerful locomotives could haul 450 tons over the Mendips unassisted, it was an onerous task for the firemen of such trains to keep their drivers supplied with a sustained full head of steam in order to do so. Therefore, in practical terms, such trains continued to be double-headed – so back to square one! There was an interesting suggestion of rostering two firemen per Class 9F locomotive on such trains, but for various reasons this proposal was not followed through.

Now reduced to a local service, by the winter of

1962 anomalies had crept in with connecting trains still being run, like the 16.13 from Evercreech to Bournemouth West, which had no connection to meet and run from a place unlikely to attract any custom. Like many of the stations on the line, Evercreech served a scattered, predominantly agricultural population, who just did not use the system, except those living nearer to Bath. As a railway operating services for this kind of community, apart from school traffic and the occasional excursion, it could not be expected to pay and survive. These circumstances were not helped by a census of passenger traffic taken during the school holidays (when it was considerably less) and in 1963 Class 9F locomotives instead of the requested Class 5MTs were sent to work local passenger services, to highlight just two cited examples of Western Region disinterest. With these factors against it, it is hardly surprising that the line soon became completely unviable and hopelessly uneconomic: its demise was well and truly under way. The coalfields were already suffering from the availability of cheaper alternatives such as oil and, ironically, were failing to attract sufficient labour to work in the pits, thus reducing potential output and perhaps hastening final closure of both line and mine (the last pit closed in 1973).

Beeching's report of 28 March 1963 entitled *The Reshaping of Britain's Railways* argued that a third of the system should be axed. Fares would rise to compensate for the loss of capacity. A point which many statisticians and economists seem to underestimate constantly is the human factor involved: the report meant that some 70,000 people would be made redundant; many would be of retiring age it is true, and the job shortage was not as acute as it is today, but it obviously had a totally demoralizing effect on the workforce. The report also envisaged that 75 per cent of the population would have a car by 1984 (later proven to be over optimistic). However, it was true that the country was becoming more wealthy – the 'you've never had it so good' era had hardly begun. People were discovering the freedom that the motor car offered and at home the washing was being done with the aid of one of John Bloom's machines. Even summer rail traffic was getting less and less. By 1966 the railways had already embarked upon a massive programme of conversion to diesel, resulting in steam engines of less than ten years of age being scrapped although still good for another 500,000 miles or more. It was this type of motive power upon which the S&D still totally depended.

Although some rail closures were inevitable, it is now generally accepted that the Beeching report was a crude cost-cutting exercise and as one commentator pointed out: "If you cut the tributaries of a river you are depriving it of the sources upon which it depends". It is an irony that in the thirty years or more since the sharpness of the axe was felt, stations and some lines closed then have been reopened around the country: Templecombe is one example and is earning good revenue in the 1990s.

The Somerset & Dorset lingered on until 6 March 1966, reprieved by two months due to a bus operator withdrawing an application for a licence. Valiant attempts to save the line were made by various bodies: two stalwarts of the S&D who played a leading part in trying to bring about a reprieve were Norman Down, the stationmaster of Binegar and Ernie Cross, the signalman. To the shame of the railway authorities and the Labour government of the day, this came to nothing. So it was that the S&D passed into history.

It was not just a railway line which came to an end: the staff, many of whose families had worked the S&D for generations with a pride and enthusiasm that was second to none, lost their jobs. A special 'family' atmosphere which had formed over the years was devastated at a stroke and a way of life had gone for ever. The *esprit de corps* S&D folk had was epitomised by the way the stations and gardens were kept. The pretty flower beds and productive allotments, which were such a joy for passengers to behold, would soon become overgrown and there would be nothing but dereliction and decay.

The Mendip Hills themselves seemed poorer for the absence of the steam engines that had toiled over Masbury Summit, at 911ft above sea level, the highest point on the line. Because of the S&D's long history of being operated as a 'joint' line, it was noted for its rich diversity of motive power and rolling stock, which attracted enthusiasts nationwide – particularly after nationalisation.

Fortunately, images of all this had been caught on film by many notable railway photographers, including Ivo Peters, Dick Riley, Derek Cross, Tony Richardson and others, who recognised the unique variety of locomotives and magnificent scenery afforded by the line; so let us remind ourselves of what the S&D was like with the aid of some of those splendid photographs taken during its last few decades and compare the same scenes today: the Somerset & Dorset then and now.

THE SOMERSET & DORSET JOINT RAILWAY

GRADIENT PROFILES

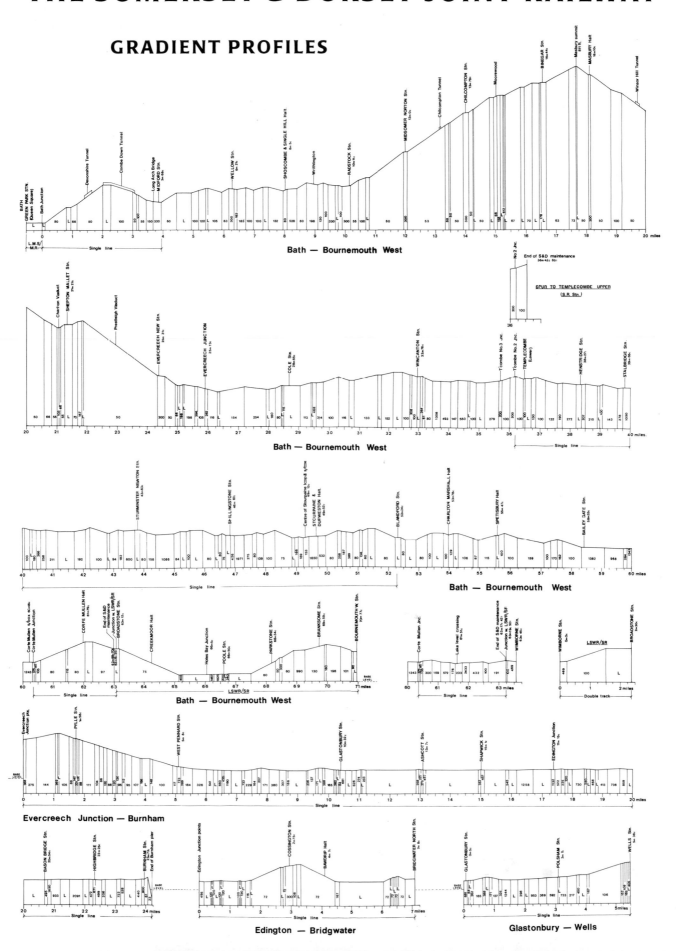

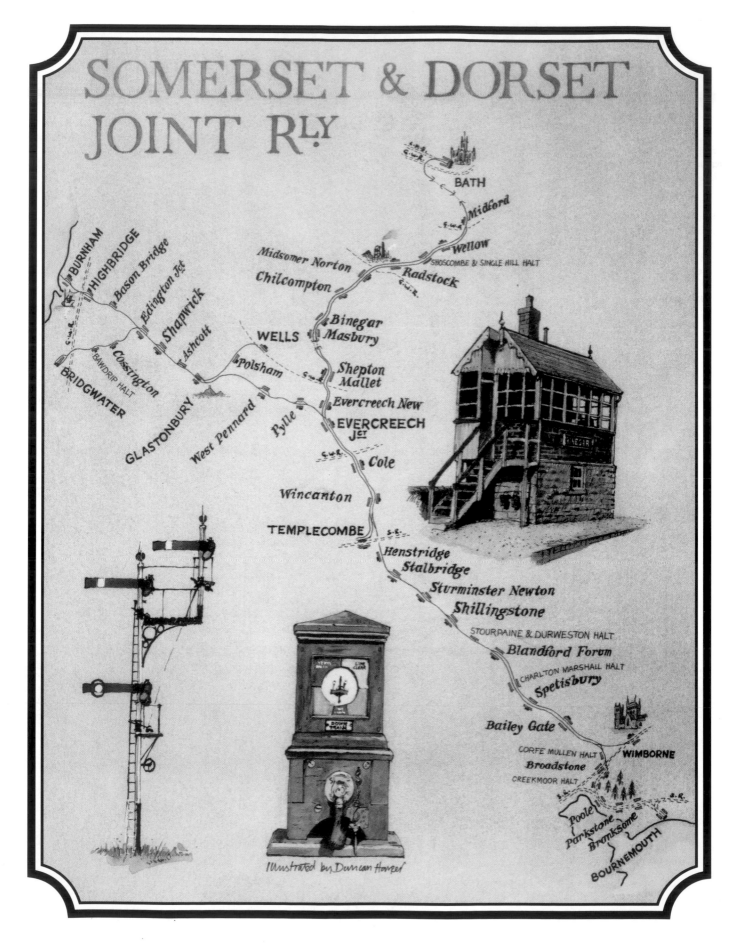

SOMERSET & DORSET JOINT Rˡʸ

Illustrated by Duncan Harper

BATH–DEVONSHIRE TUNNEL

1
**Bath Green Park
station (1)**
172 ST 746648

A 1959 view of the façade
taken in railway days: a
notable structure built of
Bath stone in Georgian
style. Like many buildings
of the period it was in
need of a good clean.
Photo: R.C.Riley.
Date: 5 July 1959.

Restored to its former
glory – its stonework
repaired and cleaned like a
new pin, the station façade
forms the pedestrian
entrance to J.Sainsbury's
supermarket. The ground
floor houses a café and
lobby area whilst the large
first floor room, the
windows of which are
draped with curtains, is
used by the Bath Society.
By coincidence, this
photograph was taken on
the same date 26 years
later. *Date: 5 July 1985
(revisited 12 March 1995).*

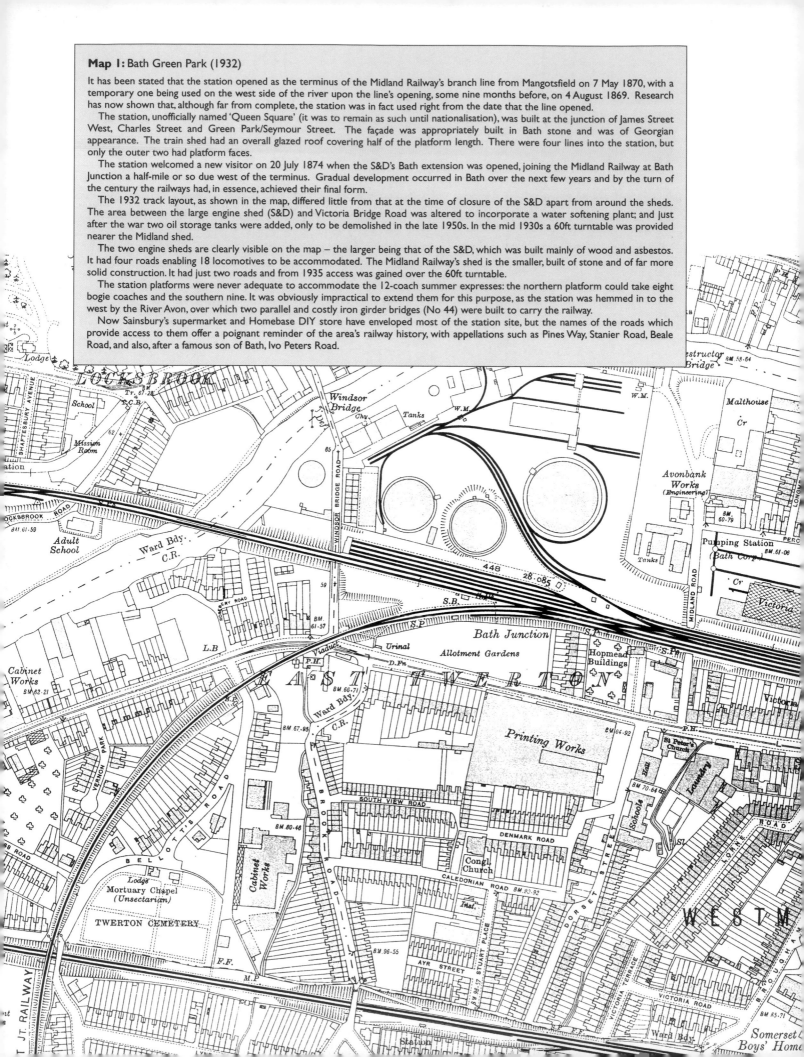

Map 1: Bath Green Park (1932)

It has been stated that the station opened as the terminus of the Midland Railway's branch line from Mangotsfield on 7 May 1870, with a temporary one being used on the west side of the river upon the line's opening, some nine months before, on 4 August 1869. Research has now shown that, although far from complete, the station was in fact used right from the date that the line opened.

The station, unofficially named 'Queen Square' (it was to remain as such until nationalisation), was built at the junction of James Street West, Charles Street and Green Park/Seymour Street. The façade was appropriately built in Bath stone and was of Georgian appearance. The train shed had an overall glazed roof covering half of the platform length. There were four lines into the station, but only the outer two had platform faces.

The station welcomed a new visitor on 20 July 1874 when the S&D's Bath extension was opened, joining the Midland Railway at Bath Junction a half-mile or so due west of the terminus. Gradual development occurred in Bath over the next few years and by the turn of the century the railways had, in essence, achieved their final form.

The 1932 track layout, as shown in the map, differed little from that at the time of closure of the S&D apart from around the sheds. The area between the large engine shed (S&D) and Victoria Bridge Road was altered to incorporate a water softening plant; and just after the war two oil storage tanks were added, only to be demolished in the late 1950s. In the mid 1930s a 60ft turntable was provided nearer the Midland shed.

The two engine sheds are clearly visible on the map – the larger being that of the S&D, which was built mainly of wood and asbestos. It had four roads enabling 18 locomotives to be accommodated. The Midland Railway's shed is the smaller, built of stone and of far more solid construction. It had just two roads and from 1935 access was gained over the 60ft turntable.

The station platforms were never adequate to accommodate the 12-coach summer expresses: the northern platform could take eight bogie coaches and the southern nine. It was obviously impractical to extend them for this purpose, as the station was hemmed in to the west by the River Avon, over which two parallel and costly iron girder bridges (No 44) were built to carry the railway.

Now Sainsbury's supermarket and Homebase DIY store have enveloped most of the station site, but the names of the roads which provide access to them offer a poignant reminder of the area's railway history, with appellations such as Pines Way, Stanier Road, Beale Road, and also, after a famous son of Bath, Ivo Peters Road.

Restoration of Bath Green Park

During the nights of 25/26 and 26/27 April 1942, Bath was the target for one of the notorious *Baedeker* reprisal raids, carried out on historic towns and cities throughout the country. The station caught the blast of the first bomb dropped on the city during the raid in which the old S&D offices in Green Park Buildings were destroyed.

After closure of the line in 1966, the station began to deteriorate rapidly: the buildings suffered considerable damage and decay, not helped by the roof lead being stolen. In November 1971 it was made a listed building, and in 1972 Bath City Council decided to purchase the site. A number of repairs were effected to prevent further decay.

During the next seven years various schemes for development were mooted, the council expressing preference for a hotel to be built, which would have meant the train shed being demolished. Then in October 1979, Bath City Council gave official support to enter into an agreement between the British Railways Board and J. Sainsbury plc to the leasing of the site, with planning permission for the erection of a retail store, which included the restoration of the building.

Late in 1979 structural surveys were carried out, which revealed the desperate condition of the building. However, restoration commenced in earnest in 1981 and involved many complex engineering and construction techniques to ensure that the essential character and appearance of the structure remained. After some £1.5 million and 44 weeks spent on restoration, Green Park was formally opened by HRH Princess Margaret on 1 December 1982. The building today reflects the splendid achievement of all concerned.

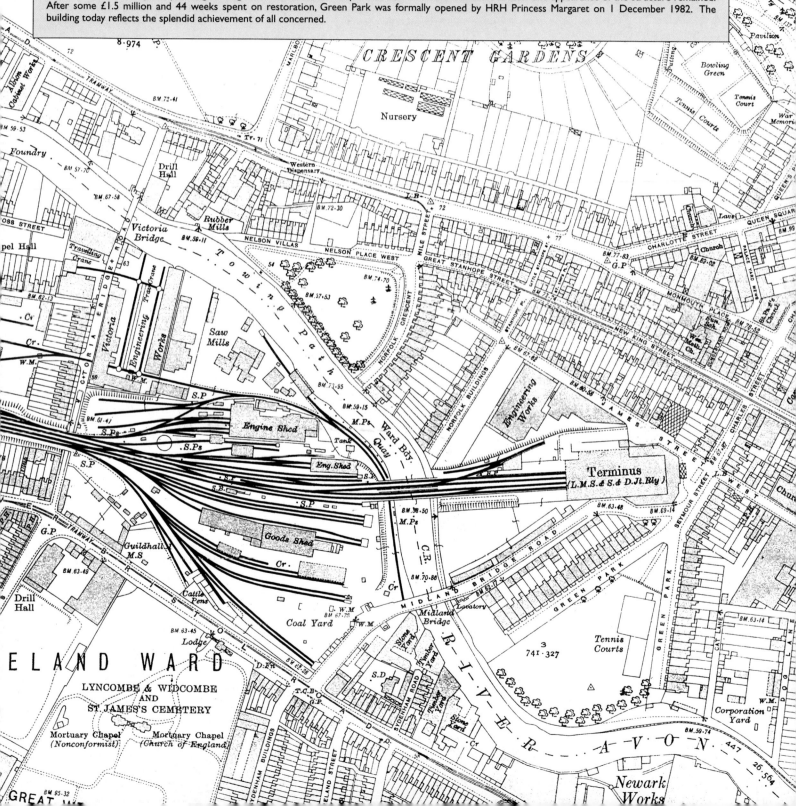

2
Bath Green Park station (2)
172 ST 745648

Drivers Dave Hadfield and Bert Brewer bring their respective charges, Class 2P No 40563 and BR Class 5 No 73050 on the up 'Pines Express', slowly to a halt at the buffer stops in the train shed. Note the familiar advertisement hoardings of the period and the war-damaged roof remaining unglazed. *Photo: Ivo Peters. Date: 3 July 1954.*

The train shed now beautifully restored and protected by a glazed roof, stands empty in the evening light after the last shoppers have left. The supermarket is seen in the background. Note the wooden floor area that once formed the trackbed adjacent to the buffer stops and also the empty market stalls used by traders under the protection of the train shed.

The station rooms have been let to a variety of craft shops and businesses, including the Egon Ronay-recommended Bath Brasserie (restaurant); Bath Enterprises (small industries group); a dance studio; and upstairs, the meeting room of the Bath Society. The latter has been the venue for several railway lectures and film shows over the years. *Date: 12 March 1995.*

3
Bath Green Park station (3)
172 ST 744647

A steamy evening scene at Bath Green Park: Class 2P 4-4-0 No 40568 prepares to get under way with a down local train, whilst a sister engine, No 40505 waits its turn of duty in one of the centre roads. Of interest is the former horsekeeper's cottage to the right of the picture.

Previously unpublished, Ivo Peters probably did not approve of this picture because of the untidy pile of timber and wheelbarrow left in the foreground – most unlike the high standard of tidiness associated with the S&D. *Photo: Ivo Peters. Date: 8 March 1952.*

The former train shed, looking majestic, provides a dramatic backdrop to Sainsbury's supermarket, which had shut its doors to the public only a few minutes earlier after a hectic Sunday's trading and the car park lies almost empty. Access is gained via one of the original railway bridges spanning the River Avon, to the north side of which a new pedestrian bridge has been constructed, using the abutments of its demolished twin. Green Park will no more be host to steam trains, but it stands as a worthy monument to them, the best possible alternative use being made of it – and it looks simply magnificent. *Date: 12 March 1995.*

4

Bath motive power depot (82G)
172 ST 741648

A fine study of Bath MPD taken from the top of the old water treatment plant set between the sheds and Victoria Bridge Road. The S&D's wooden shed in the foreground could house up to eighteen locomotives; the smaller Midland stone-built shed is seen behind the coaling plant, which itself was rebuilt in 1954. Until 23 February 1958 the shed code was 71H and 22C before that.

Taken a few months before summer through-traffic on the S&D was diverted, the scene shows considerable activity, with a bevy of Stanier Class 5 4-6-0s in residence, including Nos 44666, 44667, 44775, 44804 and 44888, together with two BR Standard Class 9F 2-10-0s, Nos 92001 and 92210. Note the reporting numbers being placed on the smokebox of 9F No 92210 and also the locomen 'chewing the fat' near the dry sand bin. Green Park's station roof can be seen in the middle distance, as can some of Bath's many church spires and the abbey.
Photo: Ivo Peters. Date: 14 July 1962.

In total contrast this photograph, taken from approximately the same place, but in pouring rain, was made possible with the kind co-operation of Messrs Stothert & Pitt, who owned the site at the time. They arranged for a large crane to be placed on the spot where the water treatment plant once stood in order that this comparison could be obtained.

A good idea of how Sainsbury's supermarket fits into the scene can be judged from this vantage point. Note the retaining wall of the former coaling plant, its south side forms part of the structure of the adjacent building. *Date: 21 May 1985 (revisited 12 March 1995).*

In the late 1980s, the site was sold by Stothert & Pitt to Sainsbury's and has now been developed by them into a Homebase DIY store and car park. It is evident from this viewpoint that an enormous change has taken place over the last 10 years.
Date: 12 March 1995.

COMMENT: *The crane and cage in which I was lifted – seemingly to embark on an upward journey to shake hands with the Almighty! However, it was made under the relative comfort of an umbrella which was kindly held over the camera equipment by John Porter of Stothert & Pitt, whilst I took the shot in relatively poor visibility.*

The 1995 picture was taken with the camera mounted on poles, with me teetering precariously on top of a pair of steps enabling a photograph to be taken at an elevation of about thirty feet; not quite achieving the same height as before, but good enough to illustrate the contrasting scenes of 1962, 1985 and the present day.

5
Bath MPD – S&D shed
172 ST 742648

A variety of locomotives on parade outside the shed on a sad but notable occasion. The line-up includes S&D 7F 2-8-0 No 53807, BR 9F 2-10-0 No 92245, BR Class 4 4-6-0 No 75073 and BR 9F No 92220, *Evening Star*, sporting the headboard of the line's premier train, the 'Pines Express'. The latter, having arrived earlier from Bournemouth, was about to haul the last down 'Pines' on the S&D line before the express was transferred to run via an alternative route to and from Bournemouth. By the end of the day there would be no further through express workings and services would, apart from occasional specials, be generally confined to local and semi-fast services only.

The climb from the S&D shed to the main line was sharp, but short, being set on a slightly lower level, causing some engines to do a bit of 'running on the spot' on the slippery rails in wet weather.
Photo: Ivo Peters. Date: 8 September 1962.

The houses in the background form Norfolk Crescent and are the only link with the former scene. Everything else has changed and the S&D shed area has been made into a car park for the Homebase DIY store, part of which is seen on the right. It occupies the spot where the coaling plant and Midland shed once stood. Since this development took place, not one railway artefact can now be found at this location, unlike in 1985.
Date: 12 March 1995.

6
**Bath – Victoria Bridge
Road (Bridge 43)**
172 ST 740648

Having just started out from
Bath Green Park, Class 4F
0-6-0 No 44417 pilots Bulleid
Pacific No 34095 *Brentor* on
the down 'Pines Express' and
crosses over Victoria Bridge
Road just a few chains west
of the station. The S&D shed
is just visible between the
leading locomotive and oil
tank on the extreme left. It
was from on top of this
storage tank that Ivo Peters
obtained his elevated view of
the shed. The busy Bath
station signal box is seen in
the background, whilst the
building on the immediate
right incorporates the railway
clearing house, time office and
yard supervisor's office,
beyond which is the goods
shed. *Photo: Ivo Peters.
Date: 9 August 1952.*

Whilst the brick parapets of
the demolished bridge
remain, the background has
changed somewhat. The rear
of the Homebase DIY store
stands in full view from this
vantage point, as does the
elegant terrace of Norfolk
Crescent. An overflow car
park is sandwiched between
the eastern abutments of the
bridge and the DIY store.
The trackbed between this
bridge and the remains of the
one that once spanned
Midland Road is relatively free
from undergrowth and is
quite walkable. Odd railway
artefacts still lie scattered
about here, and during this
visit at least
one railway enthusiast was
scouring the area for
mementoes of a bygone age.
Date: 12 March 1995.

7
Bath – Midland Road (Bridge 42)
172 ST 738648

During the first fortnight of March 1953 the Southern Region carried out a series of trial runs over the S&D with Maunsell's U and U1 class of 2-6-0s to test their suitability for use over the line. Seen on the Thursday of the second week of trials, Class U1 No 31906 is piloted by 2P 4-4-0 No 40563 with the 12-coach 16.25 Bath–Bournemouth train. The 2P assisted as far as Evercreech to await a return working over the Mendips. The other Maunsell 2-6-0 involved in the trials was U class No 31621, which worked the test trains during the first week. Both the 11.40 up from Bournemouth and the 16.25 down workings were involved; but during the first half of each week, the load comprised eight coaches.

The building to the left of the sidings forms part of Stothert & Pitt's extensive Victoria Works. *Photo: Ivo Peters. Date: 11 March 1954.*

Despite the detritus in the foreground, a distant view of the Homebase DIY store is still to be glimpsed. The parapet on the eastern side of Bridge 42 remains, but the one in the foreground has been demolished; only the abutments remain. Following its sale in 1988/9, Stothert & Pitt ceased manufacturing dockside cranes and plant equipment in Bath, for which it has gained a world-wide reputation for excellence; the Victoria Works was demolished in 1990 and now lies abandoned. The land, now owned by Sainsbury's, may be considered to be ripe for development by them at some time in the future. Many of the work's railway lines remain in the former roadways as poignant reminders of better days.
Date: 17 March 1995.

COMMENT: *Almost certainly Ivo Peters would have trimmed this photograph to eliminate the telegraph bracing wire on the right.. I hope he would have forgiven me for including it, as the building on the right was something to which easy reference can be made.*

Bath Junction and gasworks
172 ST 738648

The gasometers provide an unmistakable landmark at the S&D's junction with the Midland line to Mangotsfield and the North. It was here that the Somerset & Dorset's own track commenced and its line climbed at 1:50 on a sharp curve to head south-east towards Combe Down Tunnel some two miles distant. All down trains had to collect the tablet for the single line working to Midford from here. Nearly all S&D locomotives were fitted with a mechanical tablet catcher; those that were not collected a 'big pouch' tablet with a large metal hoop, which the signalman handed to the fireman.

A panoramic view is had of the junction and adjacent gasworks from atop a bracket signal and shows BR Class 5 4-6-0 No 73050 drifting down the S&D's single line past Bath Junction signal box with the up 'Pines' relief. The Whitaker automatic tablet catching apparatus can just be seen over the cottage and towards the rear of the train.
Photo: Ivo Peters.
Date: 23 April 1955.

The gasometers provide a tangible link with the past, as do the houses in the distance. Note the industrial development that has taken place on the site of the junction. The modern-looking building in the 1955 picture, which was then relatively new, has since been demolished and replaced by another built alongside. It is now the showrooms and garage for a local Mitsubishi dealer and part of the trackbed is used as a car compound. Over the last ten years or so this site has been tidied considerably and much of the undergrowth has been removed.
Date: 17 March 1995.

9

Bath – Lower Bristol Road (Bridge 1)
172 ST 735648

BR Class 4 2-6-0 No 76007 trundles over the Lower Bristol Road bridge on its way down the line to a point beyond Midsomer Norton, where it will be engaged in engineering works. One would wonder if the advertising standards authorities – if operating then – would have questioned the ironic slogan under the S&D's bridge, for it had earned the sobriquet, some would suggest somewhat unfairly, of being the 'Slow and Dirty'! The man seen cycling along the otherwise deserted road in his Sunday best would be a sight almost impossible to repeat in the 1990s. Note The Royal Oak public house on the left and its proximity to the line, which would have afforded an excellent view of trains when viewed from its upstairs rooms. *Photo: Ivo Peters. Date: 5 May 1957.*

The only reminder today is the Royal Oak, although it has undergone a few changes, including an upstairs window bricked in and the sign changed. Even the houses across the road have made way for modern industrial units. Judging from the amount of traffic that constantly builds up at this road junction, it suggests that it would be quicker by train! *Date: 17 March 1995.*

Bath – Bellots Road
172 ST 733646

The assault of the 1:50 climb from Bath has begun in earnest: Standard Class 4 2-6-4T No 80067, in charge of the 15.20 Bath–Templecombe down local, nears the elegant three-arch bridge (No 3) over the GWR main line, which it is about to traverse. Shortly after it will pass the site of the Victoria Brick & Tile Company's siding located on the up side of the single line (just beyond the $^1/_2$-milepost – from Bath Junction), before heading out of the city in a south-easterly direction, having curved through almost 180 degrees in the process. Vintage car buffs will recognise the Vauxhall Cresta on the right.
Photo: R.E.Toop.
Date: 13 June 1964.

COMMENT: *A man noticing me taking photographs in the direction of the garage he was building thought I was a Council official from the planning department and was most concerned at my presence. Assuring him of my innocent intentions, his curiosity was satisfied!*

The line formation has now become part of the Linear Park, which starts near this point and provides an excellent leisure amenity for local people, who now use its facilities for walking and cycling. Bridge 3 still survives in good condition over the main Bristol–Paddington railway line, but is inaccessible to the public with a stout fence preventing access. The embankment has been mostly removed, but little else has changed in this scene. The monument on the hill in the distance is Beckett's Tower.
Date: 17 March 1995.

11
Bath – Devonshire Bank (Victoria Brick & Tile Company's siding)
172 ST 733643

An express for Bournemouth, headed by Class 4F No 44560 and piloted by Class 2P No 40564, both in early BR livery, is seen rounding the long curve from Bath Junction on the 1:50 gradient of Devonshire Bank. The train is passing the site of the brickworks' (formerly May's) siding and over Bridge 4 as it heads towards the overbridge (No 5) carrying Bridge Road. Shortly it will pass the Twerton Co operative Society's siding, a quarter-mile beyond on the down side, then still climbing at 1:50 on a straight stretch of track, will duck under the Maple Grove pedestrian bridge before entering Devonshire Tunnel a few chains beyond.

Note the children sitting on the bridge abutment watching the train with interest and also the rail section onto which the bridge's number plate has been fixed, which is visible on top of the structure at the trackside.
Photo: Ivo Peters. Date: 5 August 1950.

Bridge 4 has long been demolished and a road link has been created to connect Dartmouth Avenue with Millmead Road. The houses of both Millmead Road and West Avenue on the horizon provide some continuity with the past. Although the bridge has been removed, access to the Linear Park is gained on both sides of the road. It is quite noticeable how trees and scrub each side of the old formation almost obscure it from view: a total contrast from the days when the trackside was kept clear of such, partly to avoid a fire risk – and leaves on lines!
Date: 17 March 1995.

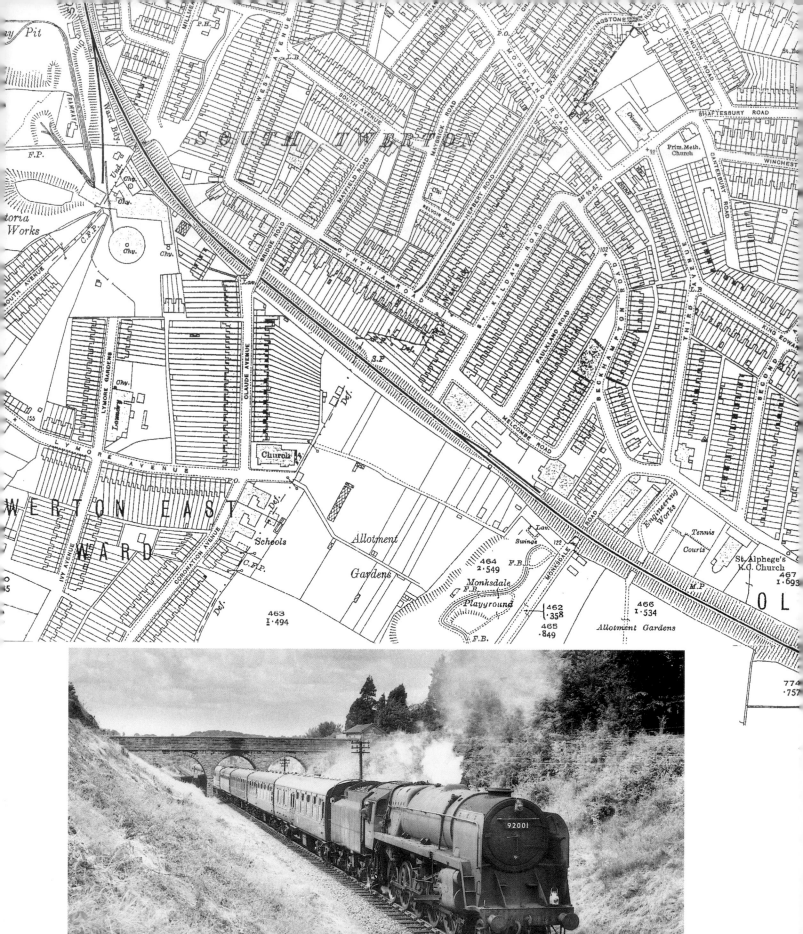

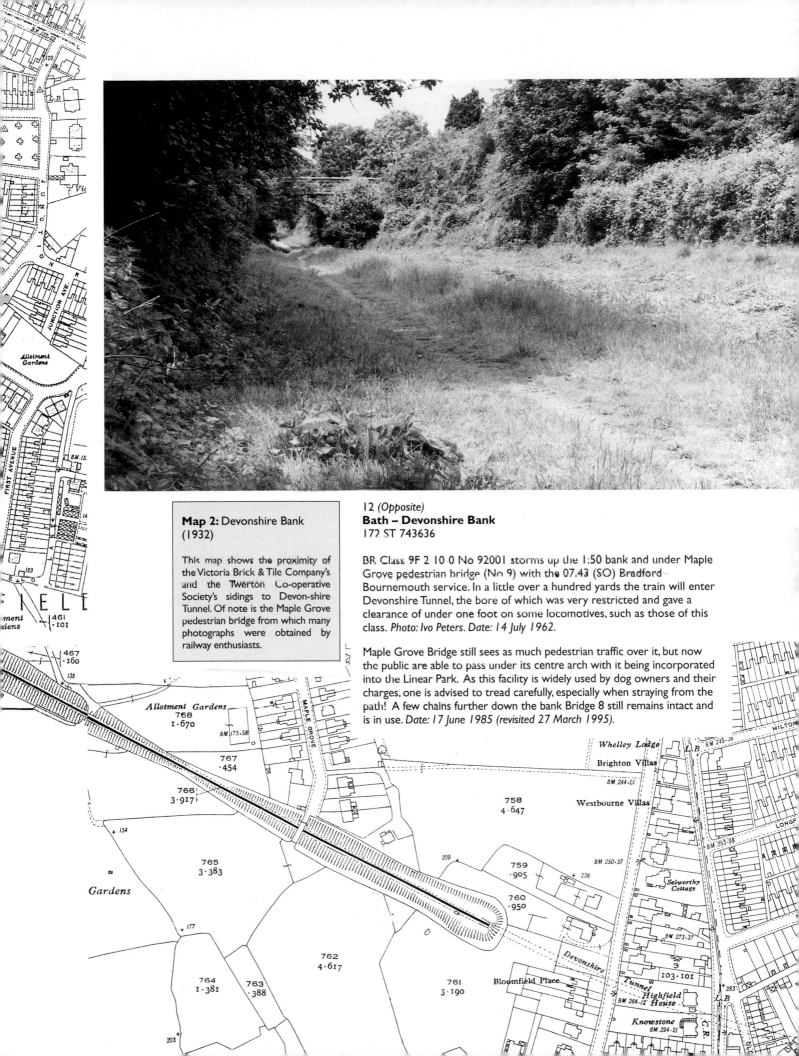

Map 2: Devonshire Bank (1932)

This map shows the proximity of the Victoria Brick & Tile Company's and the Twerton Co-operative Society's sidings to Devon-shire Tunnel. Of note is the Maple Grove pedestrian bridge from which many photographs were obtained by railway enthusiasts.

12 *(Opposite)*
Bath – Devonshire Bank
172 ST 743636

BR Class 9F 2 10 0 No 92001 storms up the 1:50 bank and under Maple Grove pedestrian bridge (No 9) with the 07.43 (SO) Bradford Bournemouth service. In a little over a hundred yards the train will enter Devonshire Tunnel, the bore of which was very restricted and gave a clearance of under one foot on some locomotives, such as those of this class. *Photo: Ivo Peters. Date: 14 July 1962.*

Maple Grove Bridge still sees as much pedestrian traffic over it, but now the public are able to pass under its centre arch with it being incorporated into the Linear Park. As this facility is widely used by dog owners and their charges, one is advised to tread carefully, especially when straying from the path! A few chains further down the bank Bridge 8 still remains intact and is in use. *Date: 17 June 1985 (revisited 27 March 1995).*

13
Devonshire Tunnel (No 10)
172 ST 743636

One of Bath MPD's double-chimney Class 4 4-6-0s, No 75073, pilots unrebuilt Bulleid Pacific No 34043 *Combe Martin* with the 12.20 (SO) Bournemouth–Nottingham and emerges from Devonshire Tunnel; the restricted bore of which is well illustrated in this view as the train emerges almost like a cork from a bottle.

The tunnel was 440yd long and had no ventilation shafts, making it extremely unpleasant for footplate crews, particularly on the second engine of a double-headed train. In the summer of 1960 a frightening experience of this nature was suffered by fireman Peter Smith when he and driver Donald Beale were on the footplate of a slipping West Country class Pacific, No 34105 *Swanage*, struggling with a train on which the brakes had bound on. Recalling the episode he likened it to being in Dante's inferno. Fortunately, they escaped relatively unscathed, if a little shaken.
Photo: Ivo Peters. Date: 14 July 1962.

Devonshire Bank has been landscaped and the cutting has also been slightly backfilled by material scraped from the embankments in order to bury the portal of the tunnel, thus preventing entry by the public and therefore direct access into Lyncombe Vale beyond.
Date: 17 March 1995.

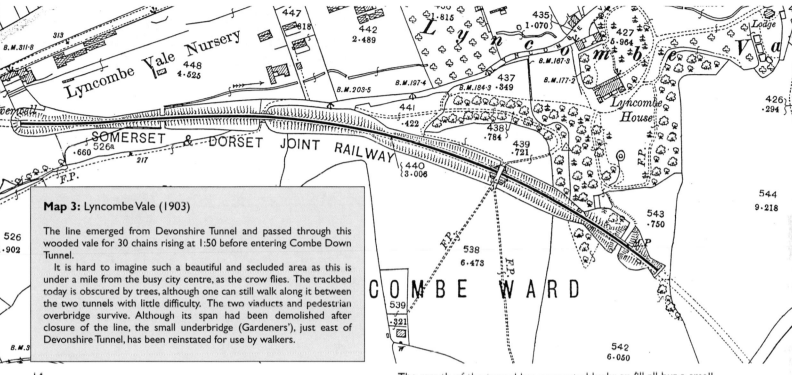

Map 3: Lyncombe Vale (1903)

The line emerged from Devonshire Tunnel and passed through this wooded vale for 30 chains rising at 1:50 before entering Combe Down Tunnel.

It is hard to imagine such a beautiful and secluded area as this is under a mile from the busy city centre, as the crow flies. The trackbed today is obscured by trees, although one can still walk along it between the two tunnels with little difficulty. The two viaducts and pedestrian overbridge survive. Although its span had been demolished after closure of the line, the small underbridge (Gardeners'), just east of Devonshire Tunnel, has been reinstated for use by walkers.

14

Lyncombe Vale – Devonshire Tunnel (No 10)
172 ST 748635

The now-preserved S&D 7F 2-8-0 No 53809, with a down goods, bursts out of the tunnel and into Lyncombe Vale. The fireman leans from the cab to gulp the fresh air and enjoy the bright spring sunlight after experiencing the stifling conditions inside the tunnel. The respite will be all too brief, for the locomotive will soon enter the much longer Combe Down Tunnel, the bore of which is equally restrictive. *Photo: Ivo Peters. Date: 15 March 1952.*

The mouth of the tunnel has concrete blocks to fill all but a small portion of the portal. Note the telegraph pole, which still survives on the right and appears in the original shot. When first visited in 1985, the portal was largely obscured by trees and undergrowth at the side of the track formation, but now is considerably clearer, some attempt having been made to remove overhanging branches and brambles. Apart from a smelly drain that appears to be from the septic tank of a house in Greenway Lane above, with its outflow dropping to the trackbed, the conditions have improved and this location is now an integral part of a footpath created along the entire line formation in Lyncombe Vale. *Date: 17 March 1995.*

15

Lyncombe Vale – Watery Bottom Viaduct (No 12)
172 ST 750634

Class 7F No 53810, with a goods for Bath, drifts down the 1:50 gradient and heads towards Devonshire Tunnel, passing over Watery Bottom Viaduct situated in the middle of Lyncombe Vale.

Due to the remoteness of this area, many non-local railway photographers, including the late Derek Cross – much to his chagrin – could never find this location and therefore were unable to capture on film locomotives working hard in this lovely setting. *Photo: Ivo Peters. Date: Winter 1955.*

When this area was first visited in 1985, the viaduct could not be seen and was completely obscured by young ash and elder trees, some of which were in danger of causing damage to the structure. Some judicious pruning was therefore necessary to obtain a partial side-on view of Watery Bottom Viaduct. However, from this acute angle, the viaduct is all but hidden by trees, although it can just be made out in the centre of the picture, which was taken in the last light of an early spring evening. *Date: 15 March 1995.*

Taken on the same occasion, a close-up shot of the viaduct, which remains in reasonable condition. *Date: 15 March 1995.*

16
Lyncombe Vale – Combe Down Tunnel (No 15)
172 ST 755632

With the dramatic lighting effect cast by a late afternoon's sun, this superb and unusual study, taken from above the northern entrance of Combe Down Tunnel, shows the rear portion of the 12.35 down goods, hauled by 7F No 53802, about to enter the portal before plunging into the narrow 1,829yd-long bore. The Class 4F banker, having given assistance from the junction, has dropped off the rear of the train at the pedestrian overbridge in the background and prepares to return to Bath, having gained a bank engine key, which offered it protection. The instructions given to crews on these duties were to see the rear of the train safely through the tunnel before reversing down the line.

This location, a favourite spot of Ivo Peters, was enhanced by the small viaduct (No 14), the gangers' hut and water trough, which made it even more photogenic. On a number of occasions, Ivo had to use a length of weighted string to snare an overhanging branch so it could be pruned before taking a shot in this thickly wooded spot. *Photo: Ivo Peters. Date: 30 October 1954.*

Over the last few years quite a bit of pruning has been undertaken and the view from on top of the tunnel is better than it has been for some time: the viaduct and water trough are still plain to see but the hut has long since gone, although its base survives. The trackbed, still indented from where the sleepers were removed, is well used as a footpath, which climbs up to the side of the tunnel and beyond.
Date: 17 March 1995.

Combe Down Tunnel

Due to its length and its restricted and unventilated bore, the tunnel presented a severe test to locomotive crews, particularly on up trains, since much of it was built on a rising gradient of 1:100 and the atmosphere inside could be choking. These conditions resulted in tragedy when on 20 November 1929, an up goods comprised of 37 wagons and hauled by the then almost new S&D 7F 2-8-0, No 89, ran out of control down the gradient and was derailed at the entrance to Bath goods yard. Those who lost their lives were driver Jennings, inspector Norman, who was in charge of the goods yard, and Jack Loader, a young LMS clerk who was taking a short cut across the track on his way home from work. The resulting enquiry came to the conclusion that the enginemen had been overcome by fumes from the hard-working locomotive in the hot and murky tunnel and were rendered unconscious; however, the fireman, Maurice Pearce, was lucky to escape with his life.

COMMENT: *In 1985 I did manage to sneak a look inside when the contractors were still working to fit the doors over the portal and found the track ballast intact. Poignantly, there were still copious amounts of soot which remained deposited on the tunnel's roof. The contractors had to reverse their pick-up truck through the entire length of the tunnel in one direction, since they were unable to turn it at the Lyncombe Vale end – not a feat to be undertaken by the timorous, or by claustrophobes!*

17 (Opposite)
Horsecombe Vale – Combe Down Tunnel
172 ST 763618

Class 2P No 40569, piloting a Standard Class 5 with the down 'Pines Express', bursts out of Combe Down Tunnel into Horsecombe Vale on a dull day. Of interest is the telephone mounted on the telegraph pole. This was used by crews in the even of a train stalling on the approach to, or inside, the tunnel and was connected to Midford box, where the signalman would authorise the train to reverse some distance before making another attempt at climbing the grade, which increased to 1:50 to a point a few chains inside the tunnel. The line then continued to climb northwards at 1:100 for near three-quarters of a mile before a level stretch of about twenty-five chains from the northern portal was reached. *Photo: Ivo Peters. Date: 8 February 1958.*

Mother Nature has almost taken over this spot now, although the trackbed remains reasonably clear, as it is occasionally used by Wessex Water as access to the tunnel, the southern portal of which has been fitted with massive steel doors for security. The remains of the lineside telephone box survives, as does the telegraph pole. The arches of the retaining wall readily identify this as the same spot. Looking in the southerly direction, the growth of trees and abundant scrub and brambles have totally obscured the view to Tucking Mill Viaduct. *Date: 17 March 1995.*

Combe Down Tunnel now belongs to Wessex Water; its northerly portal has been fitted with steel doors surrounded by precast concrete, save for a small portion at the top to allow access by bats. However, entry by the general public is not possible.
Date: 17 March 1995.

18
Horsecombe Vale – Tucking Mill Viaduct (No 16)
172 ST 764615

The impressive 96yd eight-arch Tucking Mill Viaduct, rising 63ft above the valley it spans in Horsecombe Vale, makes a splendid feature in this idyllic setting. Standing on the embankment at the southern end of the structure, the photographer has a marvellous view of an approaching double-headed express for Bournemouth, believed to be the down 'Pines' relief, piloted by Class 2P 4-4-0 No 40568 with an unidentified Stanier Class 5, which have just emerged from Combe Down Tunnel in the background. Note Midford's down distant signal, which is of SR construction. The buildings on the left are those of the water works.

The viaduct was widened in 1891/2 for double track. Its exisiting arches were encapsulated in engineers' brick, making the structure both stronger and uniform in appearance. In the event, lack of finance meant double track never extended beyond Midford. *Photo: Ivo Peters. Date: 22 May 1956.*

Standing at the same position today, the view has changed somewhat and there is not much to see: trees that have grown over the last thirty years or so have all but obscured the viaduct from view, although the concrete wall erected between the parapets to prevent access onto the structure is just visible through the thicket. There might be a good case to bring back coppicing here! *Date: 17 March 1995.*

COMMENT: *A vicious gale was blowing with frequent squally showers which necessitated my sheltering in the lee of a large tree for a half-hour before attempting this shot.*

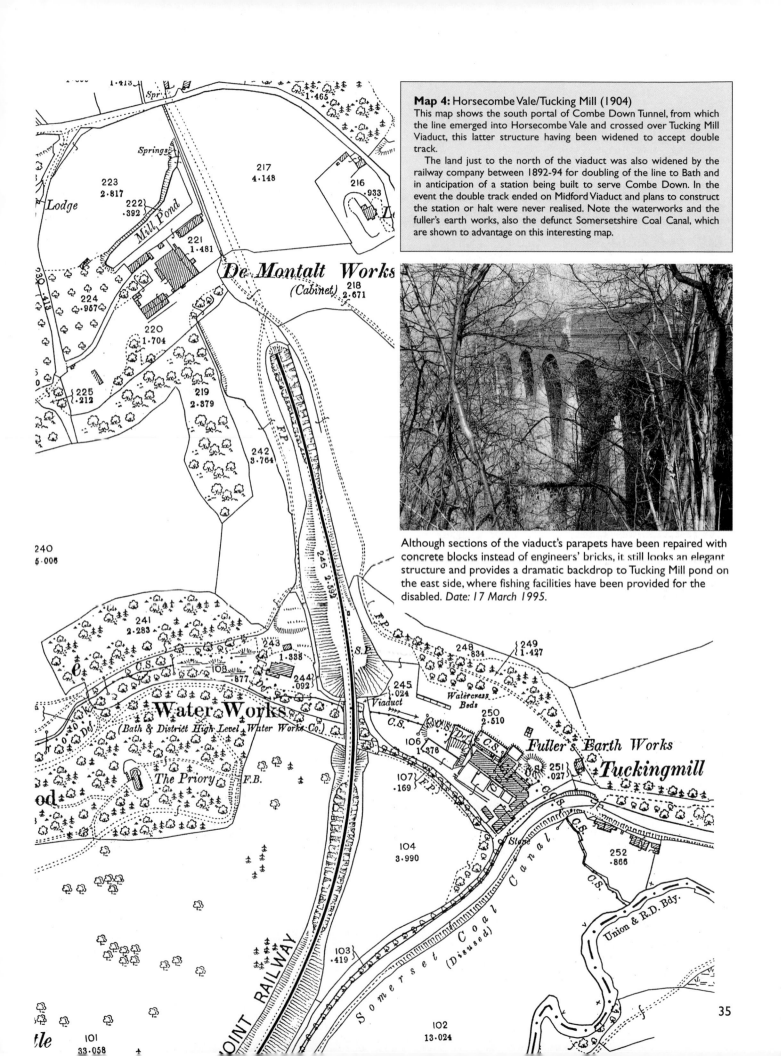

This map shows the south portal of Combe Down Tunnel, from which the line emerged into Horsecombe Vale and crossed over Tucking Mill Viaduct, this latter structure having been widened to accept double track.

The land just to the north of the viaduct was also widened by the railway company between 1892-94 for doubling of the line to Bath and in anticipation of a station being built to serve Combe Down. In the event the double track ended on Midford Viaduct and plans to construct the station or halt were never realised. Note the waterworks and the fuller's earth works, also the defunct Somersetshire Coal Canal, which are shown to advantage on this interesting map.

Although sections of the viaduct's parapets have been repaired with concrete blocks instead of engineers' bricks, it still looks an elegant structure and provides a dramatic backdrop to Tucking Mill pond on the east side, where fishing facilities have been provided for the disabled. *Date: 17 March 1995.*

19
Midford – 'Park Bank'
172 ST 762611

With the continuing demise of the S&D's 7F class, Stanier 8F 2-8-0s began to appear on the line. Coasting along 'Park Bank', as S&D men knew it, Class 8F 2-8-0 No 48737 takes the 08.15 down local from Bath to Templecombe past the grounds of Midford Castle towards Midford station. Due to lack of steam heating on all but two of the class (only one of which was allocated to the S&D), they could not be used on passenger trains after the end of September.

The white horse in the field seems unconcerned at the passing of the train. *Photo: Ivo Peters. Date: 28 September 1963.*

Photographer's luck: coincidentally, a horse browses in the same field – albeit a chestnut mare! The trees on the horizon provide the link with the previous photograph, since the trackside has become overgrown. The odd concrete post marking the boundary of the line can still be identified both here and in the original shot. *Date: 24 June 1985 (revisited 27 March 1995).*

> **COMMENT:** *When shown these comparisons, the late Ivo Peters had remarked that it was a shame I could not have arranged for a white horse to be in my shot. Apologising for the lack of attention to detail, I explained that I had left my aerosol can of paint at home!*
>
> *Ironically, during my 1995 visit, besides a chestnut, a white horse was actually in residence – but out of camera shot!*

Map 5: Midford (1904)

The line meanders southwards passing the grounds of Midford Castle (quaintly built to form the ace of clubs and set high upon the hill) and the small goods yard from which the fuller's earth sent up from Tucking Mill Works was transported. The yard is situated to the north of a 66yd tunnel known as 'Long Arch Bridge' passing under Tucking Mill Lane.

The disused Camerton arm of the Somersetshire Coal Canal can be seen running parallel to the railway until passing at almost ninety degrees underneath the eight-arch Midford Viaduct. After its completion in 1910, the GWR Camerton–Limpley Stoke branch line also passed under the S&D over another viaduct of its own (see 1930 map). The Hope & Anchor Inn is sandwiched between the old canal bed and the station located on the up side of the line above it.

The point at which the S&D's track became double, altered in the line's history, being nearer to the northern end of the viaduct in 1902: in 1933 it was moved closer to the southern end.

Midford station platform survives and has been the subject of a preservation attempt by a group of enthusiasts, whose aims were to gain planning permission for the reconstruction of the buildings. The site of the signal box, a flat-roofed affair rebuilt as such after a contretemps with a runaway train in 1936, is now part of the car park for the Hope & Anchor.

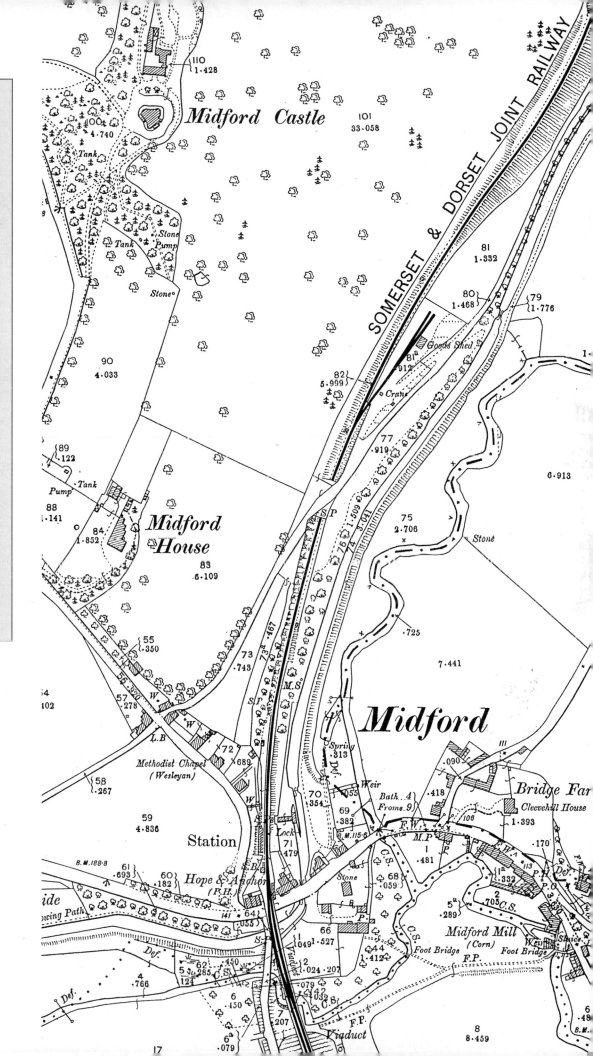

Midford

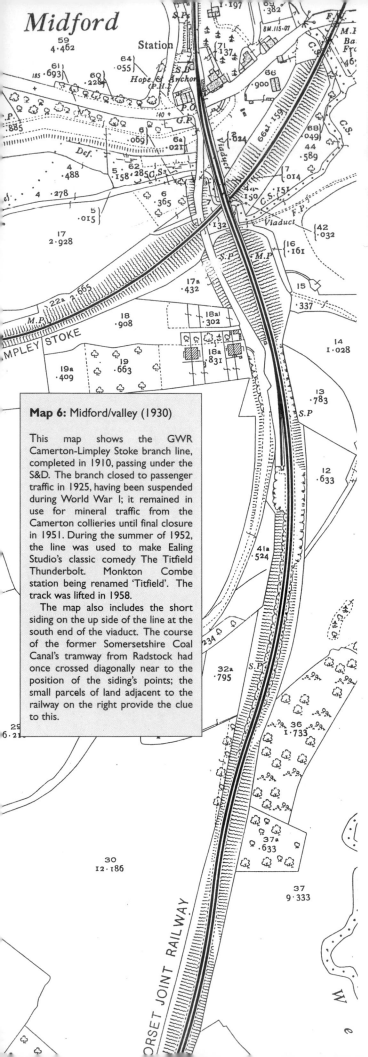

Map 6: Midford/valley (1930)

This map shows the GWR Camerton-Limpley Stoke branch line, completed in 1910, passing under the S&D. The branch closed to passenger traffic in 1925, having been suspended during World War I; it remained in use for mineral traffic from the Camerton collieries until final closure in 1951. During the summer of 1952, the line was used to make Ealing Studio's classic comedy The Titfield Thunderbolt. Monkton Combe station being renamed 'Titfield'. The track was lifted in 1958.

The map also includes the short siding on the up side of the line at the south end of the viaduct. The course of the former Somersetshire Coal Canal's tramway from Radstock had once crossed diagonally near to the position of the siding's points; the small parcels of land adjacent to the railway on the right provide the clue to this.

20
Midford goods yard
172 ST 761611

S&D 7F 2-8-0 No 53809 trundles past Midford's yard with the 15.48 goods from Bath; known to S&D folk as 'The Market', it served all stations between Radstock and Evercreech. Note the small goods shed and crane (replaced c1952) in the yard from where fuller's earth was once transported. The ground frame (Midford 'A') controlled the entrance to the goods yard. This photo was taken from the northern portal of 'Long Arch Bridge' (No 17). *Photo: Ivo Peters. Date: 21 April 1951.*

This shot could only be obtained after extensive pruning of elder and other weed-like saplings growing on the tunnel cutting's bank. The difference in the scene is plain to see in this comparison, although the trees on the horizon remain relatively unchanged. The trackbed leading under the 37yd tunnel remains reasonably clear and is used by walkers, particularly those exercising their dogs, from the station site to Tucking Mill Viaduct. The concrete base for the crane remains *in situ. Date: 10 April 1985 (revisited 15 March 1995).*

COMMENT: *Despite the vigorous pruning carried out in 1985, young trees have regrown obscuring the former goods yard from view from the same vantage point, which still remains relatively clear of undergrowth, except for piles of junk and burnt tyres left by New Age travellers who occupied the yard in recent years. They were eventually evicted and the entrance to the goods yard was then blocked with a large mound of earth and stones.*

21
Midford – 'Long Arch Bridge' (No 17)
172 ST 761609

With plenty of steam to spare, BR Class 5 4-6-0 No 73047 emerges from the 37yd 'Long Arch Bridge' with the 09.30 Whit Sunday Bath–Bournemouth excursion. Built as a cut and cover, the short tunnel carried a minor road between Midford and Tucking Mill which skewed across at an acute angle, which accounts for its length.
Photo: Ivo Peters.
Date: 21 May 1961.

With the sale of Midford station site and the trackbed to an enthusiast in the mid 1980s, fresh ballast has been laid along this section, a large pile of which has been placed at either end of the tunnel to prevent any unauthorised vehicular excursions along the same route taken by the steam locomotive in 1961! Many trees have been cut back over the last ten years and the section has been opened up considerably, having become overgrown during the previous two decades which followed closure. The 30mph signs on top of the bridge would have certainly provided a distasteful distraction for Ivo Peters, had they been present when he photographed the line!
Date: 15 March 1995.

Midford station (1)
172 ST 761607

This photograph taken from the tall backing signal on the station platform catches Class 2P 4-4-0 No 40697 drifting over Midford Viaduct on an up local, probably the 07.00 from Templecombe, and is about to catch the tablet for the single line working to Bath Junction. Note the tablet arm extended in readiness; the footplate crew of the locomotive peer over the side of the cab to see that all goes well with the transfer operation. Bob Ryan, the stationmaster, stands at ease in military style on the platform next to a mother and child, who also look on at the approaching train.

The flat roof of the signal box was the result of rebuilding after an uninvited meeting with some trucks shed from a runaway train in 1936. Note the roof of the station building and the skylight, which marked the position of the gentlemen's lavatory. The disused track of the GWR Camerton–Limpley Stoke branch, can be seen passing under the S&D's viaduct on its own structure. The roof of the Hope & Anchor is that on the left of the picture.
Photo: Ivo Peters. Date: Spring 1955.

A shot taken from the same position shows the remains of Midford's platform and the tiled floor of the gents' lavatory, which is now open to the elements. The viaduct's railings can also be spotted between the trees, to the right of which the two houses on the far side of the valley still provide good reference points to the 1955 photograph. The car park in the foreground is now that of the Hope & Anchor.
Date: 15 March 1995.

23
Midford station (2)
172 ST 761607

A view looking north, this time taken from the down starting signal seen in the previous photograph, depicts Class 7F No 53805 passing Midford station with a train of coal empties for Radstock. Note the porters' cabin in front of the lattice-construction backing, or 'wrong road' signal (the vantage point adopted by Ivo Peters) and the lamp room which can just be seen over the coal trucks towards the middle of the picture. Also of interest in this view is how the station area was hewn out of the hillside, with the stationmaster's house built on a higher level and just visible on the extreme left. *Photo: Derek Cross. Date: July 1960.*

In the mid 1980s the station was leased from BR by a group of enthusiasts and became the subject of a preservation attempt; it has subsequently been purchased. The platform was cleared of undergrowth and resurfaced through the good offices of Tarmac Ltd. Much work was done in clearing the plot land above it, so access from the road could be gained via the footpath and steps which had become overgrown.

A replica station sign was also erected at the northern end of the platform in its original position. At about the same time, a short tramway using light gauge was also laid and extended for some 30yd back towards the 'Long Arch Bridge' allowing trucks to be hauled by a hand-operated vehicle, but all traces of this have since been removed. It was hoped that planning permission would eventually be granted to allow the reconstruction of the station building and a heritage centre created; however, there has been some local opposition to the scheme and funds were raised from enthusiasts and supporters to take the case to appeal through the courts. When revisiting the site, no further work was seen to be in progress. *Date: 15 March 1995.*

COMMENT: *When I was photographing here, a car drew into the pub's car park and out stepped a pensioner who informed me he was an ex-GWR man and said that this was his first visit to Midford for over thirty-five years. Recalling the time when on his first trip to the area, he asked one of the staff if it was all right if he could look around. "Yes," said the S&D man, "providing you don't step on the stones and muck them up when crossing the line." Although the reply was somewhat unexpected, it summed up perfectly the pride staff took in the railway!*

24
Midford Viaduct (1)
172 ST 760606

S&D Class 7F 2-8-0 No 53808 crosses the 168yd eight-arch viaduct with a northbound goods. On the extreme right the remains of the GWR Camerton–Limpley Stoke branch's viaduct can be seen, which was demolished some years earlier in about 1958.
Photo: Derek Cross. Date: 29 June 1962.

Apart from the obvious growth of trees on top of its surface, there seems little difference from the former scene: the viaduct's parapets and arches are still in good condition, although the railings could do with a lick of paint. BR have recently sold the structure to a private owner, who, according to some locals, had plans to site camping coaches on the viaduct; this caused a certain amount of consternation! *Date: 17 March 1995.*

25
Midford Viaduct (2)
172 ST 761605

Class 4F 0-6-0 No 44417 on the 15.20 Bath–Templecombe takes the down line onto the double track section which was gained about two-thirds of the way across the viaduct; this also marked the point (3 miles 76 chains from Bath Junction) where the line's gradient went from 1:330 down to 1:60 up. The track and viaduct for the Camerton-Limpley Stoke branch can be seen passing underneath. The roof of the Hope & Anchor Inn is visible above the locomotive.

Signalman Percy Savage's cottage is seen nestling up to the viaduct on the left, in front of which an arm of the Somersetshire Coal Canal ran, as does Cam Brook and the Bath–Frome road. This fine study of Midford was taken from the up inner home bracket signal.
Photo: Ivo Peters. Date: 7 June 1958.

The viaduct remains intact and although the railings have lost most of their white paint, it still manages to look dignified in its retirement. The trackbed remains in reasonable condition, if a little overgrown with weeds and saplings. Surprisingly, little seems to have changed except for the occasional new house being built; however, many of the mature trees have been lost that previously obscured Midford Castle from this viewpoint. The trackbed of the old GWR Camerton branch is now hidden, although by peering over the viaduct, it can still be seen clearly.
Date: 14 June 1985
(revisited 15 March 1995).

26
Midford valley
172 ST 761601

Swinging through the reverse curves just south of Midford, Class 2P No 40563 pilots Standard Class 5 4-6-0 No 73050 on the down 'Pines Express' for Bournemouth. Midford's up outer home signal can just be discerned on the left towards the middle of the train, whilst the tall down advance starter signal can be spotted just beyond. Up trains often had to wait for the single line section from Bath Junction to Midford to clear before proceeding on their journey from here. A lineside telephone was sited at the side of the hut near the signal post to enable footplate crews to call Midford signal box to enquire as to the delay, if they had been held up for a while, as they were ever mindful of the need to keep to correct time.
Photo: Ivo Peters.
Date: 21 May 1956.

The horizon provides a very definite clue as to the location: many features are readily identified. It is noticeable how well defined the trackbed is in this section kept fairly clear, the embankments being regularly cut back with mechanical hedgecutters, as it is used as a farm track. The torched remains of the up outer home signal, together with the concrete base of the lineside hut, are still to be found in the undergrowth. Many of the mature trees have gone and have been usurped by others.
Date: 13 March 1995.

28
Midford valley – Lower Twinhoe
172 ST 756592

BR Standard Class 4MT No 75071 pilots Class 9F 2-10-0 No 92245 with the down 'Pines Express' through the lovely valley near Lower Twinhoe. The line was engineered to follow the course of the old Somersetshire Coal Canal and tramway as closely as possible, hence the severe curvature of the formation. The up distant signal for Midford can be seen above the third coach of the train and halfway round the bend. It was adjacent to this point that the Radstock arm of the Somersetshire Coal Canal ended, to continue from here to Midford as a tramway. This was due to the lack of finance to complete the system, linking it with the Camerton arm, requiring a large flight of locks to be built to take it to a lower level at Midford.

The railway also followed the course of Wellow Brook, situated just a little lower in the valley, which was incorporated into a defence line during the last war; pillboxes and anti-tank obstacles were constructed along its length.
Photo: G.A.Richardson. Date: 9 June 1962.

The line formation that is used as a private farm track extends from Bridge 21 at Wellow to a few chains short of Midford Viaduct; however, casual visitors are not encouraged, partly due to the fact that the local landowner uses much of this stretch for breeding pheasants.

The formation of the old coal canal is set against the hillside immediately to the left of this photograph, but set some ten to fifteen feet above the level of the S&D's trackbed. Note the similarities on the horizon.
Date: 8 June 1985 (revisited 13 March 1995).

27
Midford valley – Lower Twinhoe (Bridge 20)
172 ST 756594

A delightful picture which sums up the beauty of the Midford valley and Lower Twinhoe in particular. This was an excellent location to photograph trains as they swung through the reverse curves in this glorious part of the countryside. Passing over Twinhoe Bridge is Class 4F 0-6-0 No 44102 working a down local and it is captured on film for posterity by Ivo Peters, who was standing on the spoil bank left over from when the railway was built over the tramway. Of amusement is the guard leaning out of the rear coach who seems to be hailing a colleague on an up train, which is passing under Bridge 19 in the background. No doubt he was engaging in some good-natured banter!

The bridge, situated at the 4¾ milepost, marked the end of a half-mile level stretch and then the line started to climb at 1:100 towards Wellow. It was also very near here where the Somersetshire Coal Canal's terminal basin was located, but a little further up the hillside to the rear of where the photographer was standing. *Photo: Ivo Peters. Date: 3 July 1957.*

Although the bush in the foreground is preventing a good view of the bridge, the parapets are readily identifiable, as are the features on the hills in the background. The trackbed is in very good condition in this section and constantly used by a local farmer.
Date: 13 March 1995.

WELLOW–RADSTOCK

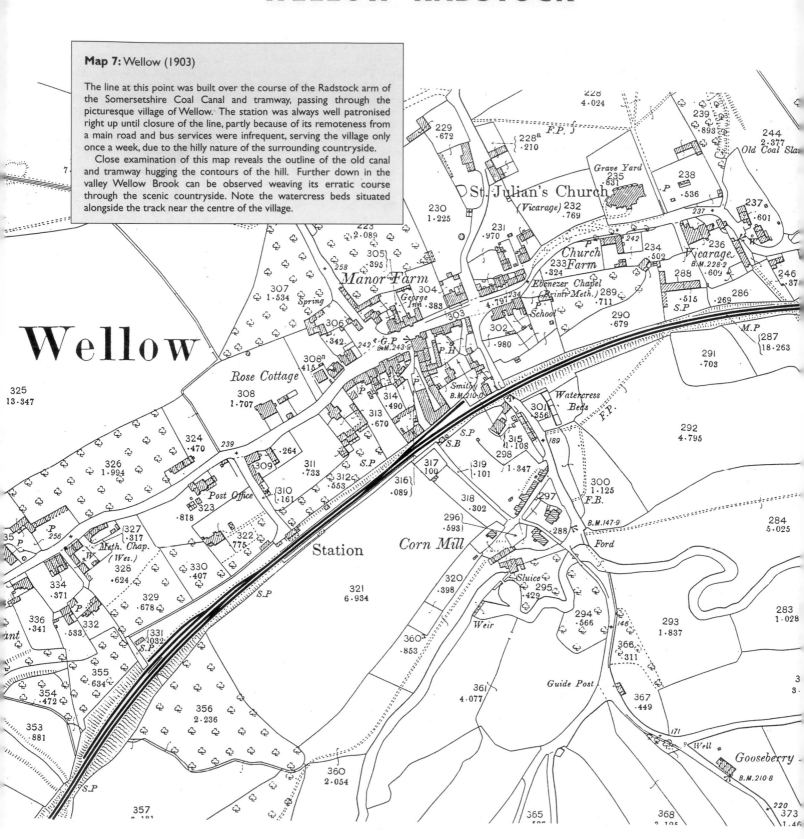

Map 7: Wellow (1903)

The line at this point was built over the course of the Radstock arm of the Somersetshire Coal Canal and tramway, passing through the picturesque village of Wellow. The station was always well patronised right up until closure of the line, partly because of its remoteness from a main road and bus services were infrequent, serving the village only once a week, due to the hilly nature of the surrounding countryside.

Close examination of this map reveals the outline of the old canal and tramway hugging the contours of the hill. Further down in the valley Wellow Brook can be observed weaving its erratic course through the scenic countryside. Note the watercress beds situated alongside the track near the centre of the village.

29
Wellow Viaduct (No 22)
172 ST 746583

On a cloudless summer's day the up 'Pines Express', hauled by 2P No 40564 and rebuilt West Country class Pacific No 34046, *Braunton*, passes over the four arches of Wellow Viaduct, seen towards the middle of the train. The viaduct spanned a small cleft in the hillside, through which the Wellow–Hinton Charterhouse road passed. The tower of the fourteenth-century St Julian's church can be seen dominating the small village, which is surrounded by hills. This shot was taken from a favourite vantage point for many photographers, being the farm overbridge (No 21) just off the Hinton Charterhouse road. *Photo: Ivo Peters. Date: 18 June 1960.*

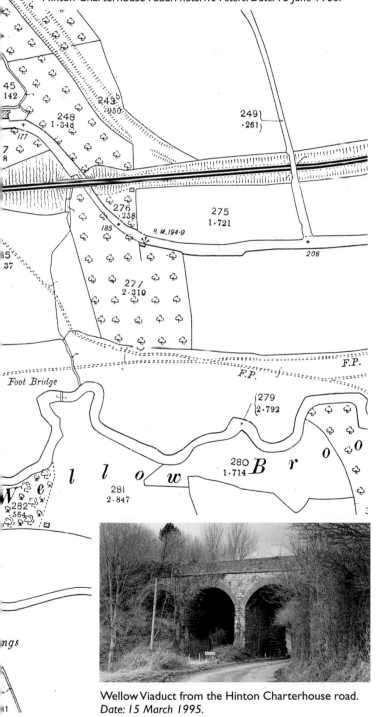

Again taken on a March day, albeit in a strong gale, the church tower still commands the view on the hill, but the area in the foreground has changed considerably and the Wellow Trekking Centre, complete with a children's play area, has been established here along with an associated company, Horsecroft Composts and Manures; previously a piggery occupied the site. A mass of bushes and young trees now cover the embankment on the up side of the formation: a vast change from the well manicured railway cutting of 1960.

The viaduct remains in good condition, but could possibly be under threat of demolition in the years to come if it is ever deemed necessary to widen the road, as the structure creates a blind corner. *Date: 15 March 1995.*

Wellow Viaduct from the Hinton Charterhouse road. *Date: 15 March 1995.*

Wellow station
172 ST 739581

A view of Wellow station and village taken from the down starting signal shows the layout to good advantage. The main building on the up platform was constructed of grey limestone and a substantial shelter built in the centre. At the western end of the platform a wooden lever cabin was sited for operating the goods yard, which was released from the signal box; at the eastern end a small metal shed was used as a lamp room. A wooden shelter was provided on the down platform, access to which was via a timber level crossing at the western end of the station. The 18-lever signal box, just visible in this photograph, was sited a few chains east on the down side of the line. Wellow opened on 20 July 1874 and remained so until closure of the line, but goods traffic ceased on 10 June 1963. The station's neat and tidy appearance was typical of the high standard associated with the S&D. *Photo: R.C.Riley. Date: 6 July 1959.*

The former station building was extended and converted into a private dwelling by the artist Peter Blake who owned it for some years. It featured in *Living Homes* magazine in an article on stations converted into dwellings. At the time of writing the property was unoccupied and offered for sale, due to the last owner's illness. A boundary fence and gate have been erected across the western end of the station, but the original railings are still clearly visible on the down side, having survived the passage of time and a replica station sign has been erected, but is in poor condition. The former lamp room now serves as a garden shed. A very attractive garden has been created on the trackbed, with a lawn laid on the infilled section between the platforms.
Date: 13 March 1995.

A close-up of the former station building and platforms. *Date: 13 March 1995.*

The last signal box to survive on the line once housed an 18-lever frame. Peter Blake owned the structure for many years until he sold it in the late 1980s. Now it is inhabited; a well designed and tasteful extension has been built, which has caused some controversy in the village and was recently an item featured on the local television news.
Date: 13 March 1995.

31
Wellow goods yard
172 ST 738580

A superb study of 7F 2-8-0 No 53809 as it trundles past Wellow goods yard with the 17.00 down freight. For a small station, the yard was quite well equipped and had a loading gauge and two sidings, one of which extended for some distance, as seen in this picture. An excellent view is had of the station in the background, also of the signal box and village, dominated by St Julian's church. Note the up home bracket signal on the left, in front of which the parapets of Bridge 24 can be seen.

Although the goods yard closed on 10 June 1963, the sidings and crossover remained in use until 30 June 1964. *Photo: Ivo Peters. Date: 8 May 1954.*

Part of the former goods yard is now used as a village car park and remains clear as far as the small underbridge (No 24), where a fence has been erected, to the west of which undergrowth and small trees have taken over, although a path has been cut which zig-zags through it and is walkable with care. Note the church in the background, which provides some continuity.

The line formation behind this vantage point has been erased and landscaped to form part of a large sloping field. However, Bridge 25 survives just beyond, but the cutting to the west side of it is largely overgrown and partly infilled.
Date: 13 March 1995.

> **COMMENT:** *This previously unprinted photograph would probably have not met with Ivo Peters' strict criteria for publication: the engineers have carelessly left sleepers alongside the goods yard siding on the left, making the scene a little too untidy — especially since the ends have been painted white!*

Wellow valley
172 ST 733576

South-west of the village, the S&D continued to snake through the lovely Wellow valley, following closely the route of the old tramway laid along the course of the former Somersetshire Coal Canal; its remnants can be seen immediately to the right of the railway line.

Perched on the brow of an adjacent hillside along the side of which the line has been cut, Ivo Peters has a commanding view. BR Class 5 4-6-0 No 73050 on the 16.45 up freight from Evercreech Junction is captured on camera as it swings through the valley, which is bathed in bright sunlight on a glorious summer's evening.
Photo: Ivo Peters. Date: 8 July 1958.

Evening shadows steal across the beautiful landscape of the Wellow valley. The line in the foreground has been obscured by trees and bushes, hiding a large poultry unit, which has been built on the trackbed; its roof is just visible through the trees. This location is a haven for many rabbits, which find cover in the thick undergrowth on the embankment. Note the remnants of the line formation in the middle distance, winding its way round the hillside towards Shoscombe and Single Hill.
Date: 25 June 1985 (revisited 13 March 1995).

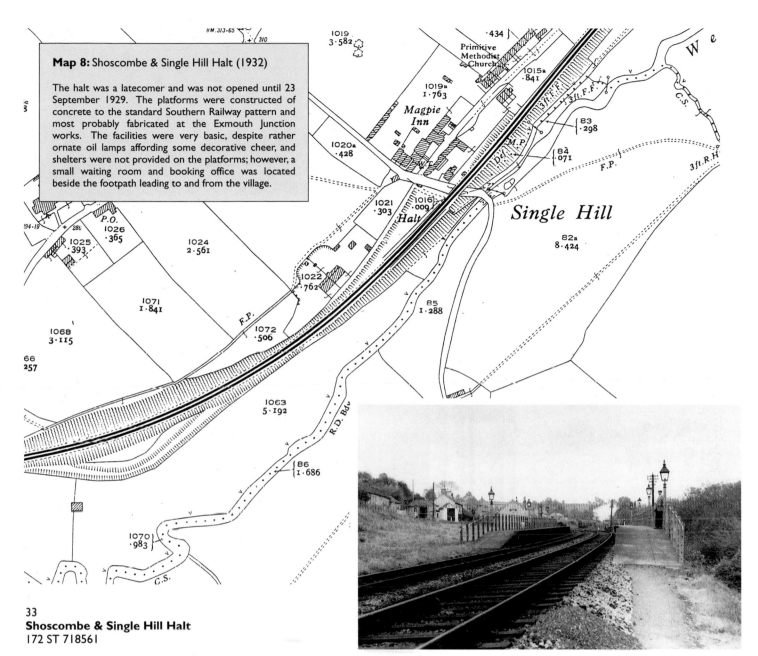

33
Shoscombe & Single Hill Halt
172 ST 718561

"If there is anyone for here – this is it!" called out the guard on an up local one dark night, as it drew into the isolated halt of Shoscombe & Single Hill. Legend has it a local man used to walk back along the line from Radstock after a night out in the town, where he played in a silver band, thus saving a considerable amount of puff by not having to climb the steep hills which surrounded the village; it also reduced the risk of getting lost if he over-imbibed, but not of being squashed by a train!

In this view, a train for Bath has just departed and is seen disappearing round the bend towards Wellow.
Photo: C.L.Caddy. Date: 18 May 1963.

The halt has been completely demolished and the site where it once stood has been made into two or three small paddocks. Apart from one or two cottages, the only reference to the former scene are two concrete posts in the middle of the picture, which mark the top of a flight of steps which led from the road below to the down side platform and survive today. *Date: 13 March 1995.*

Map 9: Paglinch Farm (1904)

The Radstock disaster of 1876 was by far the worst accident that occurred in the line's history. It happened on the night of 7 August when an up relief from Wimborne and a return excursion from Bath met in a head-on collision near Foxcote. In the crash, 13 people lost their lives.

Paglinch Farm's granary had the dubious honour of being used to lay out the bodies of the unfortunate victims for identification purposes. For reference, both the point of impact and the barn have been highlighted on this map. Paglinch Farm's former granary still stands and is virtually unchanged since the time of the accident.

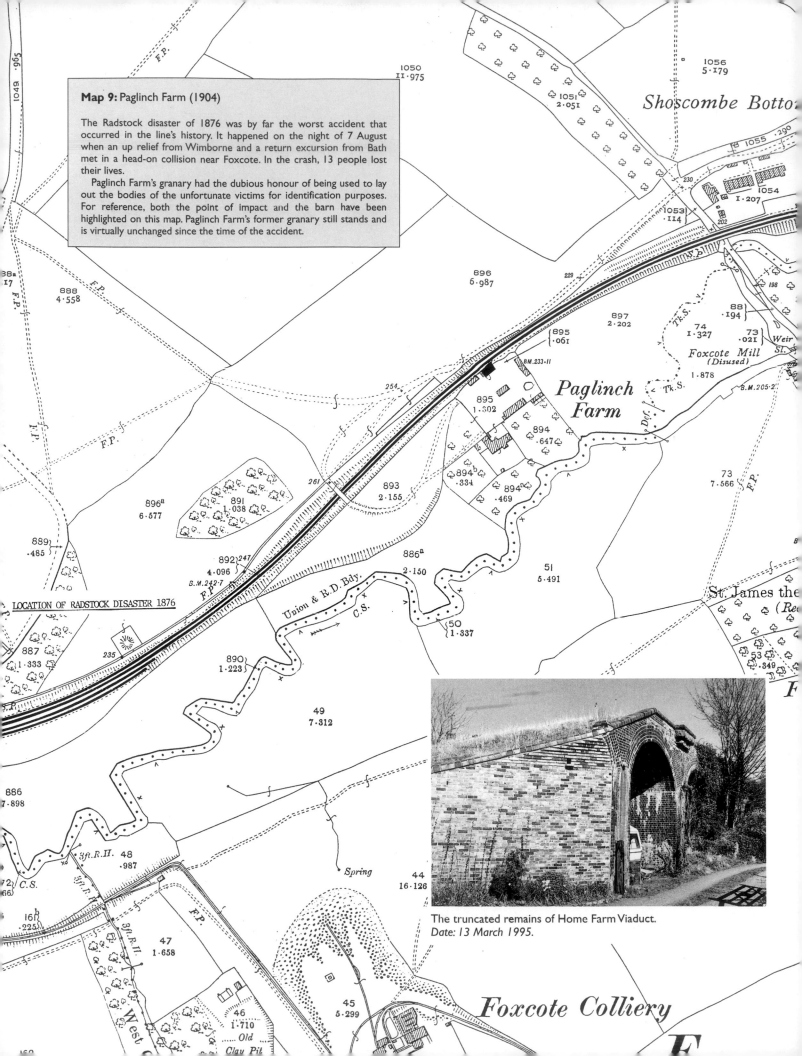

Shoscombe Botto[m]

Paglinch Farm

Foxcote Mill (Disused)

St. James the [...] (Re[...]

LOCATION OF RADSTOCK DISASTER 1876

Foxcote Colliery

Old Clay Pit

West [...]

Spring

Union & R.D. Bdy.

Weir

The truncated remains of Home Farm Viaduct.
Date: 13 March 1995.

34
Paglinch Farm
172 ST 711557

Working a southbound goods, S&D 7F No 53809 passes the granary building of Paglinch Farm. This was the barn in which the bodies of the 13 victims of the 1876 Radstock disaster were laid out for identification. This sad tale had an unfortunate twist to it, for the return excursion from Bath, in which the people were killed, was chosen in preference to them returning to Radstock via the GWR line from Bristol, which they had been visiting that day. *Photo: R.E. Toop.*
Date: 27 December 1961.

Today the barn is unchanged from 1961 and has probably remained so since it was built. Note that the yard gate seen in the original photograph is now propped up against the wall and the line of railway fence posts can be observed beyond the International fore-end loader attachment. The wooden posts carry an electric fence to restrain cattle and are actually positioned on the line of the down track's nearside rail and apparently were very difficult to drive in.

Home Farm Viaduct (No 31), located at map reference 172 ST 715559, a low structure of six arches, mostly still stands. In 1990, the low arch over the narrow lane near Paglinch Farm was demolished, along with the parapet walls, but the remaining structure was repointed to a high standard and is used by farmers for storage. Photographs showing this viaduct in S&D days have thus far proved elusive.

Paglinch Farm was for sale at the time of visiting in 1995.
Date: 2 May 1985 (revisited 13 March 1995).

COMMENT: *In 1985 it took three visits here to effect a satisfactory shot, mostly due to adverse weather conditions: on the first occasion my car's sump received severe punishment inflicted by the deeply-rutted farm track; on the second visit the Volvo was up to its hub caps in liquefied bovine fertiliser – ah well, such are the trials of being a railway photographer!*

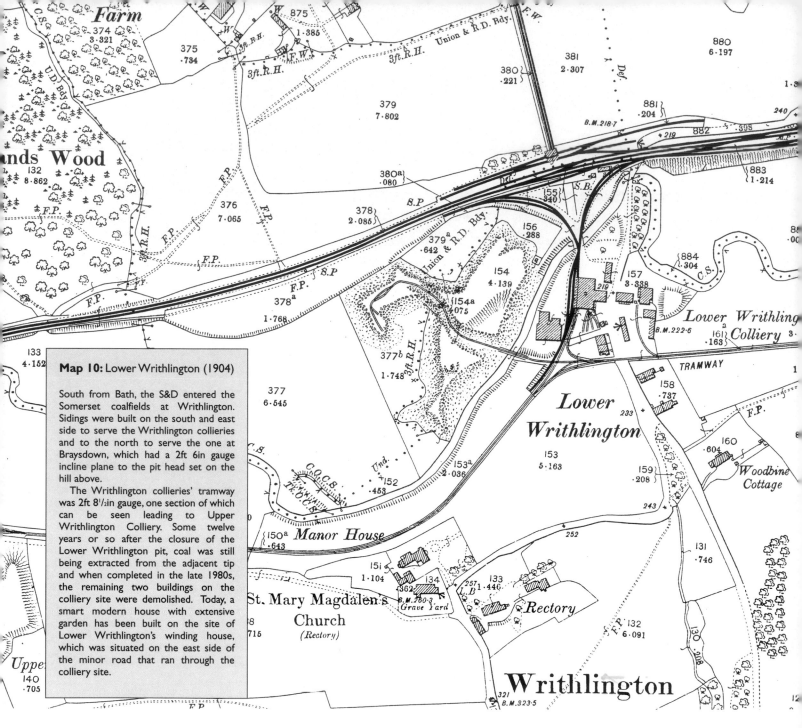

Map 10: Lower Writhlington (1904)

South from Bath, the S&D entered the Somerset coalfields at Writhlington. Sidings were built on the south and east side to serve the Writhlington collieries and to the north to serve the one at Braysdown, which had a 2ft 6in gauge incline plane to the pit head set on the hill above.

The Writhlington collieries' tramway was 2ft 8½in gauge, one section of which can be seen leading to Upper Writhlington Colliery. Some twelve years or so after the closure of the Lower Writhlington pit, coal was still being extracted from the adjacent tip and when completed in the late 1980s, the remaining two buildings on the colliery site were demolished. Today, a smart modern house with extensive garden has been built on the site of Lower Writhlington's winding house, which was situated on the east side of the minor road that ran through the colliery site.

35 *(Opposite)*
Lower Writhlington Colliery
172 ST 706555

BR Class 9F 2-10-0 No 92000 passes Writhlington Colliery with a Bournemouth to Bristol train. Using large engines rostered on such a light duty two years later did not help the cost-effectiveness of the S&D line.

Note the pithead winding wheels of Writhlington Colliery, together with trucks being loaded with coal. The signal box controlled the colliery sidings. The remains of Braysdown Colliery sidings can be seen to the right of the bridge (No 33). An incline plane from the pit at the top of the hill was used to take coal down to the screens below. *Photo: Derek Cross. Date: 15 August 1961.*

Writhlington Colliery was finally closed in 1973, but coal extraction was still taking place in the mid-1980s: some twelve to thirteen per cent of it being recovered from the tip in the background. The north Derbyshire firm of Burrows, who specialise in coal extraction, used the Barnaby Medium Washer System in the recovery of reasonable quality coking coal from the tip. On completion of the work, the slag heap was landscaped and planted with numerous trees, which in the years since have become well established. The profile of the tip has been considerably reduced as a result of the extraction and it is difficult to realise that it was only some twenty-two years ago the colliery was still in use.

The line formation to the west side of Bridge 33 has been left piled with junk and debris after New Age travellers recently vacated the area, but the the east side is still in good condition. It is ironic that the last section of S&D track to be worked was between Radstock and Writhlington sidings, lingering on until late 1975 and into the early months of 1976, when it was finally lifted. This followed the Somerset & Dorset Railway Museum Trust's relocation to Washford on the West Somerset Railway, after its attempt to preserve the section here failed, having centred its activities at Radstock North. *Date: 13 March 1995.*

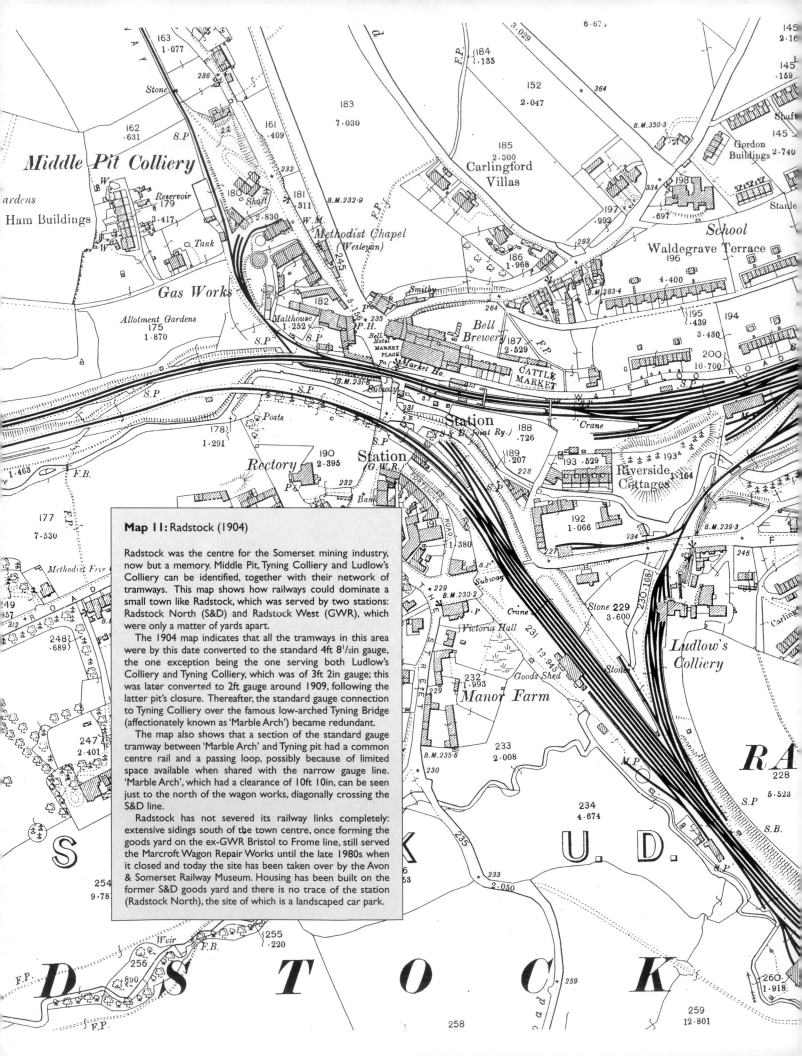

Map 11: Radstock (1904)

Radstock was the centre for the Somerset mining industry, now but a memory. Middle Pit, Tyning Colliery and Ludlow's Colliery can be identified, together with their network of tramways. This map shows how railways could dominate a small town like Radstock, which was served by two stations: Radstock North (S&D) and Radstock West (GWR), which were only a matter of yards apart.

The 1904 map indicates that all the tramways in this area were by this date converted to the standard 4ft 8½in gauge, the one exception being the one serving both Ludlow's Colliery and Tyning Colliery, which was of 3ft 2in gauge; this was later converted to 2ft gauge around 1909, following the latter pit's closure. Thereafter, the standard gauge connection to Tyning Colliery over the famous low-arched Tyning Bridge (affectionately known as 'Marble Arch') became redundant.

The map also shows that a section of the standard gauge tramway between 'Marble Arch' and Tyning pit had a common centre rail and a passing loop, possibly because of limited space available when shared with the narrow gauge line. 'Marble Arch', which had a clearance of 10ft 10in, can be seen just to the north of the wagon works, diagonally crossing the S&D line.

Radstock has not severed its railway links completely: extensive sidings south of the town centre, once forming the goods yard on the ex-GWR Bristol to Frome line, still served the Marcroft Wagon Repair Works until the late 1980s when it closed and today the site has been taken over by the Avon & Somerset Railway Museum. Housing has been built on the former S&D goods yard and there is no trace of the station (Radstock North), the site of which is a landscaped car park.

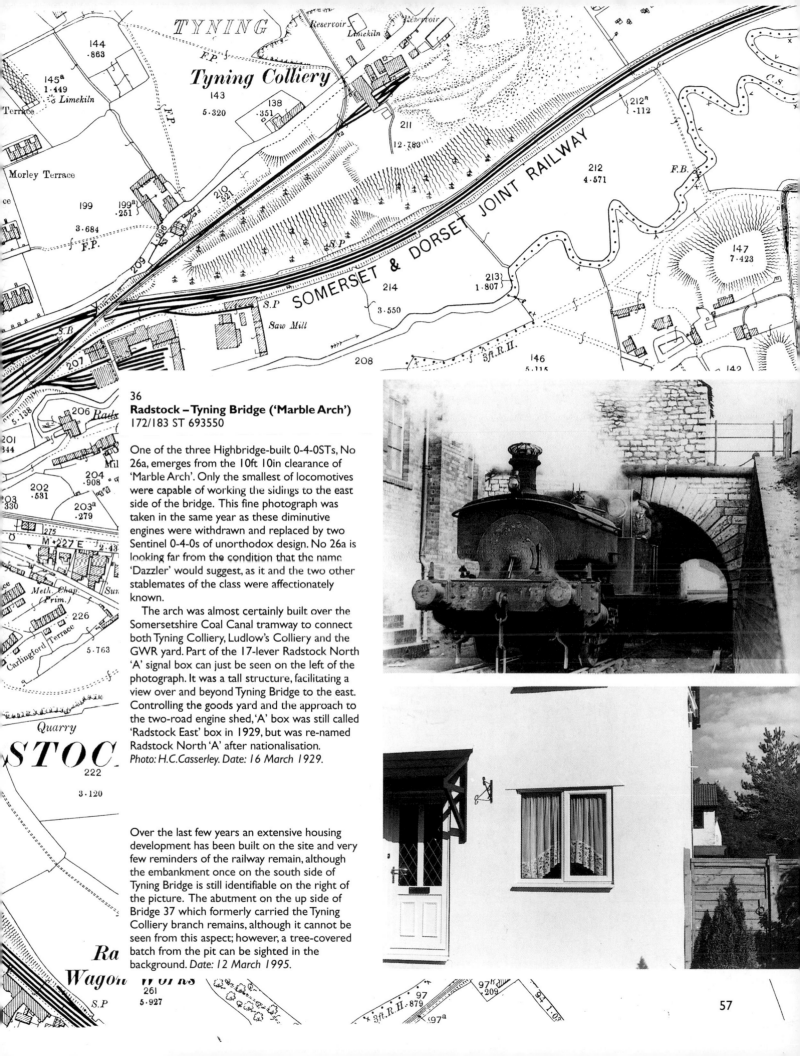

36
Radstock – Tyning Bridge ('Marble Arch')
172/183 ST 693550

One of the three Highbridge-built 0-4-0STs, No 26a, emerges from the 10ft 10in clearance of 'Marble Arch'. Only the smallest of locomotives were capable of working the sidings to the east side of the bridge. This fine photograph was taken in the same year as these diminutive engines were withdrawn and replaced by two Sentinel 0-4-0s of unorthodox design. No 26a is looking far from the condition that the name 'Dazzler' would suggest, as it and the two other stablemates of the class were affectionately known.

The arch was almost certainly built over the Somersetshire Coal Canal tramway to connect both Tyning Colliery, Ludlow's Colliery and the GWR yard. Part of the 17-lever Radstock North 'A' signal box can just be seen on the left of the photograph. It was a tall structure, facilitating a view over and beyond Tyning Bridge to the east. Controlling the goods yard and the approach to the two-road engine shed, 'A' box was still called 'Radstock East' box in 1929, but was re-named Radstock North 'A' after nationalisation.
Photo: H.C.Casserley. Date: 16 March 1929.

Over the last few years an extensive housing development has been built on the site and very few reminders of the railway remain, although the embankment once on the south side of Tyning Bridge is still identifiable on the right of the picture. The abutment on the up side of Bridge 37 which formerly carried the Tyning Colliery branch remains, although it cannot be seen from this aspect; however, a tree-covered batch from the pit can be sighted in the background. *Date: 12 March 1995.*

**Radstock goods yard
and shed**
172/183 ST 693550

Class 2P 4-4-0 No 40564 assists BR Standard Class 5 4-6-0 No 73051 on the up 'Pines' relief, passing an unidentified 'Jinty' 0-6-0T in the yard and S&D 7F 2-8-0 No 53809 waiting on the down road with a goods, and heads towards Bath past Radstock North 'A' signal box, the embankment to the side of which this panoramic view was taken. The stone-built engine shed, once the home of the 'Dazzlers', is on the left of the picture; until 1975/6 it remained in use, latterly by the Somerset & Dorset Railway Museum Trust to house its locomotives. A well-known Radstock landmark in the form of the Co-operative Society's building is seen in the background; next to it is one of the station's footbridges, which can just be spotted over the 2-8-0. The stone-built terraced miners' cottages were built to a design characteristic of this area. *Photo: R.E.Toop. Date: 8 April 1958.*

This comparison was taken from exactly the same position of the old Radstock North 'A' signal box, but one would never realise a railway ran through here if visiting the area for the first time. New housing has totally enveloped the site, but the cottages seen in the original photograph remain unaffected, although they cannot be viewed from this aspect.
Date: 12 March 1995.

38
Radstock North 'A' signal box and goods yard
172/183 ST 692550

Hauled by 2P No 40569 and West Country class Pacific No 34107 *Blandford,* the 07.35 (SO) Nottingham (Midland)–Bournemouth train sweeps past Radstock North 'A' box in the background; Tyning Bridge is just visible to its right. Of interest is a slag heap of the former Tyning Colliery poking above the row of cottages on the left. An older slag heap seen over the train has already been landscaped and is crowned with trees. The signal box closed on 23 August 1964, just over two months after goods traffic was withdrawn on 15 June. Of note is the tablet catcher on the cabside of No 40569 The train was scheduled to pass Radstock at 12.50 on this busy high-summer's Saturday. *Photo: R.E. Toop. Date: 2 August 1958.*

Sheltered housing, almost appropriately named Pine Court, was built here in the mid-1980s and apart from the connotations the name implies, there is no trace or evidence that a railway ever existed. *Date: 12 March 1995.*

39
Radstock North station
172/183 ST 689550

A view looking west through the station. the 32-lever Radstock North 'B' box is in the background and sandwiched between it and the platforms is the wall of the subway (Bridge 40). The main buildings were situated on the up side, whilst the down side had only a wooden shelter. The station once had two footbridges (Nos 38 and 39) and it was from near the site of the latter, which had been demolished some years before, this view was taken; the structure in the immediate foreground is the porters' cabin. Bridge 38 carried a footpath over the railway from Waterloo Road, which ran parallel to it on the right of the photograph. The building facing Waterloo Road just to the rear of the station is Market House behind which, and in the same complex, is the former Oakhill brewery; a public lavatory (with round windows) is on the extreme right. The roof of the Waldegrave Arms Hotel on the A367 road is seen over them and the station buildings. Just a few yards south of here was the GWR station, whose line ran parallel to the S&D's across the main road. *Photo: R.C.Riley. Date: 12 July 1961.*

The area once occupied by the station has been totally landscaped and a shoppers' car park built. The building on the right has not changed to any great degree and acts as a positive clue to the location. Of interest is a winding wheel from one of the local collieries, which stands as a monument to a long mining tradition for which this area, centred on the town, was once famous. The station was demolished in the late 1970s and the subway filled in.
Date: 12 March 1995.

40
Radstock – A367 level crossing
172/183 ST 689550

This level crossing marked the start of the southward climb of the Mendips; it also caused considerable traffic congestion, especially since the GWR Bristol–Frome line crossed the main road within yards south of this point as well. Everything has to stop to allow the passage across the A367 road of Class 2P 4-4-0 No 40563, piloting West Country class Pacific No 34108 *Wincanton* on a Bournemouth to Liverpool working, which drifts down the 1:55 gradient and into Radstock North. The West Country had almost a further nine years in service before being withdrawn at Salisbury in June 1967, having been rebuilt in April 1961. No 40563, a Templecombe locomotive, was not so long-lived and was scrapped at Crewe in July 1962, having been taken out of service two months earlier.

Of interest in this photograph, taken from the steps of Radstock North 'B' signal box, is the trackbed of the tramway (seen behind the railings in the foreground), which ran under the main line to Middle Pit Colliery. The site also marked the basin of the Somersetshire Coal Canal. *Photo: Derek Cross. Date: August 1958.*

Despite the fact that there are no level crossings to contend with, the area is still subjected to heavy traffic congestion in the centre of the town, as it is also the site of a busy multiple road junction. This comparison shows clearly the trackbed of the S&D on the far side of the road, which now marks the start of a linear park sponsored by Wansdyke District Council; it leads to North Somerset Viaduct, commonly known as 'Five Arches', where the line once crossed the GWR and the old Welton tramway a few hundred yards distant from this point. Note the old railings that once separated the line from the tramway. *Date: 30 May 1985 (revisited 12 March 1995).*

41
Radstock – Bridge 43
172/183 ST 686549

Traversing one of the bridges built over the former Welton Tramway, Class 7F No 53810, with driver Barber in charge, makes a spirited start on the 1:55 gradient of the long southbound climb of the Mendips and has assistance from a 'Jinty' 0-6-0T banking at the rear, which is just passing over the level crossing at Radstock North station, working hard to elevate the 12.35 down freight to Masbury Summit. In about a half-mile, the gradient will steepen to 1:50 on the climb to Midsomer Norton, which will surely test both locomotives on this long train. Radstock market building is clearly visible in the background. The GWR's Bristol–Frome line is on the right and it was near this point a connection was made between the two systems on 6 March 1966, the last day of operation, by slewing the S&D's down line, which facilitated Writhlington Colliery to be served by a rail link until closure of the pit in 1973.
Photo: Ivo Peters. Date: 9 April 1955.

Both the trackbeds of the S&D and GWR lines form part of the linear park and extend over and under 'Five Arches', with links between them. The land between the two former railway lines has been made into a children's playground and adventure area, now known as the Tom Huyton Memorial Park, which can just be spotted between the trees. On the day of this visit, it was packed with families enjoying a day out on this fine Sunday afternoon. Note the houses on the horizon providing some continuity and the old Welton Tramway bridge in the foreground.
Date: 12 March 1995.

Part of the children's adventure play area of the Tom Huyton Memorial Park and the S&D's formation behind.
Date: 12 March 1995.

North Somerset Viaduct (No 44) – 'Five Arches'
183 ST 678549

Class 7F No 53809 2-8-0 is seen with the 17.00 down goods to Evercreech working hard, unassisted, on the steep gradient towards Midsomer Norton and passes over 'Five Arches', as S&D railwaymen knew it, about a half-mile west of Radstock. The GWR's North Somerset line sweeps under the main arch on a sharp curve.
Photo: Ivo Peters. Date: 3 April 1956.

'Five Arches' survives in good order, having been repaired by Wansdyke District Council in 1993 and now has a plaque fixed over its main arch to commemorate this and the S&D railway itself. The trackbed of the S&D between the bridge and Radstock town centre is in particularly good condition and track aligning monuments embedded at half-chain intervals can be found along the section. Note the remains of the GWR signal post on the left of the picture.

Apart from the fact that the bridge over Somerdale Road was demolished in 1982 and reduced to its abutments only, a scheme to extend the linear park beyond this towards Midsomer Norton has been in the offing for several years, but has been delayed at the planning stage with several obstacles to overcome, including possible development of parcels of land. Doubts have also been raised about the stability of the slag heap adjacent to the S&D trackbed and the former Norton Hill Colliery, the site of which now forms an industrial estate mainly occupied by a large printing works and an ink manufacturer. *Date: 12 March 1995.*

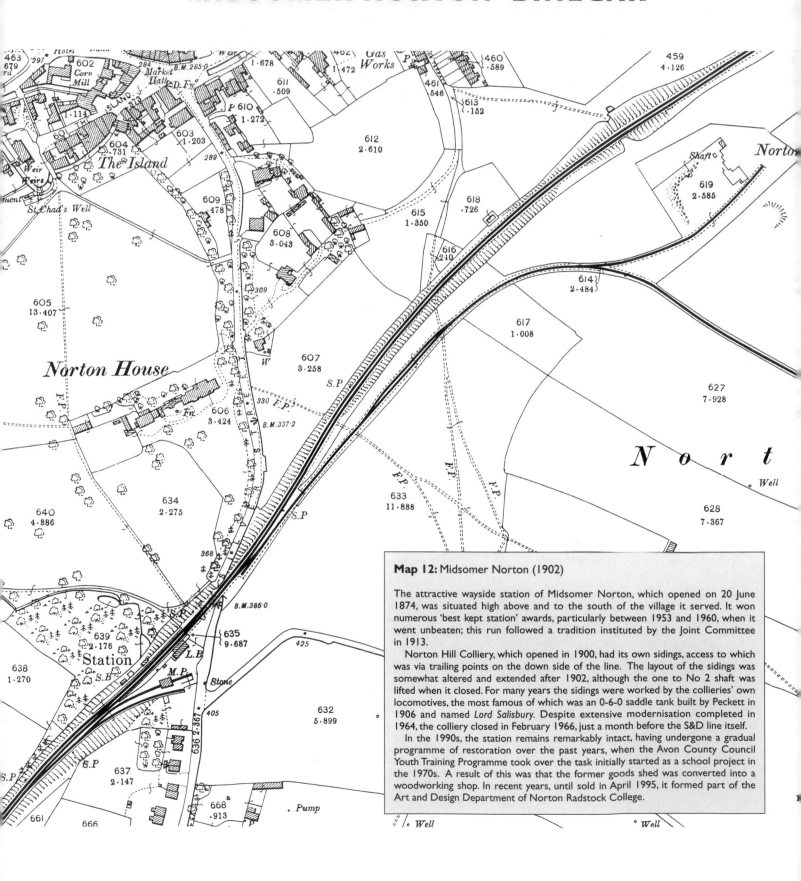

Map 12: Midsomer Norton (1902)

The attractive wayside station of Midsomer Norton, which opened on 20 June 1874, was situated high above and to the south of the village it served. It won numerous 'best kept station' awards, particularly between 1953 and 1960, when it went unbeaten; this run followed a tradition instituted by the Joint Committee in 1913.

Norton Hill Colliery, which opened in 1900, had its own sidings, access to which was via trailing points on the down side of the line. The layout of the sidings was somewhat altered and extended after 1902, although the one to No 2 shaft was lifted when it closed. For many years the sidings were worked by the collieries' own locomotives, the most famous of which was an 0-6-0 saddle tank built by Peckett in 1906 and named *Lord Salisbury*. Despite extensive modernisation completed in 1964, the colliery closed in February 1966, just a month before the S&D line itself.

In the 1990s, the station remains remarkably intact, having undergone a gradual programme of restoration over the past years, when the Avon County Council Youth Training Programme took over the task initially started as a school project in the 1970s. A result of this was that the former goods shed was converted into a woodworking shop. In recent years, until sold in April 1995, it formed part of the Art and Design Department of Norton Radstock College.

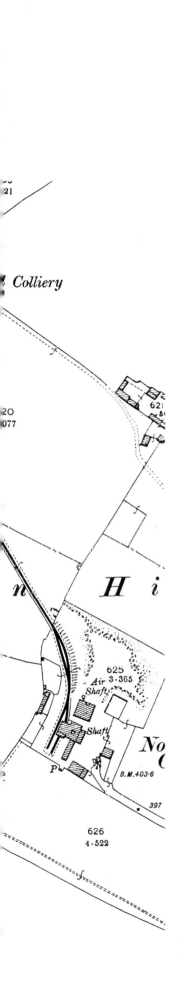

43
Midsomer Norton – Norton Hill
183 ST 665537

Unassisted, Class 7F No 53807 pounds up the 1:50 gradient towards Midsomer Norton with the 08.55 down goods and passes Norton Hill Colliery sidings and the gated entrance to them. The Welton district of Midsomer Norton is seen in the valley below. Judging from the other LSWR-built signal on the up side of the line and seen over the wagons, another train is due to pass in the opposite direction. The 7F had just over another year's work before being withdrawn in October 1964. *Photo: Ivo Peters. Date: 28 September 1963.*

The bank on which Ivo Peters was standing now forms the gardens of houses built over the last few years on the hillside above, whilst factories cover the site of the colliery. The wooden fence marks the former railway boundary line and a post of the old colliery sidings' gate can just be spotted over the greenhouse; both survive, but the other is hidden from view by undergrowth. It is quite noticeable from this comparison how Midsomer Norton and Welton have expanded: there has been a rapid expansion of building development in the area over the last decade or two. *Date: 12 March 1995.*

44
Midsomer Norton station (1)
183 ST 664537

A sad day for Midsomer Norton: spectators standing on the down platform witness the passing of the last down 'Pines Express', with Class 9F No 92220 *Evening Star* in charge and crewed by driver Peter Guy and fireman Ronald Hyde. The train is passing over Bridge 48 spanning Silver Street (B3355) adjacent to the station, whose main building, located on the down platform, can just be seen on the right. Not only was the 'Pines' diverted from the route after this day, but all other through trains, apart from the occasional excursions, were also removed, thus leaving the S&D with only a local service. *Photo: Ivo Peters.*
Date: 8 September 1962.

The platforms and building provide the instant clue, but much of the former scene has changed: the horizon is now crowned with modern housing; many of the mature trees seen in the previous photograph have been cut down and the bridge has long since been demolished, partly because of the very restricted headroom it afforded, which would not have been sufficient clearance for modern lorries plying their trade to and from the nearby industrial estates. The area beyond the road has been partly landscaped, but the formation of the S&D is just visible to the left of the street lamp, immediately to the right of which are the remnants of Norton Hill Colliery's sidings. *Date: 12 March 1995.*

The former station building and goods shed seen from the embankment on the other side of the main road. *Date: 12 March 1995.*

45

Midsomer Norton station (2)
183 ST 664536

The 12-coach train of the 10.38 (SO) Manchester–Bournemouth is brought up through Midsomer Norton by a pair of 4F 0-6-0s, Nos 44557 and 44559, struggling to haul their heavy load up the 1:50 gradient to the station, which eased to 1:300 through it, only to steepen again to 1:53 once past the platforms. By the appearance of the smoke issuing from the exhaust of the train engine, its fireman is hard at work to ensure keeping a full head of steam on the southbound assault of the Mendips, which is far from over at this point.

The attractive 16-lever signal box proves an ideal vantage point for the signalman to give the train crews a cheery wave as they pass by. The stone-built goods shed can be seen to good advantage in this photograph; it ceased to handle traffic on 15 June 1964, when the yard closed. *Photo: Ivo Peters. Date: 6 August 1955.*

The afternoon sun shines on the former goods shed and station building, which had undergone renovation in the mid-1980s with some £1,500 alone spent on refurbishing the nearest chimney. At the time this photograph was taken, the station building and goods shed still formed part of the Art and Design Department of Norton Radstock College, who were in the process of clearing it out prior to disposing of the site. The up platform cannot be seen in this view and is obscured by branches and undergrowth. *Date: 12 March 1995.*

46
Midsomer Norton station (3)
183 ST 664536

BR Class 4 2-6-0 No 76015 and BR Class 5 4-6-0 No 73050 pass through Midsomer Norton station with a Whit Monday excursion to Bournemouth from Bristol. Train travel at this time was still a popular way for the public to enjoy a day out to the seaside. Taken from fairly well up on the steep embankment, this vantage point affords a good panoramic view of the station layout; note a van is in the goods shed siding awaiting collection and just visible in the background are many trucks which await shunting at Norton Hill Colliery sidings.

The station underwent several name changes in its existence: it was 'Midsomer Norton' until 16 October 1898, then 'Midsomer Norton & Welton' until 26 September 1949; thereafter it became 'Midsomer Norton Upper' (passenger station) and from 25 September 1950 'Midsomer Norton South' (goods depot).
Photo: Ivo Peters. Date: 5 June 1960.

From the same vantage point near the loading gauge which still survives, nothing much can be seen of the station, except the up platform and wooden shelter, which has been allowed to deteriorate since being renovated in the 1980s.
Date: 12 March 1995.

COMMENT: *In 1985 two visits had to be made to this site to clear undergrowth and prune overhanging branches in order to obtain a near comparison, which was finally achieved by propping up a pair of steps with a plank of wood against a steep bank – having fallen off them during a dummy run; however, no damage was done, save to my dignity!*

In 1995 no such drastic pruning was undertaken to obtain this limited view.

The loading gauge is still visible above the spoil heap placed around it when the trackbed between the platforms was re-excavated, having previously been filled in. Note the station in the background. *Date: 12 March 1995.*

47
Chilcompton Tunnel cutting
183 ST 652523

Recently back from a works overhaul at Derby, 2P 4-4-0 No 40568, built in 1928, pilots West Country class 4-6-2 No 34093 *Saunton*, then just two years old, on the down 'Pines' relief as they climb up the 1:53 gradient and pass through the steep-sided cutting leading to Chilcompton Tunnel. Midsomer Norton lay back around the curve seen in the far distance.

This was one of Ivo Peters' favourite locations and certainly provided him with a fine vantage point from which to photograph steam in its element and full glory, working hard on the southbound assault of the Mendips. *Photo: Ivo Peters. Date: 16 June 1951.*

Thousands of tons of infilling with industrial and other waste covered with top soil have returned the land to a meadow, which it was a hundred and twenty years or so ago, making the location very difficult to pinpoint accurately. Just a fraction of the line formation is still visible sweeping around the bend in the background towards Midsomer Norton. A test of observation is to spot various trees that can be identified as the same as those in the 1951 photograph, although many look dissimilar after the passage of 34 years.
Date: 29 May 1985 (revisited 2 March 1995).

COMMENT: *When here in 1985, there was a large bull attending his cows just out of sight in the foreground, so while he was fully engaged in these pressing duties, I took advantage of his preoccupation and sat on the grass awaiting the sun to reappear before taking this photograph!*

48
Chilcompton Tunnel
183 ST 652522

Templecombe stabled BR Class 4 4-6-0 No 75007, carrying a temporary shed plate on the smokebox, having recently been allocated from 81F Oxford MPD, bursts from the 66yd tunnel with the 16.37 down stopping train from Bath. It is quite noticeable how the use of different materials used in repairs over the years have created a patchwork effect on the portals' stone facing. Clearly portrayed in this shot is the limited clearance the tunnel afforded to trains; seemingly no greater than both those of Devonshire and Combe Down at Bath. The twin bores of Chilcompton Tunnel were a reminder that the S&D was built as a single track and later doubled; its contemporaries at Bath never were, although plans had been drawn up to do so. *Photo: Ivo Peters. Date: 14 September 1963.*

A photographer has to have an element of luck on occasions and this time it is a late afternoon's sun casting a shadow across the up portal, which is virtually at the same angle and position as in the original picture! Midsomer Norton & District Rifle Club have converted the up bore into a 25yd range, whilst the down side is sometimes used by a farmer as a storage and implement shed. Because the cutting on the north side is completely filled in, it is impossible to walk right through the tunnel's one open bore. A gravel track has been hewn into the embankment leading from the road above and the area in front of the portals is kept in a clean and tidy condition. Chilcompton Bank is kept fairly clear and often used for grazing cattle or sheep. *Date: 12 March 1985 (revisited 2 March 1995).*

49
Chilcompton Bank – Redan Bridge (No 51)
183 ST 649515

Rounding the curve on the 1:50 gradient of Chilcompton Bank, Class 4 2-6-0 No 76006 hauls the 13.10 Bath to Bournemouth train over Redan Bridge just before it enters the steep-sided rock cutting on the approach to Chilcompton station and is clearly on the map. The twin portals of Chilcompton Tunnel are visible in the distance.

Of note is the pillbox on the left, which was one of many constructed during the last war along a section of the S&D from a point near Masbury and then to follow it and the course of Wellow Brook to its confluence with the River Avon. This once formed part of the defence line known as GHQ Stop Line Green, which stretched from the Bristol Channel, at Burnham-on-Sea, to the Wash. In the foreground stand several concrete anti-tank traps; these were placed at many strategic points, particularly bridges and viaducts, along the length of the line during 1940. In the event of an invasion they could have been lifted across the railway to hinder the advance of enemy forces, if necessary.

No 76006 would see out the end of steam on the Southern Region before being withdrawn at Salisbury in July 1967; it was scrapped at Bird's, Swansea, that November. *Photo: Tony Wadley. Date: 28 December 1963.*

Apart from the growth of shrubs and trees along the bank either side of the line formation, particularly over the last decade, little seems to have changed. Chilcompton Tunnel can be seen in the left background – seemingly with a patch over one of its 'eyes'! *Date: 4 March 1995.*

50
Chilcompton – 'Rock Cutting'
183 ST 645514

Emerging from what was referred to by S&D staff as 'Rock Cutting', Class 2P 4-4-0 No 40569 and Class 4F 0-6-0 No 44422 pound up the final few yards on the approach to Chilcompton station with the 07.00 (SO) Cleethorpes–Bournemouth train. The gradient eased to 1:300 at this point, only to resume at 1:50 just past the station. Bridge 52 carrying a minor road is obscured by the 4F's smoke. *Photo: G.A.Richardson. Date: 12 August 1961.*

Map 13: Chilcompton (1904)
Situated high above the valley where part of the village lies, Chilcompton station was an oasis for banking engines and allowed them to replenish their water supplies from a large water tank situated behind the main buildings before returning to Radstock for other duties.

The station opened on 20 July 1874. The up platform, which was a good deal longer than the one opposite, was only provided with a rudimentary shelter which afforded scant protection for any waiting passengers. The layout of the sidings shown in this map on the down side of the line was subsequently altered and extended to accommodate a loading dock and screens used to load coal brought by road from New Rock Colliery, a half-mile distant from the station. The yard ceased to handle goods traffic on 15 June 1964 and the signal box shut on 11 April 1965, but the station remained open until the line's closure.

Since Chilcompton station was close to Downside, the famous public school, it was used for special trains that ran to and from London via Templecombe at the beginning and end of term.

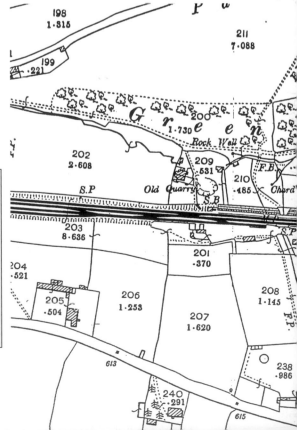

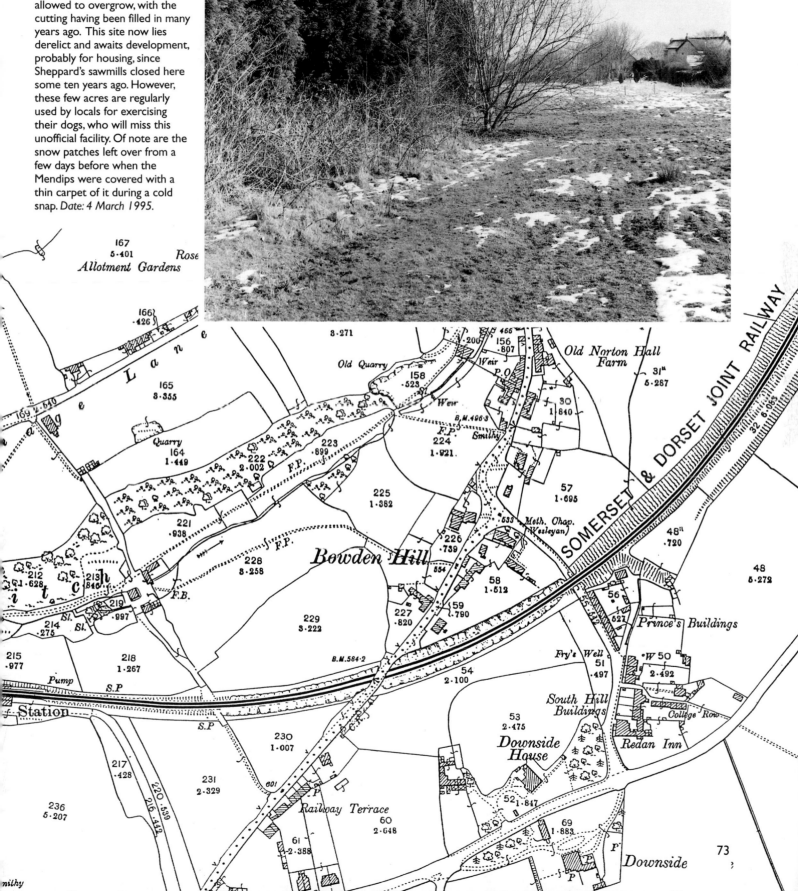

The large house on the right is readily identifiable, but the others are obscured by the recent growth of trees in the foreground planted on the trackbed, which has largely been allowed to overgrow, with the cutting having been filled in many years ago. This site now lies derelict and awaits development, probably for housing, since Sheppard's sawmills closed here some ten years ago. However, these few acres are regularly used by locals for exercising their dogs, who will miss this unofficial facility. Of note are the snow patches left over from a few days before when the Mendips were covered with a thin carpet of it during a cold snap. Date: 4 March 1995.

51
Chilcompton station
183 ST 645514

On a bright Saturday morning, with the temperature a little above freezing, S&D 7F No 53810 drifts down the gradient through Chilcompton station with the 06.05 up goods from Templecombe. Ivo Peters' midnight-blue Bentley, NHY 581, stands on the station road in front of the buildings and awaits its driver's return and the next port of call somewhere along the line.

Of note is the SR-type down starting signal situated off the end of the platform. Access to the up platform was gained via a timber crossing seen under the locomotive. Although equipped with 13 levers, the box visible in the background did not have the requisite shunting signals for controlling movements in the yard; these were governed by hand. The water tower on the left was used extensively by banking engines before returning to Radstock.
Photo: Ivo Peters. Date: 14 September 1963.

For several years the station area was used as a storage area by Sheppard's saw mills, who vacated the site in the mid-1980s, having closed their adjacent works. The remnants of the down platform are mostly hidden by the undergrowth, which has sprouted tremendously over the last ten years. Beyond the remains of Bridge 53, which once passed under the middle of the up platform and was sited off the west end of the down side, a large trailer park, belonging to Massey Wilcox, a local haulage company, has been created encompassing the trackbed. Obscured from view by tall trees on the right, much housing development has taken place on the hillside to the north of the station site.

To the west of the village, two bridges (Nos 55 and 56) remain intact, just beyond which part of the car park of a large factory built for Mulberry, makers of quality clothing and accessories, has partly encroached on the line's formation at grid reference 183 ST 635514. *Date: 4 March 1995.*

52
Emborough – Burnt House Bridge (No 57)
183 ST 630511

The worst of the southbound climb to the summit of the Mendips was over once this bridge (No 57) carrying the B3139 road over the line had been passed and was the point where the gradient eased slightly on the approach to Moorewood sidings. Despite having reached the 700ft level, it was still mostly up hill all the way to Masbury Summit, although the climb would be no more severe than 1:63. Nevertheless, driver Arthur Turner and fireman Colin Powis would still have to work hard on the footplate of S&D 7F 2-8-0 No 53807 to elevate the 08.55 down goods from Bath to the summit, about two-and-a-half miles distant. This view was obtained from Bridge 58.
Photo: Ivo Peters.
Date: 28 September 1963.

Because of the cutting, this location had been used for selective tipping over recent years – particularly in the 1980s – but has now been transformed back into a meadow, which it was prior to the Bath extension being built and opened in 1874. The fences still mark the railway's former boundaries. Bridge 58 was demolished many years ago and no trace of it remains, with the road now carried on an embankment. Court Hotel on the Emborough to Chilcompton road can just be discerned through the trees.
Date: 4 March 1995.

53
Moorewood signal box
183 ST 626509

Closure of Moorewood's compact 19-lever signal box, built in 1914 to replace ground frames operated since 1901, was effected on 21 June 1965. It had also controlled the sidings on the down side for Moorewood Colliery, but when those operations ceased in 1930, it was only used on a one-shift basis to handle stone traffic from Emborough Quarry. Access to the latter, formerly known as 'Old Down' siding, was on the up side of the line a few chains west of the bridge (No 59) over the Ston Easton–Gurney Slade road.

Class 4F 0-6-0 No 44561 passes Moorewood signal box with the 15.20 Bath–Templecombe down local. The locomotive is straddling Bridge 59 spanning the A37 trunk road. Moorewood Colliery's sidings were situated just east of the bridge and the signal box a little distance behind the train. By this date the points connection to the sidings from the down line had been removed; those in the foreground are of a trailing crossover to service Emborough Quarry. *Photo: R.E. Toop. Date: 20 May 1961.*

Bridge 59 has been demolished, but the abutments remain still restricting the width of the A37 road. There is not much to compare with the 1961 photograph, but the wooden post seen immediately to the right of the locomotive is identifiable in today's comparison. The trackbed is somewhat overgrown on this side of the bridge and falls within the area owned by Emborough Quarry, but on the east side, it is kept grazed and in good condition. *Date: 4 March 1995.*

The elusive Nettlebridge Viaduct (No 61), which stands hidden from public view within the Emborough quarry site itself, remains in generally excellent condition. It has been well maintained by its owners, helped by an isolated situation which has kept the attentions of vandals at bay.
Date: 4 March 1995.

54
Milepost 16 – Portway Bridge (No 62) between Moorewood and Binegar
183 ST 621501

The 15.45 down local goods from Bath hauled by Class 7F No 53810 approaches Binegar's down distant signal which is set on. The signal was constructed from two rail sections bolted together and had an upper quadrant arm which followed SR design practice, whilst Moorewood's up distant signal seen on the left was of LSWR lattice post construction with a lower quadrant arm.

Portway Bridge is in the background; a favourite location of Ivo Peters, he took countless shots from several vantage points near to this spot.
Photo: Ivo Peters.
Date: 30 May 1950.

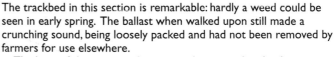

The trackbed in this section is remarkable: hardly a weed could be seen in early spring. The ballast when walked upon still made a crunching sound, being loosely packed and had not been removed by farmers for use elsewhere.

The base of the two signal posts can be spotted with a keen eye. A large stone on the edge of the track in line with the tree in the field on the immediate right marks the spot where the remains of Binegar's down distant stood, whilst Moorewood's up distant base can just be seen under the shadow in the middle distance on the left side of the formation between the branches of a sapling. *Date: 7 May 1985 (revisited 4 March 1995).*

All that remains of Moorewood's up distant signal. *Date: 7 May 1985.*

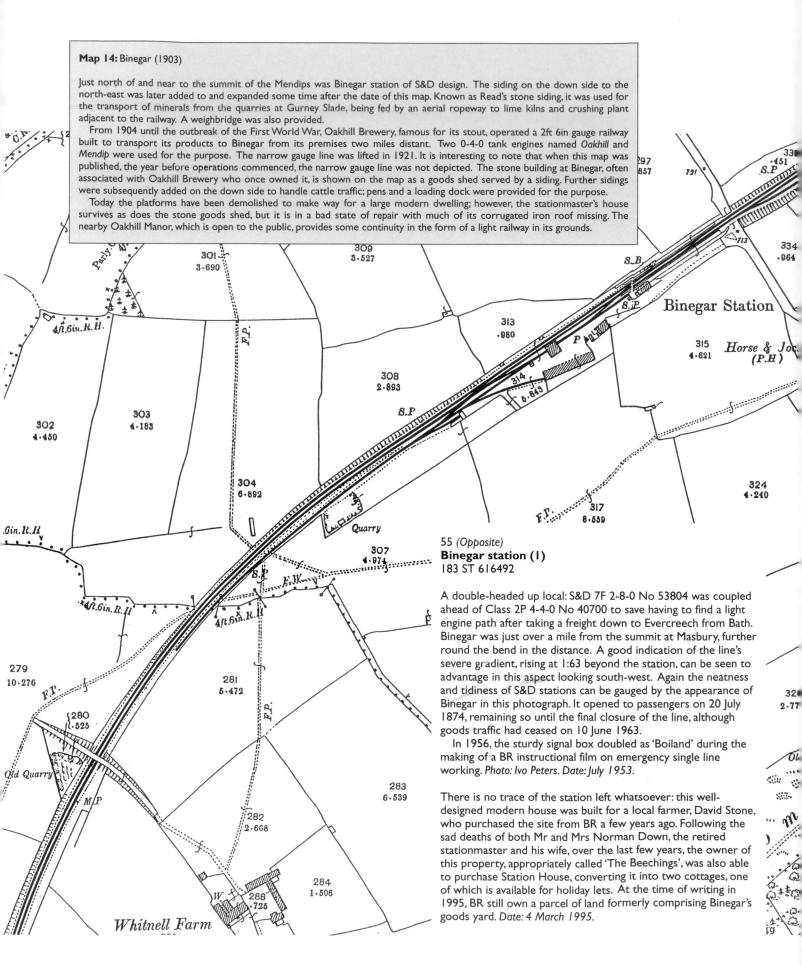

Map 14: Binegar (1903)

Just north of and near to the summit of the Mendips was Binegar station of S&D design. The siding on the down side to the north-east was later added to and expanded some time after the date of this map. Known as Read's stone siding, it was used for the transport of minerals from the quarries at Gurney Slade, being fed by an aerial ropeway to lime kilns and crushing plant adjacent to the railway. A weighbridge was also provided.

From 1904 until the outbreak of the First World War, Oakhill Brewery, famous for its stout, operated a 2ft 6in gauge railway built to transport its products to Binegar from its premises two miles distant. Two 0-4-0 tank engines named *Oakhill* and *Mendip* were used for the purpose. The narrow gauge line was lifted in 1921. It is interesting to note that when this map was published, the year before operations commenced, the narrow gauge line was not depicted. The stone building at Binegar, often associated with Oakhill Brewery who once owned it, is shown on the map as a goods shed served by a siding. Further sidings were subsequently added on the down side to handle cattle traffic; pens and a loading dock were provided for the purpose.

Today the platforms have been demolished to make way for a large modern dwelling; however, the stationmaster's house survives as does the stone goods shed, but it is in a bad state of repair with much of its corrugated iron roof missing. The nearby Oakhill Manor, which is open to the public, provides some continuity in the form of a light railway in its grounds.

55 *(Opposite)*
Binegar station (1)
183 ST 616492

A double-headed up local: S&D 7F 2-8-0 No 53804 was coupled ahead of Class 2P 4-4-0 No 40700 to save having to find a light engine path after taking a freight down to Evercreech from Bath. Binegar was just over a mile from the summit at Masbury, further round the bend in the distance. A good indication of the line's severe gradient, rising at 1:63 beyond the station, can be seen to advantage in this aspect looking south-west. Again the neatness and tidiness of S&D stations can be gauged by the appearance of Binegar in this photograph. It opened to passengers on 20 July 1874, remaining so until the final closure of the line, although goods traffic had ceased on 10 June 1963.

In 1956, the sturdy signal box doubled as 'Boiland' during the making of a BR instructional film on emergency single line working. *Photo: Ivo Peters. Date: July 1953.*

There is no trace of the station left whatsoever: this well-designed modern house was built for a local farmer, David Stone, who purchased the site from BR a few years ago. Following the sad deaths of both Mr and Mrs Norman Down, the retired stationmaster and his wife, over the last few years, the owner of this property, appropriately called 'The Beechings', was also able to purchase Station House, converting it into two cottages, one of which is available for holiday lets. At the time of writing in 1995, BR still own a parcel of land formerly comprising Binegar's goods yard. *Date: 4 March 1995.*

56
Binegar station (2)
183 ST 615492

A star is born: under the direction of Mr Fairburn, the director of the British Transport Film Unit, Class 7F No 53810 prepares to depart with a down goods on the wrong-road from Binegar during the making of a film on emergency single-line working, in which the signal box was dubbed 'Boiland' for the occasion. The other station that featured in the film was Shepton Mallet; its name was changed to 'Averton Hanger'. Since the film was to be shown all over the rail network, BR were anxious to avoid it being identified with any particular region.

Station House, the home of Norman Down, the stationmaster, is seen on the extreme right. The area in the foreground was adjacent to the goods shed. *Photo: Ivo Peters. Date: 14 October 1956.*

A view taken from the same spot shows both Station House and The Beechings, behind which a new bungalow has been built on a plot of land which would have once been at the northern end of the platforms and abutting the now-demolished Bridge 65. Both Bridges 63 and 64 (Tillet's Lane) remain on the well-defined embankment between two cuttings north of the village at Gurney Slade. *Date: 4 March 1995.*

Station House and the former goods shed, from which the one-ton hand-operated crane was salvaged and now resides at Washford on the West Somerset Railway.
Date: 28 May 1985 (revisited 4 March 1995).

57
Whitnell Farm – Bridge 66
183 ST 611489

Nearly there: large-boilered S&D 7F No 53807, with Driver Horace Clarke in charge, approaches Bridge 66 at Whitnell Farm, near Binegar, with a down goods assisted by 'Jinty' Class 3F 0-6-0T No 47557 at the rear. Only a mile to go to Masbury Summit, then No 47557 will return wrong line to Binegar, having seen the goods safely over it.

By the spring of 1955, No 53807 had been fitted with the smaller G9AS type boiler of 4ft 9^{1}/$_{8}$in diameter and in October 1964 was the last of the class to be withdrawn.
Photo: Ivo Peters.
Date: 15 March 1952.

The only visible reminder of the railway is the up side's fence line, which now forms the boundary between two meadows. A better view of Binegar church can be observed in this comparison, obscured by steam in Ivo's photograph. The farm bridge from which the 1952 shot was taken has been demolished completely and the ramps levelled – only a rail-sectioned fence support remains on the track leading to the site. *Date: 7 May 1985 (revisited 4 March 1995).*

MASBURY–WINSOR HILL

58
Masbury – Oakhill Road Bridge (No 69)
183 ST 609479

On a brilliant Saturday in high summer, Class 2P No 40564 pilots unrebuilt West Country class No 34043 *Combe Martin*, from 71B Bournemouth shed, on the down 'Pines Express' and approaches Oakhill Road Bridge on the final few yards on the 1:73 gradient, having eased from 1:63 from Binegar, on the northerly approach to Masbury Summit.

Remaining in its original condition, the Pacific was withdrawn from service just under two years later in June 1963 and scrapped at Eastleigh Works that month; however, the 2P did not even survive more than another seven months before withdrawal in February 1962, being broken up at Crewe Works almost immediately.
Photo: Ivo Peters.
Date: 5 August 1961.

When the area was first revisited shortly after the infilling of the cutting during the winter of 1983, it resembled the Somme! Although the gateway is heavily rutted, today the area has recovered and traces of the railway are becoming harder to discern.

Note how the ash tree on the left has grown over the last thirty-four years or so. The track formation in the distance is still well defined; two bridges (Nos 67 and 68) beyond survive, as does a small prefabricated concrete structure on the down side, the size of a telephone box, which was probably used as a fogman's hut.
Date: 13 March 1995.

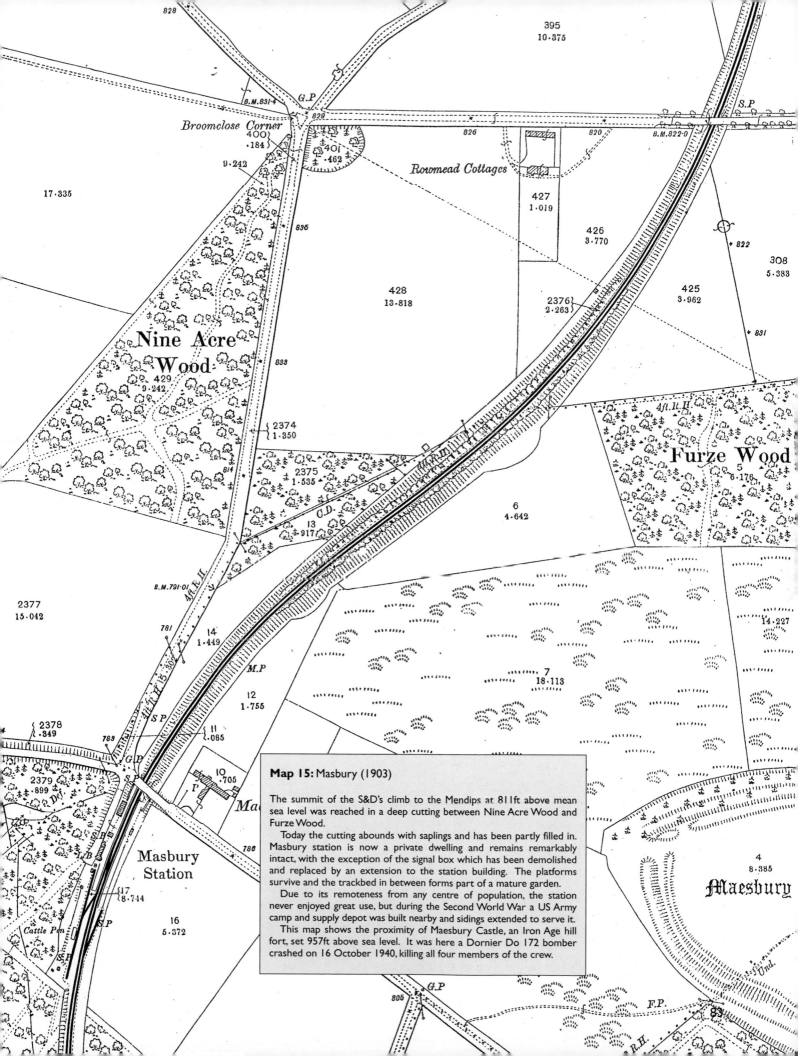

Map 15: Masbury (1903)

The summit of the S&D's climb to the Mendips at 811ft above mean sea level was reached in a deep cutting between Nine Acre Wood and Furze Wood.

Today the cutting abounds with saplings and has been partly filled in. Masbury station is now a private dwelling and remains remarkably intact, with the exception of the signal box which has been demolished and replaced by an extension to the station building. The platforms survive and the trackbed in between forms part of a mature garden.

Due to its remoteness from any centre of population, the station never enjoyed great use, but during the Second World War a US Army camp and supply depot was built nearby and sidings extended to serve it.

This map shows the proximity of Maesbury Castle, an Iron Age hill fort, set 957ft above sea level. It was here a Dornier Do 172 bomber crashed on 16 October 1940, killing all four members of the crew.

Masbury Summit (1)
183 ST 609477

The date is 8 September 1962: worked at 55 per cent cut off and with 240psi pressure showing on the gauge, Peter Smith takes BR Class 9F No 92220 *Evening Star*, on the last up 'Pines Express', over Masbury Summit, 811ft AMSL. At 426 tons, it was the heaviest load ever hauled over the Mendips unassisted – a marvellous tribute to the crew and the power of these magnificent locomotives. It is no wonder fireman Aubrey Punter, leaning from the cab, looks all in as he takes a welcome breather from his efforts.

The summit, on a level stretch of 110ft, was reached in the foreground just a little further ahead of the locomotive and was 435ft north of the 17½ milepost, which can be discerned on the left at the trackside opposite the first coach. *Photo: Ivo Peters. Date: 8 September 1962.*

Saplings and trees abound in the deep sided cutting, particularly southwards towards Masbury station; a few rotting sleepers remain among them. Foxes have made a home high up the embankment between some rocks. Notice the outcrop on the right of the picture, now partly obscured with creepers, which is readily identifiable as that in the original.

This was arguably the favourite location of the late Ivo Peters and a truly magnificent setting where he most enjoyed photographing hard-working trains. Never severing links with the S&D and his love of the line, he expressed the wish to have his ashes scattered at Masbury Summit after his death, which was in June 1989. *Date: 13 March 1995.*

60
Masbury Summit (2)
183 ST 609477

A sequence shot of the last up 'Pines': Peter Smith and Aubrey Punter have spotted Ivo Peters, both giving him a friendly wave as No 92220 *Evening Star* breasts the summit and heads towards Bridge 69 in the background. Notice the apparent emptiness of the tender, which will have to be replenished at Bath. Judging from the lack of serious steam leaks and absence of exhaust smoke, the locomotive was in fine fettle for this the final run of the up 'Pines'.

Ivo Peters used to enjoy eating wild strawberries in the season, which he found at the trackside here; he liked to think they were known only to him and S&D linesmen!
Photo: Ivo Peters.
Date: 8 September 1962.

The line formation in this short section is still quite well defined, but Bridge 69 was demolished some years ago and the road flattened out, the ramps having been removed. On visiting the area for the first time, one can easily pass by on the B3155 without realising the railway ever existed, which is partly due to the fact that the cutting on both sides of the road has been filled in and partly landscaped. The trackbed in the foreground, which also marked the actual summit, has been occasionally used for tipping building and farm waste, as is evident in this study, but this has now been ceased and the remaining portion of the cutting will be left up to nature to take its course. *Date: 13 March 1995.*

61
Masbury – Bridge 70
183 ST 604473

On a beautiful early summer's day with blossom adorning the trees, one of Templecombe's Standard Class 4 4-6-0s, No 75009, with plenty of steam to spare working the 15.20 Bath–Templecombe local, drifts down the 1:50 gradient from the summit and is about to pass under Bridge 70 adjacent to Masbury Halt. Of interest is the Masbury down home repeater signal of LSWR origin on the up side of the line. It was positioned thus to afford drivers a good view around the sharp radius curve on the descent towards the halt. *Photo: Ivo Peters.*
Date: 2 June 1962.

> **COMMENT:** *When attempting a comparison photograph two days before, in failing light and a howling gale, it was so cold that I could not even feel my finger on the camera's shutter release. Abandoning my efforts for the day, I went home for a nice hot cup of tea and a bun!*

Not such a good view is had from the same position now, because of the trees that have grown unabated in the cutting since closure of the line. With the apparent warming of the climate since 1962, blossom such as once seen in June seems now more likely in April! *Date: 6 March 1995.*

62
Masbury station
183 ST 604473

Opened on 20 July 1874, Masbury was the highest station on the Mendips and only served a scattered rural community. Viewed from Bridge 70, this 1937 photograph shows clearly the unusual layout of the station buildings: the substantial stone-built stationmaster's house was situated at the far end of the up platform; the waiting rooms and booking office are just visible on the right. Sandwiched in between them was a 20-lever signal box, complete with block switch. When the station was reduced to halt status in 1935, the box closed at night. The down side's platform was only equipped with a small wooden shelter. From 26 September 1938 Masbury became an unstaffed halt. A small goods yard was located on the up side, complete with a cattle loading dock; one short siding was initially provided on the down side. This was later added to and extended to serve the stone crushing plant seen on the left of the

picture. It was built by Mendipadam, a subsidiary of Emborough Stone Company, but was not used to any great degree. By the Second World War, it had been demolished and the down sidings were further extended to serve a nearby US Army depot.

Although the station was built on a short stretch of 1:300, northbound trains starting from here were faced with an immediate 1:50 climb just off the end of the up platform.
Photo: H.C.Casserley. Date: 23 July 1937.

Taken from the same vantage point Masbury is readily identifiable, although in summer the same view would be obscured by the foliage on the trees. Note the extension to Station House built in the years following the line's closure.
Date: 9 April 1985 (revisited 6 March 1995).

> **COMMENT:** Another photograph was taken in 1995, but the trees have grown so much in ten years that they have all but obscured the station buildings when viewed from the bridge. Since neither they nor the platforms have changed to any significant degree, the 1985 picture was retained.

COMMENT: I was talking to Mr Couling about Ivo Peters' prowess in his Bentley by racing trains up the Mendips, enabling several photographs to be taken at different locations. "Oh yes, one could do that," he said, and continued, "I could leave Evercreech Junction by car or motorcycle at the same time as the up 'Pines' and on the way home watch the train slowly crossing Prestleigh Viaduct, then on to Cannard's Grave. On arriving home at Masbury, I even had time to put my car into the garage, and then walk onto the platform to hear the train still some way off climbing the 1:50 gradient!"

63
Masbury Halt (1)
183 ST 604473

The up 'Pines Express' piloted by Class 2P 4-4-0 No 40700 and an unidentified BR Class 5 4-6-0 pass Masbury Halt on the final stretch of the northbound climb to the summit of the Mendips, a quarter of a mile away. Of note are the cinder surface of the platforms which were built of compacted clay with brick facings. The tall down starting and the up home signals on the extreme left were of LSWR design. *Photo: Lens of Sutton. Date: c1958.*

Mr Wilfred Couling, who was relief stationmaster at Evercreech Junction, has lived here with his wife since 21 January 1954, when trains still stopped at the halt. They have made the platforms and trackbed into an attractive garden by planting a variety of trees, which was undertaken with some difficulty, as every hole had to be dug into the compacted chippings and remaining ballast. *Date: 6 March 1995.*

64
Masbury Halt (2)
183 ST 604472

The passengers on the Warwickshire Railway Society's special had a lot to complain about: the weather was foul and Masbury Summit was enveloped in thick cloud, thus restricting what should have been breathtaking views of the countryside. In addition, the 'imported' BR Class 9F No 92238's performance that day was abysmal: at times the climb to the Mendips was no more than walking pace; however, No 92238 has a chance to regain some of its steam as it drifts under Bridge 70 past Masbury's down platform. Much later in the day the locomotive returned home, via the Mendips, light engine. Although obscured by the mist, Ivo Peters was standing on Bridge 70 to photograph the train as it descended from the summit.

It was very difficult to hear trains approaching from the north as they passed under this bridge, having built up speed on the short 1:50 stretch from the summit. Wilfred Couling stated that something like twenty or thirty farm cats were killed this way, having failed to hear trains coming!

Just visible is the curious stone carving of a mediaeval castle above the bay window on the stationmaster's house, inscribed with a Gothic legend, 'Maesbury Castle'. *Photo: Derek Cross. Date: 12 June 1965.*

The young trees on the platforms and trackbed provide a dramatic contrast. Still bearing the name 'Station House', the building is a constant reminder of its history. Some people have wandered along the formation and into the garden, completely oblivious to the fact that this is now a private property and not owned by BR.
Date: 6 March 1995.

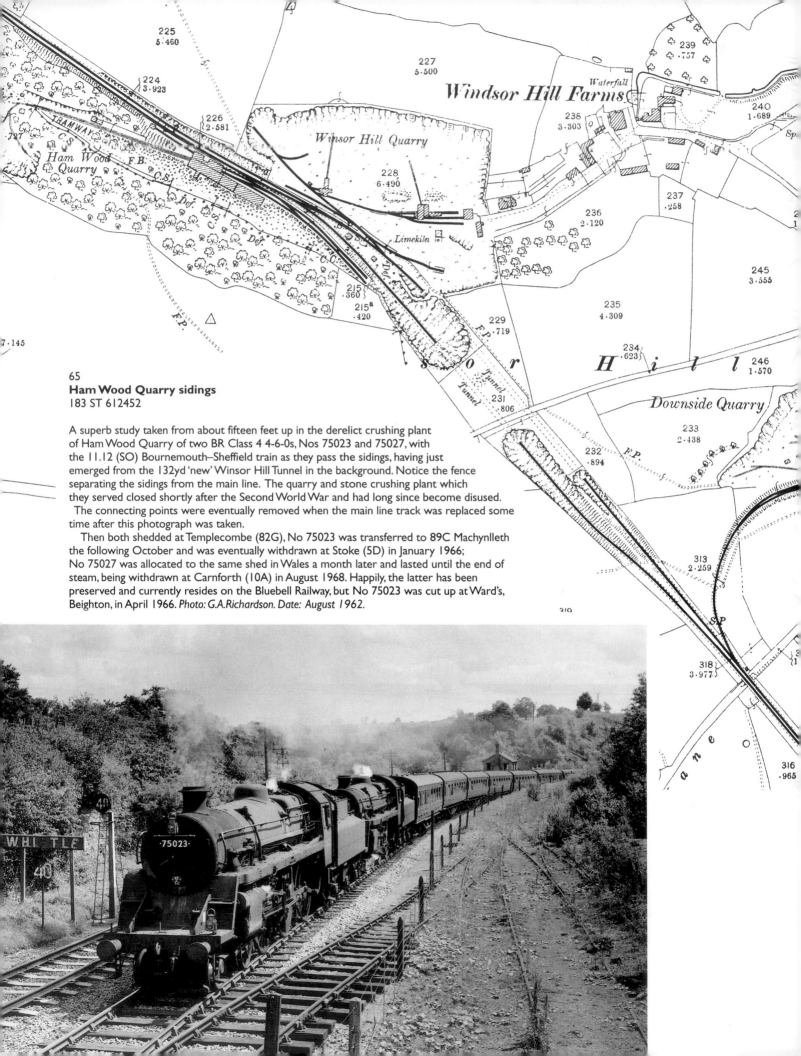

65

Ham Wood Quarry sidings
183 ST 612452

A superb study taken from about fifteen feet up in the derelict crushing plant
of Ham Wood Quarry of two BR Class 4 4-6-0s, Nos 75023 and 75027, with
the 11.12 (SO) Bournemouth–Sheffield train as they pass the sidings, having just
emerged from the 132yd 'new' Winsor Hill Tunnel in the background. Notice the fence
separating the sidings from the main line. The quarry and stone crushing plant which
they served closed shortly after the Second World War and had long since become disused.
 The connecting points were eventually removed when the main line track was replaced some
time after this photograph was taken.
   Then both shedded at Templecombe (82G), No 75023 was transferred to 89C Machynlleth
the following October and was eventually withdrawn at Stoke (5D) in January 1966;
No 75027 was allocated to the same shed in Wales a month later and lasted until the end of
steam, being withdrawn at Carnforth (10A) in August 1968. Happily, the latter has been
preserved and currently resides on the Bluebell Railway, but No 75023 was cut up at Ward's,
Beighton, in April 1966. *Photo: G.A.Richardson. Date: August 1962.*

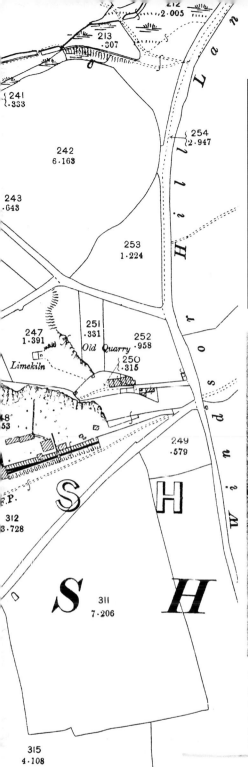

It is interesting how the map denotes two spellings of Winsor Hill: one version for the hill and one for the quarry! The modern OS 1:50,000 Landranger map (sheet 183) shows it as 'Windsor' Hill. On checking with the Somerset Local History Library, there seems to be no obvious reason for the differences, apart from the inability to be consistent; however, the accepted version today seems to be 'Windsor', but as the alternative spelling is used in most reference works on the S&D, so it will be in this volume.

The two tunnels of different lengths are clearly depicted on this map. The original bore was on the down side and longer, being 242yd long; the one on the up side, built in 1892 on doubling of the line, was shorter at 132yd long. It was found that by slightly deviating the new (up) line, it would save 110yd of tunnelling, thus representing a considerable reduction in the cost of construction.

The extent of the stone extraction industry on the Mendips can be gauged by this map, where three quarries are shown: Ham Wood on the west side of the line, Winsor Hill (which opened in 1875) and Downside on the east, together with their attendant sidings, tramways and crushing plants. All three quarries had closed long before the line. The stone-built signal box which controlled the sidings (seen between the tracks just north of the tunnels) closed in 1948.

Only the indentations of sleepers from the sidings now mark this spot. The trackbed is still in good condition, being regularly used by walkers. Remains of the Ham Wood stone crushing plant can still be found: various pieces of twisted corrugated iron, an old water tank and stonework lie scattered at the trackside. The line formation north of this point back towards Masbury Summit is still well defined, although Bridge 72 (183 ST 605465) that once spanned the Croscombe to Masbury road has been removed and only the abutments remain. *Date: 6 March 1995.*

COMMENT: *A howling gale and difficult lighting experienced on this day made photography very tricky, so the results may be deemed as being 'curate's egg': bad, but good in parts – maybe!*

A little further up the line, the five-arch Ham Wood Viaduct (No 75) spans a thickly wooded ravine and remains in fairly good condition, although its parapets have been repaired by BR with concrete blocks, where vandals had removed the capping stones from the walls. The viaduct is almost totally obscured by trees and difficult to view. It is now privately owned by a Mr Weeks, who purchased it along with Winsor Hill tunnels and a quarter of a mile of trackbed, as a wildlife conservation park. *Date: 12 March 1985 (revisited 6 March 1995).*

66
Winsor Hill Tunnel – north portals
183 ST 613452

The up 'Pines Express', hauled by 2P 4-4-0 No 40697 and Bulleid Pacific No 34042 *Dorchester,* emerges from the north end of the 132yd up tunnel, built when the line was doubled in 1892. This was shorter than the original bore seen on the left, which was 242yd in length. During the construction of the first tunnel, four navvies lost their lives in a rockfall; they now lie buried in the cemetery at Shepton Mallet.

The train is seen passing the derelict stone signal box, the windows of which have been smashed. The 16-lever box, built in 1892 and the only one of its construction on the line, became redundant in August 1948 following the closure of both the Ham Wood and Winsor Hill sidings. The points to the latter are still seen to be *in situ* in this study, but the sidings had already been removed. *Photo: Ivo Peters.* *Date: 18 September 1954.*

Although the tunnel mouths appear overgrown in this shot, both portals remain clear and can easily be seen further round the bend. Their condition is good and they are used constantly by walkers, particularly the up bore. The down tunnel is rather sinister by comparison and its cuttings are somewhat overgrown. Up until the late 1980s its portals were obscured by massive steel doors, built a little in front of the stonework and supported by a frame. These were constructed as an anti-blast measure by Rolls-Royce in 1968, who used the tunnel for destructive tests on the Olympus jet engine for Concorde. They ran an engine without oil, expecting it to blow up within twenty minutes or so, but in the event it apparently lasted for well over two hours! The tunnel's use for this purpose was only over a few days, planning permission having been sought from Shepton Mallet RDC as a matter of course, in case an explosion caused a change in the local topography! *Date: 28 May 1985 (revisited 6 March 1995).*

Left: The north portal (down side) of Winsor Hill Tunnel. *Date: 6 March 1995.*

Right: The north portal (up side) of Winsor Hill Tunnel. *Date: 28 May 1985 (revisited 6 March 1995).*

67
Winsor Hill
183 ST 613450

With its exhaust drifting away from the line in a stiff westerly breeze, an unidentified Class 7F 2-8-0 toils northbound with an evening goods on the 1:50 gradient towards Winsor Hill Tunnel. This view from the south side of Winsor Hill summarises perfectly the pastoral pleasures of the S&D which could be enjoyed by the lineside photographer. *Photo: Ivo Peters. Date: 29 September 1956.*

COMMENT: *Visiting here ten years before, with a flask of coffee at my side, I took a welcome break from the exertions of a hard day's photography and lay back against the gently sloping meadow to doze, reflecting on the scenes of yesteryear. It is incredible now to think of this area bearing witness to the sight and sounds of heavy trains pounding up the southern slopes of the Mendips, their exhausts echoing in the tunnel cuttings at the base of the hillside.*

'So I awoke, and behold it was a dream'
John Bunyan (1628-88)

The track formation is still quite distinct; some trees have grown markedly, others have succumbed to the passage of time – and to Dutch elm disease, which was prevalent during the 1970s, as testified by the huge stump in the field at the foot of the hill.

A post and rail fence has now been erected across the sloping field in the foreground.
Date: 28 May 1985 (revisited 6 March 1995).

68
**Winsor Hill Tunnel –
down portal (south
side)**
183 ST 616449

Grazing cows remain oblivious to S&D 7F 2-8-0 No 53805 as it emerges from the original south portal of Winsor Hill Tunnel with the 10.45 down coal train from Norton Hill Colliery, Midsomer Norton. It will be braking most of the way down to Charlton Viaduct, some one and a half miles distant, before the driver opens the regulator to climb the short stretch of 1:55 gradient to Shepton Mallet station. The guard in his van will have his brake applied at the rear of the train helping to control the descent and by keeping the couplings tensioned. The braking properties of the 7Fs were excellent – and these were further enhanced when they were fitted with Ferodo brake blocks, which were more effective and lasted longer than the standard cast iron variety. *Photo: Ivo Peters. Date: 27 March 1954.*

The tunnel mouth is almost obscured by trees, particularly when in full leaf. On the first visit here, it was quite noticeable how the cutting was littered with polythene and paper blown down from the tip at the top of the hill. Now closed and landscaped, the rubbish tip and the surrounding area have been cleaned up.

With the removal of the steel doors in front of the down portals during the late 1980s, the trackbed on this side is also used by walkers and is clearer than this comparison shot would suggest.
Date: 6 March 1995.

69
Winsor Hill Tunnel – south portals
183 ST 616448

BR Class 9F No 92212, with the 09.35 (SO) Sheffield–Bournemouth service, drifts out of Winsor Hill Tunnel towards the twin-deck iron bridge (No 78) over Forum Lane. The catch points on the left were strategically placed to deal with possible breakaways from northbound goods trains climbing the 1:50 gradient towards Masbury Summit. Until 1940, there was a siding, controlled by a ground frame (the key to which was collected from Winsor Hill box) to Downside Quarry (latterly used as a rubbish tip), situated higher on the hill. The trailing points to the siding were located in front of the Class 9F, but had been removed by this date. Note the divergence of the up line before it enters the 'new' tunnel in a deep cutting. *Photo: Ivo Peters. Date: 26 August 1961.*

With the demolition of Bridge 78 in the early 1990s, much of the rubble and earthworks have been bulldozed back towards the tunnel, raising some of the formation by about a metre. Bricks from the base of the permanent way hut can still be found, but these amount to no more than a small pile of rubble and are difficult to spot in the undergrowth. Individual trees are easily identifiable, although many of them have grown quite considerably over the ensuing years. South of here the trackbed is still distinct and often used for the keeping of cattle and also by walkers from the Shepton Mallet district, who frequently utilise the area as a leisure amenity – particularly for exercising their dogs. *Date: 6 March 1995.*

70
Bridge 79 – between Winsor Hill and Shepton Mallet
183 ST 618446

The embankment near this small occupation bridge, situated a few hundred yards south of the twin tunnels, provided a good vantage point from which this fine study was obtained of BR Class 4 2-6-4T No 80059 working the 16.15 up local from Templecombe, where it was shedded and carries the 82G plate on its smokebox. Judging from the drifting exhaust, a stiff north-westerly wind is blowing on this fine early spring day with hardly a cloud in the sky. Of note is the occupation bridge (No 80) in the background, a few chains beyond which is Bath Road Viaduct in Shepton Mallet.

The locomotive was withdrawn from Bath MPD only seven months later, having spent May on temporary allocation to Bristol Barrow Road (82E). Languishing for a time in storage at Bath Green Park, it was eventually scrapped at Buttigieg's, Newport in March 1966, the same month the S&D line closed. *Photo: Ivo Peters. Date: 10 April 1965.*

The same scene depicted almost thirty years later on the 29th anniversary of the line's closure shows how things change – and grow – in a relatively short period of time and this photograph, taken in a howling westerly gale, vividly illustrates the point: the bridge parapet can easily be made out beyond the thicket, although the view towards Shepton Mallet has been obscured. Bridge 80 still stands, as does Bath Road Viaduct, but its future is far from secure. On the day of this visit, following a prolonged period of heavy rain, the trackbed was like a black morass, trampled by the hooves of cattle which are often kept on this section. *Date: 6 March 1995.*

SHEPTON MALLET–EVERCREECH JUNCTION NORTH

71
Shepton Mallet – Bath Road Viaduct (1)
183 ST 620443

Shortly after crossing over the 27-arch Charlton Viaduct, the longest on the line, Standard Class 4 4-6-0 No 75072, possibly with the 15.40 up mail, passes over the 118yd Bath Road Viaduct (No 81) spanning the Fosse Way and climbs up the 1:50 gradient towards Winsor Hill Tunnel a half-mile distant. This view from the occupation bridge (No 80), seen in photograph 70, provided an excellent vantage point to capture locomotives as they pounded up the southern slopes of the Mendips.
Photo: G.A.Richardson. Date: c1962.

One of the hazards of retaking photographs where commanding views were previously obtained is that more often than not it is impossible today to achieve, as well illustrated here. Young trees have all but obscured the view of the viaduct, but the fencing on the right remains as tangible evidence this is the same location. The trackbed is still well defined and is used for cattle; the bridge and short cutting provide them with excellent shelter and a convenient place for their feeding and watering.
Date: 6 March 1995.

COMMENT: *I took this comparison to accompany another 1962 photograph by Tony Richardson. In the event, he provided this superb example which was taken two feet further to the right, hence the slight disparity in alignment of the fence line – however, the limited view would be the same!*

Shepton Mallet – Bath Road Viaduct (2)
183 ST 620442

The new (up) side of Bath Road Viaduct, built during widening in 1892, collapsed during a winter gale on 2 February 1946, but was not repaired until the following August and is shown here during the course of this work.

Since funds were always in short supply, the viaducts on the S&D's Bath extension were generally built to meet tight financial constraints and this was more often than not reflected in the standard of work and materials used during construction, particularly on the widened sections.
Photo: LRGP/Real Photographs.
Date: 1946.

Bath Road Viaduct is again in need of repair: it is ironic that in 1995, the structure again has scaffolding under its main arch, but this time it is to prevent masonry falling on people walking underneath due to its dilapidated state. The viaduct has been listed as a Grade 2 building, so cannot be demolished easily, despite BR's wish. Access over it has been prevented by the erection of steel mesh gates topped with barbed wire.
Date: 2 March 1995.

Map 17: Shepton Mallet–Charlton Viaduct (1903) *(Opposite)*

Entering from a north-westerly direction, then swinging southwards to skirt the east side of the town, the S&D crossed over two notable structures in the process: the 118yd Bath Road Viaduct (No 81) of six spans and the 317yd Charlton Viaduct (No 84) of 27 spans; the latter is shown clearly on this map.

The viaduct was bought from BR for £5 by Showerings, famous for the manufacture of Babycham, who, during the following few years, spent over £30,000 on it, including £13,500 tarmacing the surface as a precaution against water ingress and resultant damage.

In 1992, Showerings, then still owned by Allied Breweries, was subjected to a management buy out and today forms part of the Matthew Clark Gaymer Group. In October 1994, the Silver Street offices and gardens were vacated and put up for sale, but are still being maintained and at the moment four gardeners are employed to look after the latter; however, the Hiram Walker division of the Allied group still own the Grade 2 listed viaduct and it was not part of the deal.

At the time the 1995 photograph was taken, an 18-month programme of maintenance and restoration was being implemented, reputing to be costing something in the region of £250,000, towards which English Heritage were contributing £100,000. The contractors, Messrs Foreman, Ellis & Co of Shepton Mallet, are constructing new drainage channels to facilitate the rapid dissipation of water from the surface, which itself is being replaced with a much less porous material. In addition, the parapets are being capped with high quality engineers' bricks replacing those previously used, which were inferior and did not stand up well to the elements. Of interest, sections of the viaduct's brickwork were found to have been built using the Flemish garden wall style, which is apparently most unusual for a structure of this kind. Despite its future ownership being uncertain, the viaduct is likely to survive for a long time to come, due to its listed status and generally good condition.

The last rays of the late afternoon sun catch the viaduct in this view taken from a little further down the embankment, with the magnificent Showerings' gardens seen below. *Date: 8 March 1995.*

Contractors' vehicles on the viaduct during repairs. *Date: 6 March 1995.*

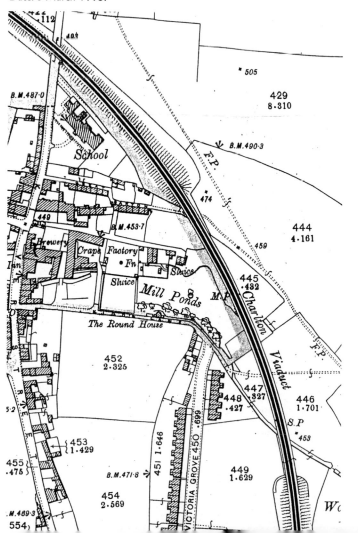

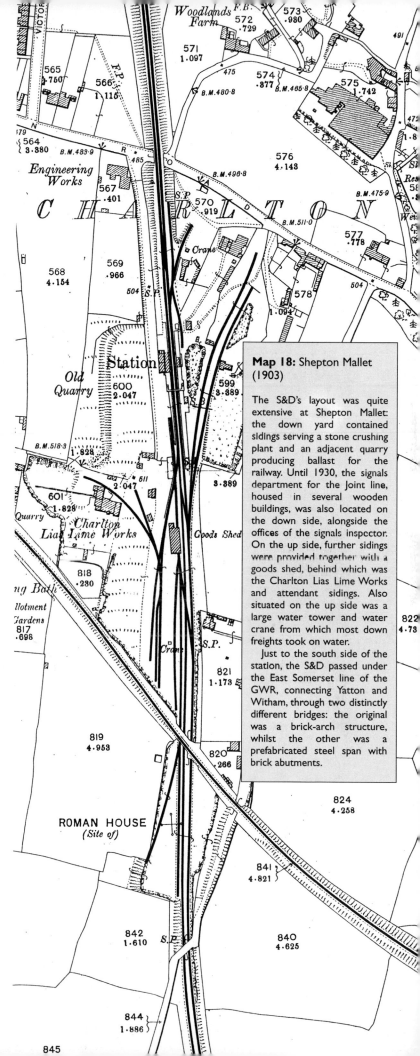

Map 18: Shepton Mallet (1903)

The S&D's layout was quite extensive at Shepton Mallet: the down yard contained sidings serving a stone crushing plant and an adjacent quarry producing ballast for the railway. Until 1930, the signals department for the Joint line, housed in several wooden buildings, was also located on the down side, alongside the offices of the signals inspector. On the up side, further sidings were provided together with a goods shed, behind which was the Charlton Lias Lime Works and attendant sidings. Also situated on the up side was a large water tower and water crane from which most down freights took on water.

Just to the south side of the station, the S&D passed under the East Somerset line of the GWR, connecting Yatton and Witham, through two distinctly different bridges: the original was a brick-arch structure, whilst the other was a prefabricated steel span with brick abutments.

73
Shepton Mallet – Charlton Viaduct (No 84)
183 ST 627437

Described as the S&DJR's architectural masterpiece, the curved structure of the 67ft-high Charlton Viaduct of 27 spans was unusual in so far as the line dipped at 1:55 towards the centre, easing to 1:66 and then rose briefly at 1:103, before increasing to a 1:55 gradient in the up direction. This in particular enabled trains to take 'a good run at it' when starting out from the station to continue the challenging northward climb to the summit of the Mendips some three and a half miles away.

Just four days after working the last 'Pines Express' to run over the S&D line and the end of all other through services, BR Class 9F 2-10-0 No 92220 *Evening Star* is relegated to much more humble but nevertheless important duties as it brings the up mail over the viaduct. Leaving Bournemouth at 15.30 every afternoon except Sundays, the up mail had priority over all other services, including the down 'Pines', as it had to make the connection at Mangotsfield on the Midland line with the evening mail train from Bristol to the North and was usually given a clear run through on the single sections of the S&D.
Photo: Ivo Peters. Date: 12 September 1962.

There is not much to see from almost the same perspective today, except the parapet on the down side: the viaduct, now gated to prevent casual access, is all but obscured from view by young trees growing on the embankment. *Date: 8 March 1995.*

74
Shepton Mallet – Charlton Road Bridge (No 85)
183 ST 628431

Having just crossed the 317yd Charlton Viaduct and traversed the main A361 road bridge, BR Class 4 4-6-0 No 75007, with the 15.20 Bath–Templecombe local, approaches Shepton Mallet station, where it was booked to stop. Of note is the tall up advanced starting signal, which was visible to drivers of up trains from beyond the bridges south of the station. A small part of the down goods yard is seen on the right of the photograph, which was taken from the station footbridge (No 86). On the immediate left is the distinctive building of the town's bacon factory with its vented roof; the station approach road is sandwiched between it and the railway line. *Photo: R.E.Toop. Date: 22 June 1963.*

COMMENT: *To obtain this view, I stood on a pair of steps borrowed from the company and hoisted the camera aloft on poles to simulate the height of the footbridge, from which the previous shot was taken. Being able to peer inside a trailer right in front of me, I was able to see its contents of waste products from the factory. Yuk!*

One of the dramatically different S&D scenes today: the station site has been developed into an industrial estate and the unit in the foreground is Perimax's meat products plant which is being extended, thus obscuring the view of the viaduct. The bacon factory building just visible on the left is owned by Framptons, an egg processing, packing, storage and freight distribution group of companies. *Date: 8 March 1995.*

75
Shepton Mallet – Charlton Road station (1)
183 ST 629430

Standard Class 5 4-6-0 No 73049 enters Shepton Mallet station with a down local and draws to a halt opposite the substantial signal box on a dull spring day. The locomotive's bent running plate bore testament to its involvement in a minor collision at Bath Green Park shed.

The station, situated on the east side of the town, opened on 20 July 1874. From 26 September 1949 it was renamed Shepton Mallet (Charlton Road). Goods traffic ceased to be handled from 10 June 1963, although most of the sidings remained until 1964.

The main building, with a substantial wooden canopy and fitted side screens, was situated on the up platform, whilst the down side had only a small shelter and a gentlemen's urinal, behind which was a tall water tower supported by a stone-built base, serving an adjacent water crane. Also on the down side, an attractive S&D-designed 26-lever signal box was sited in the middle of the platform. *Photo: C.L.Caddy. Date: 18 May 1963.*

The units of Tachograph Services, a commercial vehicle repair and maintenance company, span the area where the train once stood. Sad to relate, there is not one shred of evidence from the original photograph to support the fact that the railway ever existed. *Date: 2 March 1995.*

76
Shepton Mallet – Charlton Road station (2)
183 ST 628430

This was a landmark occasion for the S&D for three brand-new BR Standard Class 5 4-6-0s, Nos 73050, 73051 and 73052, were allocated to Bath in May 1954. Here No 73051, with driver Walt Jeans in charge, enters Shepton Mallet on its first run up the S&D with the 15.35 from Bournemouth to Bath. The locomotive had worked light engine from Derby to Bournemouth via Brent, Willesden and Basingstoke. Of note is the down starter signal, constructed from two rail sections bolted together, and the small stone-built goods shed on the right with a loading gauge strategically sited near its door. The cattle loading dock is in the immediate foreground.

The now-preserved No 73050 worked on the S&D until it was transferred to 87E Landore (Swansea) shed in April 1965 and eventually withdrawn from BR service at 9H Patricroft in June 1968. Both Nos 73051 and 73052 worked throughout their careers on the line before being withdrawn at 82F Bath Green Park in August 1965 and December 1964 respectively; the latter was broken up at Buttigieg's, Newport, the following April. *Photo: Ivo Peters. Date: 29 May 1954.*

Both the cottage in the middle of the picture and the features on the horizon are the instant clues to the location. Constructed in the late 1980s, a unit belonging to a builders' and plumbers' merchant dominates the background obscuring the view of the second cottage, the roof of which is seen over the first coach in the previous photograph.

This aspect was gained from a compound belonging to Messrs Framptons, whose freight division runs 48 lorry units which operate from the site, part of which is used as a car park for employees, as seen here; in previous time most of the goods transported from Shepton Mallet might have gone by train! Impossible now. *Date: 2 March 1995.*

77

Shepton Mallet – Charlton Road station (3)
183 ST 629429

The 09.03 Bristol–Bournemouth gets underway from Shepton Mallet, with BR Class 4 2-6-0 No 76015 coupled ahead of BR Class 9F 2-10-0 No 92220 *Evening Star*, to save a light engine path down to Evercreech Junction, as was common practice on this working, which departed from Bath at 09.55; later the Mogul would assist an up train over the Mendips.

Having been transferred to Bath during August, No 92220 – being the final steam locomotive built for BR – had appropriately been selected by the shedmaster, Harold Morris, to work the last 'Pines Express' exactly a week later, providing it was serviceable. Luckily it was in fine fettle for the occasion, but it was a sad day for the S&D when all other through workings also ceased. From that day on, an important cross-country railway would become little more than a branch line.

Note the stone-built goods shed on the immediate left, whilst the signal box and water tower are seen on the right in the background. *Photo: Ivo Peters. Date: 1 September 1962.*

The old bacon factory chimney provides the only identifiable link with the previous photograph (partly obscured by steam) – otherwise it would be virtually impossible to associate the two views! *Date: 2 March 1995.*

COMMENT: *On arriving at this location, I discovered to my horror that my clipboard and photographs of West Pennard, temporarily left on the car roof whilst loading my camera there, had been forgotten. Driving at top speed several miles back to where I had parked, I found the remains of the clipboard in a gateway at the side of the road some two hundred yards from the spot where it had obviously fallen off the roof of the car, then been smashed into a dozen pieces by countless juggernauts running over it. To my great relief, the photos were found to be completely undamaged in their plastic sleeve!*

78

Shepton Mallet – Bridge 87
183 ST 628425

The GWR's Witham–Yatton branch, also known as the 'Strawberry Line', crossed the S&D at this point. The twin bridges of different construction are clearly seen in this view: the original one was the brick-arch structure, whilst the other was erected on doubling of the line in 1892.

Having worked hard on the ruling 1:50 gradient from Evercreech, Standard Class 5 4-6-0 No 73052, with the up relief 'Pines', heads towards the bridge and gathers speed on the short level stretch through the station before taking advantage of the downhill plunge towards the centre of Charlton Viaduct, at which point the uphill slog is on again to the summit of the Mendips. *Photo: R.E. Toop. Date: 19 May 1959.*

The short cutting between Bridges 87 and 88 has been turned into a compact industrial estate called The Centurion Business Centre, which has a dozen or so small units occupied by a number of different companies. The embankment from which Ron Toop took the 1959 photograph has been gouged away to allow an access road to the estate.

This elevated view shows that Bridge 87 still survives and is used for storage, but Bridge 88 has long since been demolished when the road was widened some considerable time ago, on the south side of which at grid reference 183 ST 629424 a large warehouse has been built on the infilled cutting and is occupied by BOC Interbrands. *Date: 8 March 1995.*

79
Cannard's Grave Summit and cutting
183 ST 629413

The variety of the S&D's locomotive power and rolling stock can be judged by this photograph: working hard on the 1:50 gradient, large-boilered S&D Class 7F No 53806 approaches Bridge 92 near Cannard's Grave with the 12.20 (SO) relief, Bournemouth–Walsall, made up of ten ex-LNER coaches. This was a heavy load for the 2-8-0 to take over the Mendips unassisted. The train is entering the cutting which extended northwards for a mile from here to Bridge 87 at Shepton Mallet. It would breast Cannard's Grave Summit in the cutting at Bridge 89, about a half mile from this point, then drop at 1:157 and 1:70, before reaching Shepton Mallet station on a level stretch. Whitstone Hill Farm, set high on the hill to the left out of camera view, provided a landmark at night for driver Donald Beale, who was able to use its light to gauge his position. *Photo: Ivo Peters. Date: 15 August 1953.*

The mile-long cutting has been completely filled in with builders' waste and non-toxic materials, covered with top soil, from here to the site of Bridge 88, where the link road between the A371 and A361 has been widened. Over forty acres have been reclaimed and turned back to pasture and arable land. The local landowner/farmer is Chris Norman, whose great-grandfather, Richard, farmed here when the railway was constructed, as generations of the family have since the 1820s. Interesting comparisons were made between the manpower needed to excavate the deep cutting and the horsepower of the bulldozers and mechanical loaders to fill it back in! *Date: 20 March 1995.*

80
Prestleigh Viaduct
183 ST 633406

Struggling with an Evercreech–Bath goods, Class 4F 0-6-0 No 44561 crawls up the 1:50 gradient and crosses Prestleigh Viaduct, located at about the halfway point between the stations of Shepton Mallet and Evercreech New, some 23 miles from Bath Junction.

Sometimes the forward progress of such trains on the severe gradients was barely discernible from a distance. The eleven arches of the graceful viaduct are shown to good advantage in this splendid view. *Photo: Ivo Peters. Date: 30 April 1955.*

Sadly, the tranquillity of the area was shattered on 16 January 1993, when BR put into effect a demolition contract and the viaduct was blown up. A combination of poor quality limestone used to build the original structure and shoddy workmanship, which was evident by the standard of brickwork on the widened portion of the viaduct and had been carried out between 1888/9, followed by years of neglect and lack of maintenance, led to its deterioration. A report submitted early in 1991 suggested that the viaduct would soon become dangerous, so there was little option but to have the structure demolished. Now the valley is shorn of its structure – but perhaps not of its sheep!

All traces of the line formation between here and the start of Cannard's Grave cutting have been turned back into farmland. South of here the formation is still distinct and a few occupation bridges survive, but Bridge 99 over the B3081 Evercreech road has been demolished. *Date: 10 March 1995.*

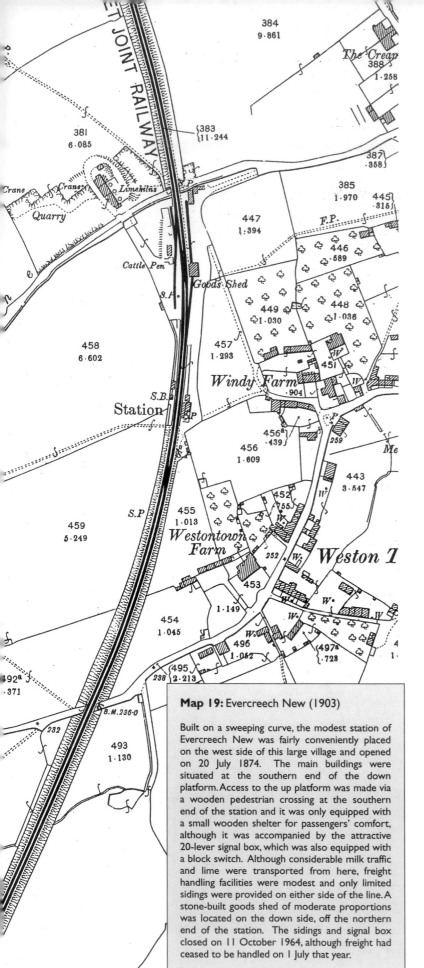

81
Evercreech New station
183 ST 645386

This elevated view of Evercreech New, taken from the down starter signal, shows the layout of the station and goods yard to advantage. The edifice on the left is the remains of a lime works and kiln. The camera also captures a quiet moment during a break in traffic on a sultry summer's afternoon and the stationmaster, Reg Jeans, who is seen standing in the field on the right, has time to enjoy a game of cricket with two small boys! This tranquil scene seems far from the realities of the ulcerative pace of modern life...how much we have lost since then. *Photo: David Milton. Date: Summer 1961.*

If it were not for the hill in the background this location would be extremely hard to recognise. Some of the railings from the up platform can still be found and now form boundary fences to gardens and a car park. The public footpath, just visible in the foreground on the 1961 photograph, crosses in front of the shiplap fencing. The entire site has been built upon, but the trackbed immediately south of this point forms part of a garden. Either side of the station site, bridges (Nos 101 and 102) have been demolished and only the north abutment remains of the former in Leighton Lane; however, both those of the latter are extant.

Considerable housing development has taken place over the last ten years, including a number of dwellings built on much of the former goods yard, now called Kiln Drive. Even the house in the immediate foreground has had an extension added to it during the last few years. *Date: 10 March 1995.*

Map 19: Evercreech New (1903)

Built on a sweeping curve, the modest station of Evercreech New was fairly conveniently placed on the west side of this large village and opened on 20 July 1874. The main buildings were situated at the southern end of the down platform. Access to the up platform was made via a wooden pedestrian crossing at the southern end of the station and it was only equipped with a small wooden shelter for passengers' comfort, although it was accompanied by the attractive 20-lever signal box, which was also equipped with a block switch. Although considerable milk traffic and lime were transported from here, freight handling facilities were modest and only limited sidings were provided on either side of the line. A stone-built goods shed of moderate proportions was located on the down side, off the northern end of the station. The sidings and signal box closed on 11 October 1964, although freight had ceased to be handled on 1 July that year.

82
Evercreech – Pecking Mill curve
183 ST 638374

This severe curve had a 25mph speed restriction and on up trains required careful handling by such locomotives as the Bulleid Pacifics, which had a propensity to slip. No such trouble is experienced here by Class 2P No 40696, crewed by driver Fred Wotley and fireman White, piloting 7F No 53803, with the celebrated partnership of driver Donald Beale and fireman Peter Smith on the footplate, with the 10.35 (SO) Bournemouth–Manchester.

In the background behind the locomotives is the guards' cabin and mess room adjacent to the down goods yard, on the Highbridge and Burnham branch, which is just visible. Note the refuge built into the retaining wall. *Photo: Ivo Peters.* *Date: 3 August 1957.*

This untidy scene was taken from a three-arched farm bridge (No 107) spanning the old line. This once-attractive structure has seen better days and the small arch on the down side has collapsed onto the embankment making it dangerous to cross, which only can be achieved by inching forward alongside the parapet. Note the refuge is still visible just to the right of the building. Some twelve chains northwards from this location the remaining arches and piers of Pecking Mill Viaduct, once a structure of six spans, can still be seen either side of the A371 road which it straddled. *Date: 10 March 1995.*

The remains of 5-span Pecking Mill Viaduct. *Date: 10 March 1995.*

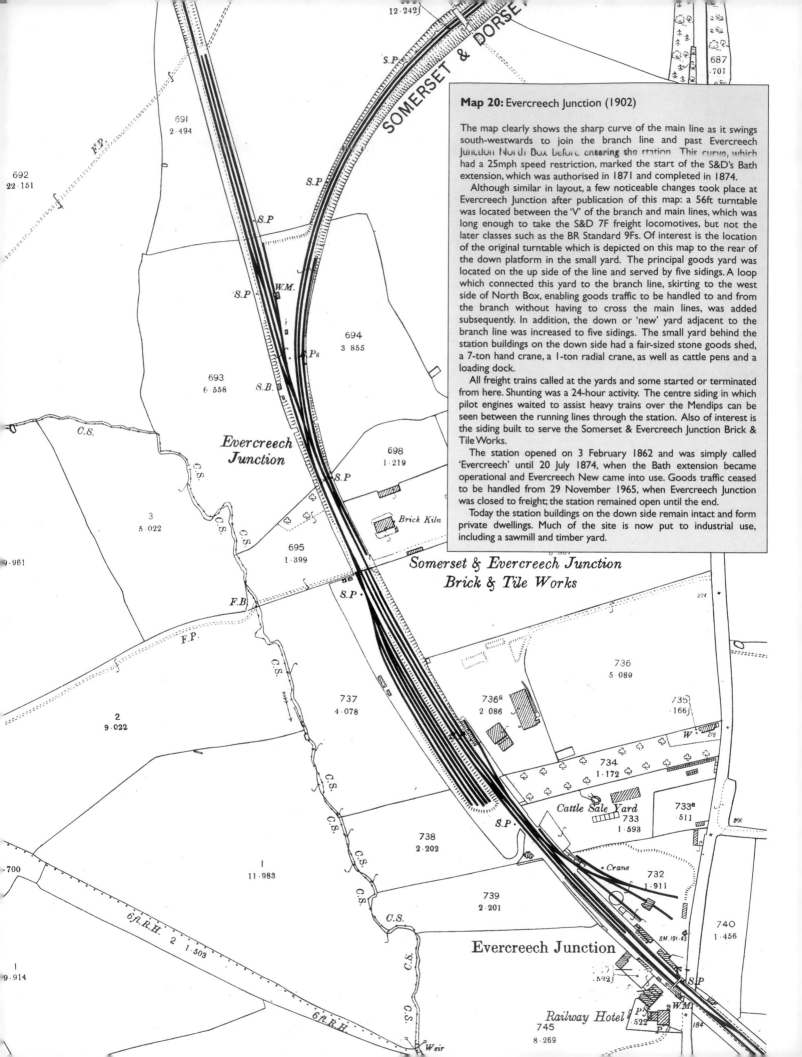

Map 20: Evercreech Junction (1902)

The map clearly shows the sharp curve of the main line as it swings south-westwards to join the branch line and past Evercreech Junction North Box before entering the station. This curve, which had a 25mph speed restriction, marked the start of the S&D's Bath extension, which was authorised in 1871 and completed in 1874.

Although similar in layout, a few noticeable changes took place at Evercreech Junction after publication of this map: a 56ft turntable was located between the 'V' of the branch and main lines, which was long enough to take the S&D 7F freight locomotives, but not the later classes such as the BR Standard 9Fs. Of interest is the location of the original turntable which is depicted on this map to the rear of the down platform in the small yard. The principal goods yard was located on the up side of the line and served by five sidings. A loop which connected this yard to the branch line, skirting to the west side of North Box, enabling goods traffic to be handled to and from the branch without having to cross the main lines, was added subsequently. In addition, the down or 'new' yard adjacent to the branch line was increased to five sidings. The small yard behind the station buildings on the down side had a fair-sized stone goods shed, a 7-ton hand crane, a 1-ton radial crane, as well as cattle pens and a loading dock.

All freight trains called at the yards and some started or terminated from here. Shunting was a 24-hour activity. The centre siding in which pilot engines waited to assist heavy trains over the Mendips can be seen between the running lines through the station. Also of interest is the siding built to serve the Somerset & Evercreech Junction Brick & Tile Works.

The station opened on 3 February 1862 and was simply called 'Evercreech' until 20 July 1874, when the Bath extension became operational and Evercreech New came into use. Goods traffic ceased to be handled from 29 November 1965, when Evercreech Junction was closed to freight; the station remained open until the end.

Today the station buildings on the down side remain intact and form private dwellings. Much of the site is now put to industrial use, including a sawmill and timber yard.

83

Evercreech Junction – North Box
183 ST 637370

A good view of the 32-lever North Box and the branch line to Highbridge and Burnham heading into the distance.

Cautiously negotiating the sharp curve around North Box are Class 2P No 40563 and Bulleid Pacific No 34042 *Dorchester* in charge of the 09.40 (SO) Sheffield–Bournemouth service. The curve was a legacy of the extension built to Bath in 1874 which diverted from the then main line to Glastonbury and Highbridge.

The loop around North Box can be seen to advantage, which meant shunting operations in the up yard could carry on without encroaching on the main running lines.

Note the crossed-arm calling back signal on the right of the picture; this was used for authorizing down freight trains to reverse on the down main line and then back into the up goods yard adjacent to the branch.

North Box closed on 31 May 1965, but burnt down on the night of 5 March 1966 in mysterious circumstances. *Photo: Ivo Peters. Date: 8 August 1953.*

'The storm has gone over me and I lie like one of those old oaks which the late hurricane has scattered about me. I am stripped of all my honours, I am torn up by the roots, and lie prostrate on the earth!'
Edmund Burke (1729-97).

What more can one say?
Date: 10 March 1995.

84

Evercreech Junction – up goods yard
183 ST 637370

BR Class 4 4-6-0 No 75073 on the 15.30 up mail passes the up goods yard and Evercreech Junction North Box's bracket up home signal and is about to negotiate the sharp right hand curve on the start of the 8½ mile climb up the Mendips. Having priority over the other traffic on the line, everything was done to ensure no delay occurred and the up mail arrived on time. Of note is the calling back signal seen to the left, which also controlled the loop to the 'new' yard alongside the branch line. *Photo: Ivo Peters. Date: 25 July 1964.*

There is little if anything left which bears a relationship to yesteryear's scene and small industrial units have been built on the site of the up goods yard. Bradfords (formerly Slades), the builders' merchants, have a premises on the left and the rather untidy mess behind the fence includes a scaffolding stock yard. *Date: 10 March 1995.*

1 *(Opposite)*
Bath – Devonshire Bank
172 ST 742636

On the penultimate day of working on the S&D line, the immaculately prepared Bulleid Pacifics, No 34006 *Bude* and No 34057 *Biggin Hill*, with 'The Somerset & Dorset Rail Tour' – a farewell special run by the LCGB – coast down Devonshire Bank and pass under the Maple Grove pedestrian bridge, where a number of spectators and photographers, including Ivo Peters, had gathered to witness the passage of the train.

The special had run down the main SR line to Templecombe, where the Pacifics had taken the train over for the trip to

Evercreech Junction. From there two Ivatt 2-6-2Ts then hauled the train up the branch to Highbridge and back, before the Pacifics took over again for the journey to Bath, returning in the late afternoon. *Photo: Angela O'Shea. Date: 5 March 1966.*

Apart from Maple Grove Bridge in the middle foreground, the roof of the house on the extreme left and the church spire on the horizon on the right give the clues that this is the spot where the two Pacifics drifted down the 1:50 bank some twenty-nine years earlier. The sign on the left indicates that this is now part of The Linear Park, a well-used walking facility in the city's suburbs. *Date: 27 March 1995.*

2
Devonshire Tunnel
172 ST 743636

BR Class 5 No 73049 and unrebuilt West Country class 4-6-2 No 34043 *Combe Martin*, with the 12.20 (SO) Bournemouth–Nottingham, emerge from the Devonshire Tunnel and into the sunshine. The restricted clearance over the train can be gauged well in this dramatic view. Typical of many in Bath, the row of terraced houses in the background is in Bloomfield Road.

No 34043 was reputed to be an erratic steamer and one of the less popular members of this class to run over the S&D. *Photo: Norman Lockett. Date: 18 August 1962.*

3
Horsecombe Vale – Combe Down Tunnel
172 ST 763618

Looking reasonably clean, Class 4 2-6-4T No 80138 bursts out of Combe Down Tunnel and into Horsecombe Vale. Southern-type discs have been used for the headcode instead of lamps to indicate an S&D passenger working. The shadows of an afternoon's sun would indicate that this is most likely to be the 16.21 Bath–Bournemouth West semi-fast. The locomotive was based at Bournemouth (70F) shed to where it had been transferred the month before, having come from 75B Redhill; it was finally withdrawn in October 1966. *Photo: Angela O'Shea. Date: March 1965.*

4
Horsecombe Vale – Tucking Mill Viaduct
172 ST 763618

Having just crossed Tucking Mill Viaduct in the background, Standard Class 4 2-6-0 No 76025 from 70F Bournemouth shed, approaches the southern portal of Combe Down Tunnel in Horsecombe Vale. This mid-afternoon shot would suggest the locomotive is working the 13.10 service from Bournemouth West. From 1955 these Class 4 2-6-0s were often rostered for duties over the S&D and were usually supplied by Bournemouth Central, but occasionally by Eastleigh MPD. No members of this class were allocated to S&D sheds.
Photo: Angela O'Shea. Date: March 1965.

The last rays of an afternoon's sun cast shadows on an entirely different scene: the embankments have been scooped away to infill part of the tunnel's cutting to create a footpath along the Linear Park. A small manhole above the buried portal allows access for maintenance of the tunnel. The terraced houses in Bloomfield Road can just be made out behind the small trees on the right, but are difficult to see. There has been some new development over the ensuing years and the modern houses in the background are in Hensley Gardens. Date: 27 March 1995.

There is not much to which reference can easily be made in this comparison that resembles anything from the 1965 photograph except, perhaps, the bank on the left and the tunnel mouth, which is all but hidden by trees and undergrowth when viewed from this perspective. Although it was obscured by the locomotive in the previous shot, the remains of the lineside telephone can be seen in the centre of the picture beyond the derelict farm trailer. Date: 27 March 1995.

The view towards the viaduct is now totally obscured by bushes and trees, although the visible part of the trackbed provides access into an adjoining field on the east side of the formation. A track leads from the water works at the base of the viaduct to the tunnel, so access can be gained should maintenance be necessary by Wessex Water, who now own it.

The stile on the right of the picture can be identified with that in the original view. Date: 27 March 1995.

5
Midford – 'Park Bank'
172 ST 762611

Both Ivo Peters (on the right) and his friend Norman Lockett capture one of the two final August bank holiday excursions to run over the S&D from Bath to Bournemouth Central. Here one of Bath MPD's few surviving Class 5s, No 73001, with an eight-coach train, drifts down 'Park Bank' to pass Midford goods yard, which has a fine display of rosebay willowherb. By this date, Bournemouth West had closed to traffic whilst electrification work took place in the area, but in the event it never reopened. *Photo: Angela O'Shea. Date: 30 August 1965.*

6
Midford station
172 ST 761607

Class 4 2-6-4T No 80147 draws into Midford with the 13.10 down local from Bath. The view from the steps of the signal box across the valley was superb, as illustrated here. The curvature of Midford's platform which nestled into the hillside is also plain to see. Immediately below the line is a former lock keeper's cottage on the course of the old Somersetshire Coal Canal, which passed to the east side of The Hope & Anchor Inn and then under the Hinton Charterhouse road before swinging westwards beneath Midford Viaduct towards the nearby basin.

No 80147 had not long to remain in service, for it was withdrawn from Bournemouth shed just three months later, where it was stored until scrapped by Bird's, Morriston, Swansea, in January 1966. *Photo: Angela O'Shea. Date: March 1965.*

7
Midford valley (1)
172 ST 762602

BR Class 5 No 73051 sweeps round the bend from Midford with the 07.43 (SO) Birmingham–Bournemouth on a glorious summer's day. Note the high retaining wall under which used to be a short siding, which had been lifted by this date, together with its points. Midford Castle can be seen on the hill in the background. On the extreme right Midford's down advance starting signal can be spotted, which was a Western replacement for a much taller and more elegant structure that was previously sited nearby. *Photo: R.C.Riley. Date: 12 August 1961.*

Mike Arlett stands in approximately the same position as Ivo Peters and Norman Locket almost thirty years before. The contrasting scene is self-evident: the embankments on either side of the line formation are largely overgrown, but the trees and fields on the horizon provide some continuity.

Regrettably, the goods yard site is rather untidy, having been left full of debris following the removal of New Age travellers from there some time ago. It is ironic that many of these people who are so active in environmental issues, particularly concerning road building schemes, often choose to leave their previous encampments in the countryside littered with refuse from their stay. *Date: 27 March 1995.*

The platform has received attention from a preservation group in the last few years and remains in reasonable condition. The trackbed, too, has benefitted, having had several hundred tons of ballast deposited on its surface extending back to 'Long Arch Bridge', which marks the northern boundary of this privately owned section of the S&D's formation. This view was taken from a pair of steps erected in what is now the Hope & Anchor's car park; no trace is left of the signal box. Trees on the embankment have obscured the view across the valley and also of the former lock keeper's cottage. *Date: 27 March 1995.*

A virtually unscalable chain-link fence placed across the formation here a few years ago has all but prevented access by the public and has enabled a variety of shrubs and trees to prosper together with an abundance of undergrowth, which provides excellent cover for rabbits and pheasants, the latter being reared in large numbers by the landowner. The formation between this point and Wellow is remarkably clear, as it is used as a farm track to service outlying fields either side of it. Midford Castle can just be made out on the horizon, but it will not be many years before it is hidden from view from here. *Date: 27 March 1995.*

8
Midford valley (2)
172 ST 761601

On a bright and crisp spring day, BR Class 4 2-6-4T No 80067, with only three months to go before its withdrawal, swings through the reverse curves in the Midford valley with a down local comprised of Bulleid set No 553.

    A year or so to closure of the line, a high standard of track maintenance is still being achieved, as can be judged from the tidy appearance of the ballast neatly aligned alongside the linesmen's footpaths.
Photo: Angela O'Shea. Date: March 1965.

9
Wellow station (1)
172 ST 740582

A fine study taken from the verandah of the signal box at Wellow of S&D Class 7F 2-8-0 No 53807 with the 06.05 Templecombe Upper–Bath pick-up goods, which it is about to reverse through the station and into the yard beyond to allow the passage of the 09.30 Bournemouth–Birmingham and also the up 'Pines Express', which left 15 minutes later at 09.45. The ground frame controlling the points to the yard was released by the box and the reversing procedure would have then been aided by hand signals from the guard.

    To complete this pastoral scene, a large herd of dairy cattle crowd the fence near the goods yard entrance, probably intrigued by the goings on.
Photo: R.C.Riley. Date: 6 July 1959.

10
Wellow station (2)
172 ST 739581

On a cloudless spring evening the rather grubby BR Class 3 2-6-2T No 82004 briskly sets off from Wellow with the 18.05 (SX) Bath–Binegar local. By this date the service had been reduced to a single coach and was usually worked by one of this class of locomotives. Judging from the up starting signal, a train is due in the other direction, probably the 15.40 up mail from Bournemouth, although if the down local was running to time, it would not be due for another twenty minutes or so. No 82004 was withdrawn five months later at Bath shed, where it was stored until closure of the line.
Photo: Angela O'Shea. Date: 25 May 1965.

A lovely spring day thirty years later; the scene is a little different now, but nevertheless unmistakable: the hillside in the background offers the instant clue to the location. Since the formation is used as a farm track, the banks are periodically trimmed with a mechanical hedgecutter keeping the way clear of undergrowth and bushes. The torched remains of Midford's up outer home signal can be found at the side of the trackbed in the background. It does not take too much to imagine fresh ballast and track being laid here for steam trains to trundle through this lovely valley once again. *Date: 27 March 1995.*

The building on the right offers some continuity with the past, although almost every other aspect has changed, with the exception of the gate beyond the parked car. A small orchard has been planted on the trackbed here and forms part of the garden of the former station, now a desirable residence.

Having once been owned by the artist Peter Blake, who used it as a studio and for storage, the signal box has been tastefully converted into a small dwelling, but it has been the subject of criticism from some of the village's inhabitants. However, others, including an ex-S&D staff member who still lives around here, have praised the well-designed conversion.
Date: 2 November 1985 (revisited 13 March 1995).

The former station building is still easily identifiable in the background. Previously used for vehicular access to the goods yard via the gate near the station, the road now leads to a car park from which this comparison was taken. As part of a landscaping scheme to enhance the derelict station area, the trees and bushes were planted by artist Peter Blake, who once owned the station property before selling it. At the time of this visit the building was unoccupied, although the gardens were still being tended.

Close observation will reveal the railway boundary fence seen through a gap in the trees on the right; beyond it are the fields across the valley, which can be identified with those observed in the 1965 view. *Date: 27 March 1995.*

11
Wellow goods yard
172 ST 738580

On the last Saturday of operation, the 16.25 Bath–Templecombe heads southwards from Wellow and passes the site of the goods yard, the sidings of which have already been lifted. The train was crowded with people taking a final chance to have one last ride over the S&D. It was also the swansong for No 80043, for it was withdrawn from service on closure of the line and stored at its home shed of 83G Templecombe for a month before being sent for scrap. *Photo: Angela O'Shea. Date: 5 March 1966.*

12
Midsomer Norton station
183 ST 664537

Before proceeding to Bath, Class 7F No 53810 backs onto the up line with a coal train from Norton Hill Colliery. Out of camera sight 'Jinty' No 47316, having helped with shunting duties, is waiting to be coupled ahead to save a light engine path to Radstock.

The station has been embellished by hanging baskets adorning the shelter on the up platform. Ivo Peters related that one year Midsomer Norton, after a long run of successes, did not win the annual 'best kept station' competition, which amazed all and sundry. Expressing complete surprise as to the outcome, one person learnt the possible reason for its failure, when asked: "Ah, yes, but didn't you see the copper pipework in the toilets?" This summed up the fierce pride S&D staff had in the appearance of their stations and the stiff competition in vying for the accolade of being judged the best. *Photo: R.C.Riley. Date: 3 July 1961.*

13
Moorewood – Burnt House Bridge (No 57)
183 ST 632513

Working a down local with Bulleid set No 813 in tow, BR Class 4 2-6-4T No 80043 draws near Moorewood and is about to pass under the twin-arch bridge carrying the B3139 road. Once this point had been reached, having passed the 700ft contour, the stiffest part of the southbound climb of the Mendips was over and the gradient eased to 1:67. However, there were still some two-and-a-half miles to go before the summit was reached at Masbury. *Photo: Angela O'Shea. Date: 31 August 1965.*

With many changes to the former railway line, St Julian's church is unaffected by the passage of thirty years. Much of the former goods yard this side of Bridge 24 is largely overgrown, but a footpath has been hacked through so walkers can pass with relative ease. One item of note is the gate on the right, which can be identified as that in the 1966 picture, but is in appreciably a worse condition today! Aside from the railway, it is interesting to see how many hedgerows and trees have been removed over the ensuing years. This is equally applicable to many of the comparison views.
Date: 27 March 1995.

Some time after closure the trackbed between the platforms was filled in as part of a project for the nearby Somervale School. This situation was reversed in the early 1980s, having received attention during a YTS scheme to enhance and renovate the station area, during which the wooden shelter was re-clad and painted. The railings on the down platform also received a lick of paint.

By 1995 the shelter was again to be found in a dilapidated state and in need of repair, as can be judged from this view; however the platforms remain in reasonable shape.

At the time of the visit the station was up for sale by tender, having been deemed surplus to requirements by Norton Radstock College, whose art and design department have occupied the buildings for a number of years.
Date: 12 March 1995.

Three sheep graze peacefully in the paddock formed by the infilling of the cutting. The tree line and wall are readily identifiable and the small shed seen on the left of the original picture is extant, but obscured by a small tree. The bridge has long since been demolished, the road levelled and trees planted to form a new hedge line on the north verge.

Unlike much of the former line, there has been very little change to this scene over the last ten years.
Date: 5 October 1985 (revisited 4 March 1995).

14
Moorewood sidings
183 ST 628510

West Country class No 34043 *Combe Martin* and Class 5 No 73051 on the down 'Pines Express' pass the disused Moorewood Colliery sidings. The colliery had closed in December 1932. It was served by a light gauge railway (trucks were winched up an incline plane from the pithead), meeting the S&D here. The 2ft gauge line, worked by diminutive 0-6-0 locomotives, was still being used in 1933 for the transference of coal remaining at the pithead and the removal of artefacts still left at the colliery following its closure.
Photo: R.C.Riley. Date: 5 September 1959.

15
Masbury – Oakhill Road Bridge (No 69)
183 ST 609479

A Bath to Bournemouth excursion, with BR Class 5 No 73051 in charge, nears Masbury Summit as it pounds up the final stretch of 1:73 gradient and is about to pass under Bridge 69 carrying the B3155 road. Note that some passengers' penchant for catching smuts and flies in their faces is being satisfied as they lean from the carriage doors on this hot summer's day! Bridge 68 over a minor road to Gurney Slade can be seen just to the rear of the train.

Having spent all its working life on the S&D, the omnipresent Class 5 locomotive was finally withdrawn from service two months later.
Photo: Angela O'Shea. Date: 7 June 1965.

16
Prestleigh – Bridge 94
183 ST 633408

The eight-coach LCGB farewell special, 'The Somerset & Dorset Rail Tour', was one of the last trains to traverse the S&D system. Hauled by the immaculately prepared West Country class No 34006 *Bude* and Battle of Britain class No 34057 *Biggin Hill*, the train approaches Bridge 94 shortly after crossing Prestleigh Viaduct on the 2½-mile climb at 1:50 from Evercreech New to Cannard's Grave.

Both engines failed to see out the end of steam on the Southern Region: No 34006 survived another year and No 34057 only outlasted it by a further two months; both were scrapped towards the end of 1967.
Photo: Angela O'Shea. Date: 5 March 1966.

Like the original, this comparison photograph was taken from the embankment of the old colliery railway, where coal used to be transferred to S&D trucks in the sidings below.

The trackbed has been grassed over and is used as a paddock. The old bridge (No 58) has been demolished, the lane to Downside now passing over an embankment built to replace it. The impressions of the sleepers that once formed the Moorewood Colliery sidings can still be made out, as can the retaining wall of the old embankment of the narrow gauge railway from Moorewood Colliery, which ran parallel to the S&D at this point. *Date: 2 November 1985 (revisited 4 March 1995).*

The last rays of an afternoon's sun casts shadows which steal across a somewhat different landscape today. It is becoming increasingly difficult to realise a railway ever existed here: if it were not for the tell-tale signs like the railway fence on the former up side of the line and the ash tree, which has grown slightly taller and wider, it would be hard to tell this is where No 73051 pounded its way up the gradient towards the summit with its excursion some thirty years before. However, the trackbed just north of here is still quite distinct for a distance towards Whitnell Farm, about a half-mile distant and Bridge 68 still survives intact. *Date: 27 March 1995.*

Late autumn sunshine highlights the hill that once provided a magnificent backdrop to the S&D line's passage through this lovely bit of countryside. The last remaining section of the line's embankment adjacent to Prestleigh Viaduct is clearly visible to the right of the photograph. It was on this section that one of the final scenes of the BBC's film *Return to Evercreech Junction* was shot.

The greater proportion of the line's formation has been wiped off the face of the earth, the embankment flattened and the land put back to agricultural use. The two pylons, which rather blighted both views, provide a good reference point; the one in the foreground was fortuitously obscured by steam in the 1966 photograph.
Date: 15 November 1985 (revisited 10 March 1995).

17
Evercreech Junction North
183 ST 636371

On a glorious hot summer's day, fireman Keith Conibear gets ready to hand the single line token from West Pennard to the signalman at North Box, as Class 3F 0-6-0 No 43436, with the 14.20 ex-Highbridge, prepares to run down to Evercreech Junction station on the main line. The weighbridge hut, shunters' cabin and lamp room can be seen on the right of the photograph, behind which was the 56ft turntable located in the centre of the 'V' formed by the divergence of the main line and the branch. *Photo: R.C.Riley. Date: 6 July 1959.*

18
Cole station
183 ST 671334

The rather grubby BR Class 4 4-6-0 No 75073 departs from Cole with the 13.10 Bath–Templecombe down local.

Cole was particularly photogenic in railway terms and able to provide great variety for the enthusiast: the neat and tidy station and small goods yard could be viewed well from this bridge (No 121), which provided an excellent vantage point from which to photograph trains. As seen, Cole Viaduct was also well within view from here.

This photograph was taken exactly a week before the end of through services; soon S&D staff at Cole would not witness the passage of expresses running through their station at speed. However, No 75073, then based at 82G Templecombe, would soldier on for another three years until it was withdrawn in December 1965. *Photo: R.C.Riley. Date: 1 September 1962.*

19
Wincanton station
183 ST 710282

S&D Class 7F No 53810 in charge of an engineers' train, consisting of a mess coach and ballast wagons, stands in the yard at Wincanton on a Sunday whilst maintenance work is undertaken on the running lines through the station. The goods shed in the background was on the down side of the line and directly opposite the up platform. The platforms were staggered and did little to enhance the station's appearance. The large Cow & Gate milk factory, which once provided the line with much traffic, is just visible in front of the locomotive. *Photo: R.C.Riley. Date: 16 July 1961.*

The whole area has been returned to pasture, but the solitary tree provided a tangible reference point which was visible in the 1959 photograph. The guards' cabin-cum-mess room, seen in the middle distance, has since been knocked down. Just visible between it and the tree, some two-and-a-quarter miles away in the distance, is Prestleigh Viaduct, but this structure has also since been demolished. *Date: 2 November 1985 (revisited 10 March 1995).*

COMMENT: *The audience was herded and positioned by Mike Arlett; they had refused to co-operate and insisted on licking my legs and rear!*

The dark satanic sky, heavily laden with rain, provides a dramatic backcloth to Cole; the scudding clouds part just enough to allow the buildings to be briefly illuminated by sunshine before the onset of another squally shower. Some rubble and spoil from Cole Viaduct can be seen on the trackbed in untidy piles, beyond which are the last remnants of the platforms. It is evident that many trees have been lost around here over the years and how it has affected the view of the landscape.

At the time of the 1995 visit the scene remained largely unaltered, but if planning permission is granted to build houses on the site of the former goods yard, it will undoubtedly change. *Date: 5 November 1985 (revisited 10 March 1995).*

The contrast could not be more stark: the premises of Hopkins Bros, a ready-mixed concrete company, dominates the foreground and a loading shovel momentarily occupies the spot where the 7F once stood in the goods yard. The former Unigate factory, which closed in the late 1980s, is still to be seen in the background, but has been split into several industrial units. Houses in 'Pines Close' can just be made out in the left background and are built on the site of the former station. *Date: 20 March 1995.*

20
Horsington
183 ST 709243

'The Southern Wanderer', a special organised
by the Southern Counties Touring Society,
ran from London Victoria to Bournemouth
and over the S&D to Evercreech Junction
from where it went up the branch to Highbridge and back. Engines had been changed
at Templecombe, where Class 4F No 44560,
once shedded there, but borrowed from
Gloucester shed for the occasion, took over
from BR Class 5 No 73022.

   The excursion is seen on the return
journey as it nears Templecombe, where
the 4F was exchanged for Merchant Navy
class No 35023 *Holland Africa Line* for the
run back up the SR main line to London.
Photo: Angela O'Shea. Date: 28 March 1965.

21
Templecombe (82G) shed
183 ST 709228

Class 4F 0-6-0 No 44559 heads past
Templecombe shed and towards
Henstridge with the 16.16 Evercreech
Junction–Bournemouth, a connecting
service with the 'Pines Express', which
stopped at intermediate stations.

   This splendid photograph was taken
from a signal halfway along the spur to
Templecombe Upper station and
provided a panoramic view of the
shed. Templecombe Lower can be
spotted between Combe Throop Road
Bridge (No 152) and the SR line bridge
(No 153). The buildings of the old
Dorset Central station are visible
adjacent to three other Class 4F
engines standing in the siding alongside
the shed. *Photo: R.C.Riley.*
Date: 12 July 1960.

22
Sturminster Newton – Bridge 171
194 ST 783143

Having worked the 09.55 semi-fast from
Bath to Bournemouth earlier in the day,
Standard Class 9F No 92220 *Evening Star*
rumbles back over the bridge spanning
the River Stour just north of Sturminster
Newton with the 15.40 Bournemouth–
Bristol up mail. The locomotive was
specially allocated to Bath MPD on 8
September 1962 in order that it would be
available to work the last 'Pines Express',
following which it was transferred to 88A
Canton a few days later, on 13 September.
A year later, due to locomotive shortages,
No 92220 was transferred back to the
S&D for a time and employed hauling
three or four coach local trains up and
down the line. *Photo: R.C.Riley.*
Date: 1 September 1962.

A rather desolate scene almost thirty years later to the day: the line's formation in this section is still quite distinct and is used occasionally as a farm track, although it appears to be rather waterlogged in this view, judging from the ruts. A few of the mature trees in the background can be identified with those seen in the 1965 picture, although many others have since been felled, or succumbed to disease, particularly Dutch elm.
Date: 20 March 1995.

The old spur to Templecombe Upper has been made into a slip road to GEC Marconi's underwater systems' factory now located here, which has meant most of the embankment being removed to provide site access. The former engine shed is still a useful part of the complex and over the years the factory has provided employment for many ex-S&D staff.

In 1995, there have been few changes to the building itself, although cars are no longer allowed to park to the side of it. Date: 12 November 1985 (revisited 20 March 1995).

COMMENT: To take this view I commandeered a lorry-mounted elevating platform, the crew of which had been busy changing street light bulbs in the village. They kindly agreed to render assistance in my quest to be raised to 30ft, the height of the former signal!

The River Stour is quite unchanged by the passage of time as it flows on its meandering course to the sea. The bridge's girder span has been demolished, but the brick arches remain intact and are likely to provide a reminder of a great past for some considerable time into the future. Date: 21 March 1995.

85
Evercreech Junction (1)
183 ST 639366

The classic S&D scene for which the line will be remembered: the 8½-mile assault of the Mendips is about to begin, as Class 7F No 53800 blasts away from Evercreech Junction on the 1:105 gradient to take the 15.35 up mail, made up of ancient stock, northwards. Over the first coach an engine waits in the centre siding to work the 18.02 to Highbridge on the branch, whilst the 16.37 Bath–Templecombe local stands at the down platform behind. The goods shed and down yard are seen in the background, in which 2P 4-4-0 No 40569 is standing awaiting a light engine path back to shed, having finished its banking duties for the day. The roof of the Railway Hotel facing the main A371 road can be discerned on the right. *Photo: Ivo Peters.*
Date: 16 August 1952.

23 *(Opposite)*
Shillingstone station
194 ST 825116

The end of the line? With the official closure scheduled for 3 January, a number of specials ran over the S&D. Prior to the eleventh-hour announcement of a temporary reprieve, which was to last a few weeks, due to a bus operator withdrawing an application for a licence, the Locomotive Club of Great Britain had arranged a special to run over the line for the last time. Due to their axle loading, Merchant Navy Pacifics had been barred from working over the S&D system, but with closure imminent, nothing seemed to matter and so the spectacle of seeing one of these magnificent engines on the line became a reality. Here Merchant Navy class 4-6-2 No 30511 *General Steam Navigation* passes through Shillingstone with the LCGB's 'Mendip Merchantman Rail Tour'. The sidings in the goods yard have already been lifted; dereliction and decay are setting in. *Photo: Angela O'Shea.*
Date: 1 January 1966.

Shillingstone today: the station building is used as a MENSA workshop, but the majority of the site, particularly the area of the former goods yard, is used as a car park for a number of small factory units built here. Now partly obscured by bushes along the old railway fence line, the slopes of the National Trust-owned Hod Hill, on which there is an Iron Age fort, later used by the Romans, can still be seen on the extreme left of the picture.
Date: 21 March 1995.

The main station buildings on the down side remain intact and form private dwellings, now rented. Much of the site covering the trackbed and down goods yard, including the surviving goods shed, forms part of a sawmill and timber yard. A small industrial estate has been built on the up sidings and a waste disposal company, Cleanaway, have a depot at the southern end. Beyond the units towards the site of North Junction, the land has been completely returned to agriculture. *Date: 19 March 1995.*

86
Evercreech Junction (2)
183 ST 640365

A sledge hammer to crack a nut: BR Class 9F 2-10-0 No 92220 *Evening Star* returns to the S&D for a few months due to the shortage of motive power caused by several locomotives being away and under repair. A request was made for two Class 5s, but Bath received two 9Fs instead. The length of the Class 9Fs precluded their use on freight trains to Evercreech as they could not be turned on the turntable. Their heavy use of coal on three or four coach trains did not help the cost effectiveness on what by now was a purely local service run on the S&D line, through traffic having ceased in 1962.

The station layout is seen to good advantage. Of note is the centre siding in which pilot engines and waiting branch line trains were kept; by this date they were seldom used in comparison with a few years before. *Photo: Ivo Peters. Date: 12 September 1963.*

With the kind help of Mr and Mrs Nash, who own the Evercreech Junction site and live in a purpose-built timber house alongside the former down goods yard, the footbridge was recreated for the day in the shape of a fork-lift truck fitted with a large box from which this comparison was obtained. No prizes are offered for guessing the meaning of 'Le Guichet' and 'Sdoog Dray', which the former station buildings are now named: the first is French for 'Booking Office'; some reverse thinking is necessary for the second! Note the extension built onto the old ticket office on the down platform and the small industrial estate built on the up goods yard.

In 1995, planning permission was being sought to extend this back towards the station with the erection of further units. *Date: 15 June 1985 (revisited 19 March 1995).*

00 (Right)
Evercreech Junction (4)
183 ST 640365

This photograph taken from near the centre of the footbridge offers a good view northwards and shows the neat wooden building on the up platform adorned with colourful hanging baskets. An up train is about to get under way with a flurry of activity on the platform, whilst a Class 4F simmers at the end of the up yard in the distance. The steepish gradient northwards from the station can be judged by the sidings in the background, being on level ground.

   Evercreech Junction was a Mecca for steam enthusiasts, particularly on a summer Saturday, to savour the tremendous variety of sight and sound that it could offer. *Photo: R.C. Riley. Date: 22 July 1958.*

87 (Left)
Evercreech Junction (3)
183 ST 639365

Class 3F 0-6-0 43218 arrives with a stopping train from Highbridge, bringing it to a halt adjacent to the water column and in front of the station footbridge, beyond which the level crossing over the A371 and large water tower can be observed. The tall LSWR lattice post of the down starter signal can be seen over the locomotive's chimney.

   The up platform, from which this photograph was taken, appears to be neat and tidy as one would expect of an S&D station. The station's staff always had a generous supply of magazines in the waiting rooms – a nice gesture which typified their friendly and thoughtful attitude towards passengers shown by many of the other employees who also worked on the S&D.
Photo: R.E. Toop. Date: 1 June 1957.

A garage has been built on the up platform, but 'Sdoog Dray' remains practically unchanged. The trackbed between the platforms has been filled to form a lawn, but the down side's edge can still be seen. *Date: 15 June 1985 (revisited 19 March 1995).*

The platform edges are a little cracked now, but still quite distinct; although heavy shadows on a late March afternoon make it difficult to judge, the roof of the garage built on the up platform can just be spotted over the cypress trees planted where the timber platform building was formerly to be seen. *Date: 19 March 1995.*

89
Evercreech Junction (5)
183 ST 640365

West Country class Pacific No 34041 *Wilton*, furiously blowing off at 250psi, gets under way from Evercreech Junction with a southbound express for Bournemouth. Besides the level crossing over the A371 road here, in the next couple of miles the train would have to pass over two others, Bruton Road and Lamyatt, which were less than a half mile apart.

A good view of the tall south signal box which housed a 26-lever frame and controlled the crossing over the A371 road seen in the foreground. The large water tower dominates this view looking south-east. The line stretches into the distance and on towards Lamyatt Crossing. *Photo: David Milton.*
Date: August 1961.

A farmer clears the trackbed, which has been used as a cattle feeding area. The base of the old water tower is seen surrounded by bushes. The A371 road is devoid of any railway artefact, thus denying the observer any clue as to its past except the old Railway Hotel just to the right of the picture which had been appropriately renamed 'The Silent Whistle' but which is now called 'The Natterjack'. Slowly but surely the S&D is disappearing into pastoral tranquillity, but two bridges (Nos 110 and 111) survive in the middle distance, the former spanning the River Alham. Much of the formation between here and Lamyatt Crossing is used as a farm track. *Date: 15 June 1985 (revisited 19 March 1995).*

The recreated footbridge with the author aboard. *Photo: M.J.Arlett. Date: 15 June 1985.*

90
Bruton Road Crossing
183 ST 654352

A gentleman's elegant horseless carriage stands at the crossing awaiting its owner, who takes a photograph of an approaching train made up of five coaches! This is thought to be the 13.10 up local from Templecombe, with Standard Class 4 2-6-0 No 76018 in charge. To the rear of the train and seen over the roof of Ivo Peters' Bentley, is a 'sound whistle' sign on the approach to an occupation crossing used by farmers, beyond which the line curves towards Bridge 115 at Wyke Champflower. *Photo: Ivo Peters. Date: Summer 1957.*

A ponyless trap temporarily awaits its dishevelled occupant, who placed it in the same position for comparison purposes! There is nothing obvious to indicate that the railway ever existed here: the landscape has been completely returned to agricultural use and changed dramatically; many of the mature trees seen in the 1957 view have not survived, making it difficult to realise this is the same location. An item of evidence found was one of the stout fencing posts, seen behind the Bentley, which can just be made out in the hedge in front of the author's Metro. The crossing keeper's cottage was demolished many years ago. *Date: 10 March 1995.*

The keeper's cottage at Lamyatt Crossing today. *Date: 10 March 1995.*

133

91
**Wyke Champflower –
Bridge 115**
183 ST 660344

This stone bridge was unique as it was constructed to span double track and the last built by the Somerset Central Railway before connecting with the Dorset Central's system. All the others on the S&D were built to span only a single track, but when the line was doubled between 1892 and 1894, second spans were built alongside.

Popping out from under the bridge is an afternoon local train from Templecombe to Highbridge, with Ivatt 2-6-2T No 41296 in charge; the next stop will be Evercreech Junction, just over two miles distant. *Photo: Ivo Peters. Date: 15 May 1965.*

Many bridges on the system which once spanned cuttings have been almost obscured from view due to infilling, as in this case, and here a pony paddock has been created from the couple of acres of reclaimed land. It is quite noticeable how the pine trees have thinned over the years. A little further north from here, the line formation has been obliterated with the land being returned to agricultural use and there is no trace whatsoever of the occupation crossing between here and Bruton Road.
Date: 10 March 1995.

COMMENT: *Without deference to middle age and almost vaulting the post and rail boundary fence in true style, my joie de vivre was short-lived: it had just been freshly creosoted...arrgh!*

92
Wyke Champflower – Cole curve
183 ST 661343

This is arguably one of the most photogenic locations on the S&D and many superb shots were obtained at this spot, which is also of considerable historical interest: it was just south of this bridge that the Somerset Central Railway's Glastonbury to Bruton extension and the Dorset Central Railway's Templecombe to Bruton extension met, formally opening on 18 January 1862. Later that year the two companies amalgamated to form the Somerset & Dorset Railway. A link had been finally created between the Bristol and English channels for the rapid conveyance of produce from South Wales to ports on the South Coast, particularly Southampton. The prospect of the trade it would generate was never entirely fulfilled, despite its early promise.

The sharp bend in the line here prevented any fast running, the speed limit being 45mph around Cole curve seen in the background. This scene shows Ivatt 2-6-2T No 41216 on an up local train from Templecombe to Highbridge.
Photo: Derek Cross. Date: 12 June 1965.

The trees are instantly recognisable although one or two have disappeared, whilst others have thinned somewhat. Note the house extension built encroaching onto the trackbed in the background, also the buildings of Bruton School for Girls (formerly Sunny Hill) visible on the horizon. Bridge 116 just around the corner beyond the house is still standing – but only just; the embankments to the south have been cut away and the land turned back to agriculture. *Date: 10 March 1995.*

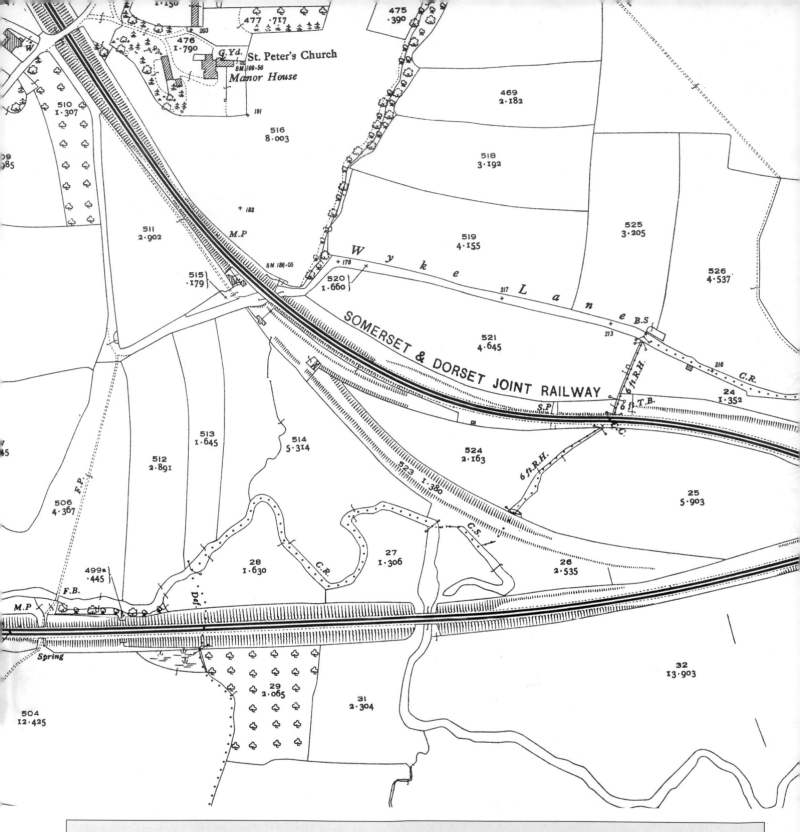

Map 21: Wyke Champflower (1930)

This map is of particular interest because it shows that the Wyke Lane bridge (No 115) marked the point at which the line diverged from the originally planned route of the Somerset Central (broad gauge) to its proposed connection with the Wilts, Somerset & Weymouth Railway (GWR line). The link, which had won the support of the majority of shareholders and was a cheaper option than the scheme initially empowered in 1855 to be made via Glastonbury, Wells and Frome, was finally abandoned during the early 1860s in favour of the narrow gauge union with the Dorset Central. The embankments of the proposed connection to the Wilts Somerset & Weymouth Railway can be seen clearly on the map. The junction, which apparently was never used nor completed (but may also account for the fact that Bridge 115 was constructed to span double track), was said to have been removed in 1878.

Today all traces of the embankments have disappeared, save for a small section, as has much of the S&D line itself between Wyke Lane and the GWR/West of England main line from Paddington, over which it crossed.

93
Cole – Bridges 117, 118 and Cole Viaduct (No 119)
183 ST 666339

A superb study of Class 9F No 92220 *Evening Star* working the last up 'Pines Express' as it accelerates away from Cole and crosses over three structures north of the station: Bridge 117 over Wyke Lane in the foreground, Bridge 118 over the main WR line (in the centre) and Cole Viaduct (No 119) at the rear of the train.

The up 'Pines' had been stopped at signals at Cole for over ten minutes, due to the preceding train, the 9F-hauled 09.25 from Bournemouth, exceeding the booked time for stopping at Evercreech Junction, due to insufficient coal needed to tackle the climb of the Mendips unaided. Assistance was therefore requested and a Collet 0-6-0 detailed for the duty; but the 9F's driver was not happy with such a light engine being coupled ahead of the much heavier 2-10-0 and insisted on exchanging places before proceeding. Driver Peter Smith and his fireman, Aubrey Punter, on the up 'Pines' would find it impossible to make up the delay and arrive at Bath 'right time'. *Photo: Ivo Peters. Date: 8 September 1962.*

All three structures have gone: both Bridge 117 and Cole Viaduct were demolished in September 1984 (along with No 120 adjacent to the station) and Bridge 118 over the ex-GW line many years before that. The railway boundary fence still survives, but provides no functional purpose, as stock can roam freely between the two fields it supposedly divides. Bruton School for Girls provides a readily tangible link, as do the trees on the hillside and in the middle of the picture the abutments of Bridge 118 are seen on the Plymouth–Paddington main line. *Date: 10 March 1995.*

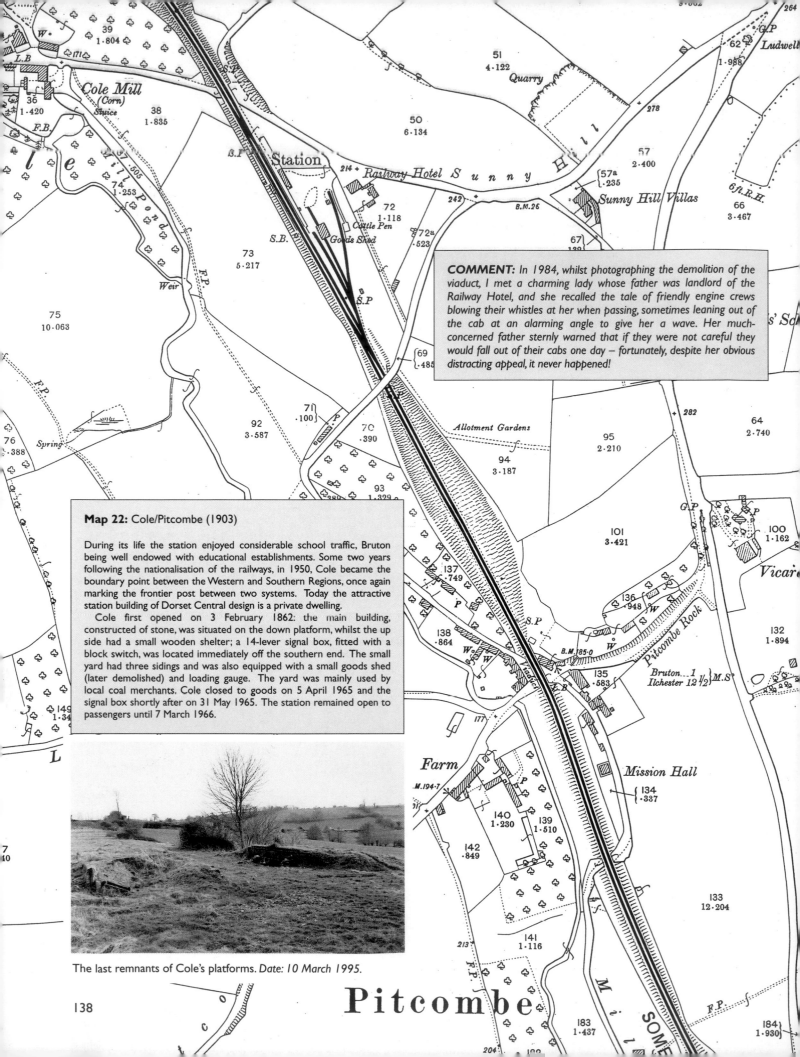

Map 22: Cole/Pitcombe (1903)

During its life the station enjoyed considerable school traffic, Bruton being well endowed with educational establishments. Some two years following the nationalisation of the railways, in 1950, Cole became the boundary point between the Western and Southern Regions, once again marking the frontier post between two systems. Today the attractive station building of Dorset Central design is a private dwelling.

Cole first opened on 3 February 1862: the main building, constructed of stone, was situated on the down platform, whilst the up side had a small wooden shelter; a 14-lever signal box, fitted with a block switch, was located immediately off the southern end. The small yard had three sidings and was also equipped with a small goods shed (later demolished) and loading gauge. The yard was mainly used by local coal merchants. Cole closed to goods on 5 April 1965 and the signal box shortly after on 31 May 1965. The station remained open to passengers until 7 March 1966.

The last remnants of Cole's platforms. *Date: 10 March 1995.*

Pitcombe

94
Cole station
183 ST 671334

Bridge 121 carrying Pitcombe Road over the line just to the south of the station provided an excellent vantage point from which to photograph trains as they passed through it on their journey southwards. Here the down 'Pines' hauled by Bath's omnipresent Class 5 4-6-0, No 73051, has traversed the four-arch viaduct seen in the background and passes the attractive Dorset Central-designed station. Of interest are the bales of hay stacked to form stook-like structures; some hard work will be necessary to fork them onto a trailer in due course! The building seen over the locomotive was the stationmaster's house, whilst the one on the extreme right was the former Railway Hotel. *Photo: Ivo Peters. Date: 8 June 1957.*

The trackbed in the foreground has been backfilled to the bridge (No 121) so that only the parapet shows, which was brought about by spoil and rubble removed after Cole Viaduct's demolition. Having remained empty for many years after the line's closure, the station building was converted into a desirable residence and an attractive garden has been created around it. Planning permission is currently being sought to erect at least three executive-style houses on the site of the goods yard, but not on the backfilled portion of the trackbed towards the bridge, south of which the deep cutting has been totally filled in. Pitcombe Viaduct (No 122) and Bridge 123 still straddle the road in the small hamlet set in an attractive valley 14½ chains south of this point, but the bridge (No 124) just beyond over the main A359 Bruton–Yeovil road has long since been demolished. *Date: 10 March 1995.*

Shepton Montague (1)
183 ST 685317

With stretches of level track and gradients no steeper than 1:100 in the section south of Cole towards Wincanton, some fast running could be achieved through this glorious countryside. Seen here are the very grimy BR Class 4 4-6-0 No 75027 and somewhat cleaner Bulleid Pacific No 34043 *Combe Martin* heading southwards with the 10.38 (SO) Manchester–Bournemouth, passing over Bridge 126. In the background is Bridge 125, beyond which a corrugated iron barrier was erected alongside the down line to separate the railway from a minor road which ran parallel to the junction with the A359 some chains north.

To the north-east of this location the passengers would be able to see the beautiful mansion and grounds of Redlynch House set on a hill.
Photo: Ivo Peters.
Date: 7 July 1962.

The early summer's blossom adorns the trees and shrubs which now envelop the banks of the track. It is obvious how many hedgerows have been removed in the 23 years between the photograph dates. Conversely it is noticeable how the wood on the right hand side has grown.

Much of the trackbed north of here towards the A359 is a haven for rabbits and is kept fairly clear with ballast still in evidence in some parts, particularly near the corrugated iron fence barrier which survives. *Date: 1 June 1985 (revisited 20 March 1995).*

96
Shepton Montague – Rock Cutting Bridge (No 127)
183 ST 687315

Class 9F No 92212 sweeps under the tall twin-arched overbridge, some two and a half miles north of Wincanton, with the 07.43 (SO) Bradford–Bournemouth train. The bridge, which carried the road between Shepton Montague and Stoney Stoke, was notable for the clearance it afforded from rail level to the soffits of the arches, which was 21ft 2in, unlike many of the other bridges and tunnels on the S&D system, where the headroom was much more restricted. *Photo: Ivo Peters. Date: 2 September 1961.*

A mixture of trees encroach the rock cutting sides, but the bridge still stands out defiantly. The trackbed is occasionally used as a farm track, but most of the ballast has been removed and in winter large pools of water collect either side of the structure, which provide ideal depositories for frogs to spawn. South of this point the line formation is still quite distinct for some distance, but sections of it have been blended into adjacent fields, although much of the original fencing survives on one side or the other. *Date: 20 March 1995.*

97
Wincanton – Bridge 131
183 ST 709291

This attractive setting just north of Wincanton town was a favourite spot for lineside photographers. The sight of a heavy train coming round this bend against a backdrop of trees on the hill, perfectly summed up the line's many charms. On its final run over the Somerset & Dorset line, BR Class 9F No 92214, working the 15.40 up mail from Bournemouth, rounds the bend just north of Wincanton. Soon the line would straighten out, on a falling gradient towards Shepton Montague, and enable some speed to be built up.

It was on this long stretch that the line ran parallel to the minor road from Wincanton to Shepton Montague for over a mile. Ivo Peters was able to film a train from out of the sunroof of his car, which was being driven by his son Julian, by issuing instructions either to speed up or slow down, as required, to keep the train in frame. *Photo: Ivo Peters. Date: 20 June 1964.*

The backdrop has not changed to a significant degree; the foreground has, although its heritage is left in no doubt. Despite the recent backfilling on the south side of the bridge making the foreground appear rather untidy, a neat paddock-cum-garden has been created and forms part of an adjoining property. The attractive twin-arched bridge from which this photograph was taken remains in fair condition. Just south of here, Bridge 132 has been demolished, as has Bridge 133 at 32 miles 52½ chains, such is the extent of new housing development in the town. *Date: 20 March 1995.*

98
Wincanton station
183 ST 710282

Class 7F 2-8-0 No 53810 is engaged in engineering duties on a Sunday and stands opposite the up platform upon which the small wooden shelter can be seen, together with the 14-lever signal box with a block switch which controlled a fair-sized layout. The main buildings on the down platform are mostly obscured by the goods shed in the foreground. This was a substantially built stone structure, with a loading gauge suspended from its northern door, and housed a 30cwt hand crane; a seven-ton version was sited in the yard on the south side of the building. Goods ceased to be handled from here on 5 April 1965. The staggered platforms overlapped for only 120ft or so; access across was gained via the footbridge (No 136), just seen in the background. The up platform was 450ft in length, the down one 210ft shorter. *Photo: R.C. Riley. Date: 16 July 1961.*

It is very difficult to imagine a station ever having been here. One or two houses seen on the hill in the background can be identified as those featured in the 1961 photograph, but extensive modern development has made them difficult to spot. In 1985 the last remnants could still be found of the station, but in the ensuing years all remaining traces, including sections of the up platform and lamp posts have been swept away.

Housing built over the last few years has supplanted the station and covers the entire site, part of which is the development in the background, which constitutes 'Pines Close', with, from right to left, Nos 40, 41 and 42 in view from this vantage point in the middle of an adjacent industrial and commercial complex. The foundations of the old signal box have been incorporated into the garden of No 42 and fencing has been erected around making it into a feature.

There is nothing left whatsoever of Bridge 137 over the former main A303 road through the town; the line's formation immediately south of this has been submerged by industrial development and beyond the bypass it has largely disappeared into farm land. *Date: 20 March 1995.*

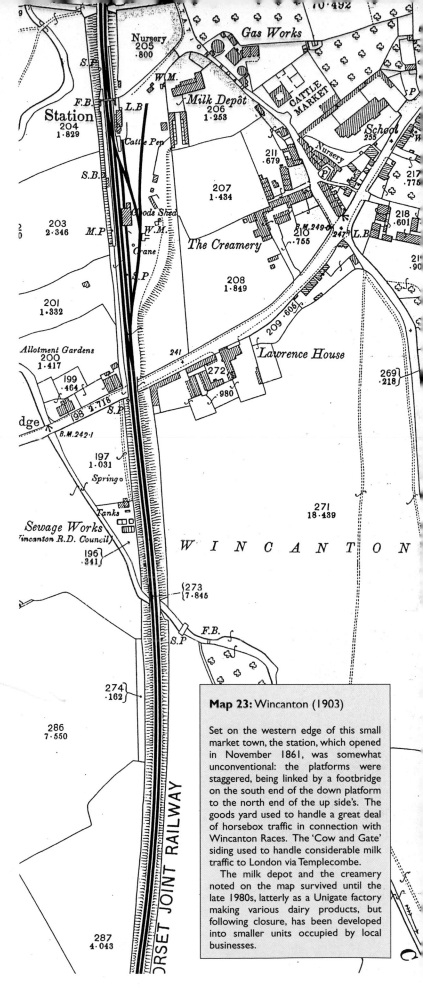

Map 23: Wincanton (1903)

Set on the western edge of this small market town, the station, which opened in November 1861, was somewhat unconventional: the platforms were staggered, being linked by a footbridge on the south end of the down platform to the north end of the up side's. The goods yard used to handle a great deal of horsebox traffic in connection with Wincanton Races. The 'Cow and Gate' siding used to handle considerable milk traffic to London via Templecombe.

The milk depot and the creamery noted on the map survived until the late 1980s, latterly as a Unigate factory making various dairy products, but following closure, has been developed into smaller units occupied by local businesses.

Map 24: Templecombe (1903)

Although situated in a small village in the heart of rural Somerset, Templecombe was a busy interchange station with the Somerset & Dorset Railway, which arrived here as the Dorset Central in 1862, just two years after the LSWR, and the majority of the local population was connected with the railway to some degree. Although an improvement over the previous method used to gain access to the LSWR, from 1870 S&D trains arrived at the north face of the up platform of the 'upper' station by a still rather complicated method via Templecombe No 2 Junction. A down train from Bath would enter the station via a spur, then be hauled out by another locomotive attached to the rear to a point just beyond No 2 Junction, where it was uncoupled. The train then continued its journey south to pass the shed, Templecombe lower platform and then under the LSWR/SR main line. With up trains the procedure was reversed: the second engine was coupled to the rear just beyond No 2 Junction and having hauled it up the spur to the SR station, it would then be detached and left standing alongside Templecombe's No 3 platform, whilst the train continued its journey northwards.

Templecombe Upper station was extensively rebuilt in 1938; the platforms were also lengthened to take 14-coach trains and the track layout redesigned. The original Dorset Central station building can be seen on this map just south of the 50ft turntable and the two-road engine shed, a wood and asbestos structure, was replaced in 1950 with a red-brick building.

The LSWR/SR line from the east of the station inclined for some distance at 1:80, which eased to 1:150 past the platforms. Even this sometimes proved a little difficult for locomotives of heavy westbound trains to restart with an immediate increase in the gradient to 1:100 for about a mile and a half. The extensive yards situated on the west side of the station were always a centre for protracted activity and handled many trains in a 24-hour period, particularly those to and from the S&D line. However, all this came to an end on 5 April 1965 when the yards and goods sheds were closed, after the Western Region had over the previous few years diverted much of the freight traffic away from this and the S&D line.

When the Somerset & Dorset line closed on 7 March 1966, so did the station here along with others on the Waterloo–Exeter route, but like a phoenix rising from the ashes, Templecombe was reopened on 3 October 1983 for a three-year trial period. The up platform had to be reconstructed to cope with the diesel-hauled eight-coach sets that initially would be required to stop here. This all came about due to the good offices of Somerset County Council and the Templecombe Station Working Committee, a pressure group formed from local residents and enthusiasts. The scheme proved successful and today the station has a promising future.

When reopened, half the upper floor of the signal box doubled as a ticket office and waiting room, but from 1988 a small platform shelter was built; this was added to in 1990 by the construction of a new building with provision of toilets and other facilities. At the same time, a footbridge which had been in use on the former LBSCR at Buxted in East Sussex was re-erected here, thus removing the need for passengers to cross the line at the west end of the station. Somewhat shorter than before, the up platform finishes just to the west of the road bridge (SR No 326). The signal box retains a 16-lever electro-mechanical frame (at one time there were 60 levers). The double track section from Sherborne ends just west of the station at a crossover which provides access to a siding occasionally used by engineers' vehicles and finishing level with the east end of the goods shed, now occupied by a small business. There are plans in the offing to extend the double track section through the station, thus bringing the former down platform back into use. Templecombe shed survives, together with a couple of other buildings from railway days which have been incorporated into a factory of GEC Marconi Naval Systems, manufacturers of sonar equipment, now occupying the site.

Through the hard work of dedicated volunteers of the Station Promotion Group, Templecombe has won awards for the best kept small station. It now sports well-tended flower beds and a lawn, upon which an attractive sundial sculpture, commissioned by British Rail and titled 'Tempus Fugit', is placed. The inscription on the pages of the 'book' held by the bronze figure is well worth reading for its humour and apposite observations on train timetables!

Standing on the station platform today, it is difficult to imagine the scene just over thirty years ago: trains coming and going, north and south, east and west; the 'Atlantic Coast Express', the fabled SR service (run in as many as five separate portions on summer Saturdays) loaded with excited holidaymakers; the S&D going about its awkward business of getting trains in and out of No 3 platform, such variety – what a spectacle it all was. Today, it is nothing more exciting than the Class 159 units that stop here, normally comprising three coaches, which provide South West Trains West of England line's service, soon to be franchised.

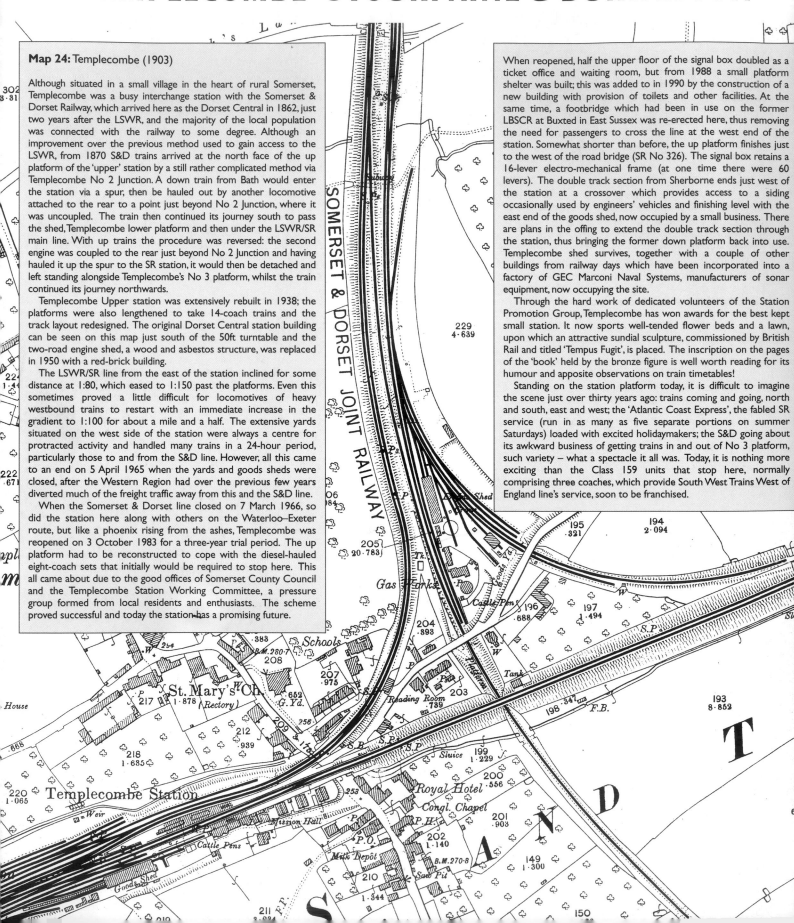

99

Templecombe – No 2 Junction (1)
183 ST 710231

Having called at Templecombe Upper station, S&D 7F No 53807, with the 07.43 (SO) Birmingham–Bournemouth, is hauled back down the spur to No 2 Junction (from 1933 just known as Templecombe Junction) before proceeding on its way to Bournemouth down the single line section to Blandford Forum, where double track was gained once more. The 44-lever wooden signal box, the largest on the line, which controlled No 2 Junction and the former No 3 Junction (38 chains north) after its box closed in 1933, is seen in the background. To the right is a diminutive ex-SR G6 0-6-0T No 30274 returning to shed after station pilot duty. Two distinct signal designs can be judged either side of the train: on the left an SR/S&D-type

constructed from bolted rail sections and on the right the LSWR lattice-type. *Photo: Ivo Peters. Date: 16 July 1955.*

This area towards the top end of GEC Marconi's site, which ends at Bridge 148 adjacent to No 2 Junction's down home signal and seen over the train in the top photograph, looks rather like a tank training area: spoil has been dumped here over the years from building work carried out on site over the years. In 1985, bases from two signal posts were still to be found discarded by the side of the formation, but they have since been removed for scrap. To the right, the formation of the lower spur and sidings serving the shed from No 3 Junction is used as a farm track accessed from under Bridge 148, which is still intact, although the parapets are totally obscured by brambles. *Date: 20 March 1995.*

100
Templecombe – No 2 Junction (2)
183 ST 709231

BR Class 9F 2-10-0 No 92205 in charge of the 08.40 (SO) Bournemouth to Bradford train, sweeps up the sharp rise to No 2 Junction. Templecombe MPD, usually a hive of activity, can be seen in the distance. It is at a lower level than the spur to Templecombe Upper pictured over the rear of the train, seen curving sharply to the right and around in front of the school building in the middle of the picture, which was taken from the signal box at No 2 Junction. *Photo: Ivo Peters. Date: 13 August 1960.*

From a position near to where the signal box stood there is not much in the foreground to which a reference point can be made, but the horizon reveals the church and school, seen clearly in the 1960 study. The view of Templecombe shed is now obscured by a dramatic new building with tinted glass windows, which has been constructed in the last few years. The remains of the trackbed fall away sharply in the foreground to form a car park. Extensive levelling has been undertaken here in the process of which the spur to Templecombe Upper has been removed almost completely. The far end is now made up as an access road from the village to the factory site. *Date: 20 March 1995.*

101
Templecombe Upper (SR) station – Bridge 151
183 ST 709226

Appearing to be running 'wrong-road', Collett 0-6-0 No 3206 departs with a three-coach up local for Highbridge from the north face of Templecombe's island platform (No 3) and down the spur towards No 2 Junction; it will shortly gain the up road via a crossover sited to the rear of the photographer. The line on the right was chiefly used for transference of S&D goods traffic to and from the main upper yard situated to the west of the station on the up side of the line. Until 1933, when its function was taken over by Templecombe 'A' box on the station, there was a small 13-lever signal box, Templecombe 'B', positioned on the spur just off the end of the platform, that controlled movements to No 2 Junction. The A357 road passed under two bridges carrying the spur (No 151) and platforms (No 326), visible on the extreme left. The extensive canopies of Templecombe Upper are clearly seen in this intereting photograph. *Photo: E. Wilmshurst. Date: 16 June 1962.*

It is the wooden building on the right which provides an instant clue as to the location, but nothing much can be seen from this aspect of the revitalized station, almost totally obscured by the wooden railings on the abutment, which remains following the demolition of Bridge 151, leaving the main A357 road clearly exposed. Both the retaining wall and bridge abutment from the S&D's spur have undergone repairs over the last few years, but the embankment has been removed and a narrow grassed area now separates the small car park in front of School Lane from the access road to GEC Marconi's factory, which follows the course of the old trackbed.

On Templecombe station itself, the former Platform 3 has been fenced off, but the old S&D trackbed is still visible, despite becoming overgrown. *Date: 21 March 1995.*

102
Templecombe Upper (SR) station – No 3 platform
183 ST 707225

By this date, there were only five surviving Class 7F 2-8-0 locomotives from the 11 built, which were often employed on passenger duties on busy summer Saturdays. The now-preserved No 53808, working the 07.35 Nottingham–Bournemouth, stands at Platform 3 and awaits to have the station pilot attached at the rear to haul the train back to No 2 Junction before resuming its southward Journey. Templecombe's 1930s-style signal box on the right housed a 66-lever frame. Beyond the coal trucks in the siding is St Mary's church. *Photo: C.L.Caddy. Date: 4 August 1962.*

Platform 3 is now derelict, although some of the edging slabs are still in place and most of it has been fenced off from the functioning face. The signal box is outwardly the same, although it has only a 16-lever frame today. St Mary's church is unchanged by the passage of time.

Owned by the Somerset & Dorset Railway Trust, No 53808 resides on the West Somerset Railway and still is in fine fettle, providing many reminiscences of a much-lamented cross-country railway line, which itself is slowly returning to nature. *Date: 21 March 1995.*

Templecombe station today. A three-coach Class 159 unit, No 159006, arrives on time with the 08.35 Waterloo–Exeter service. *Date: 21 March 1995.*

103
Templecombe shed (1)
183 ST 710228

A splendid shot taken of 71H Templecombe shed (formerly 22D), as rebuilt in 1950, which provides an excellent indication of the variety of motive power to be seen on the line: Class 7F No 53800 is engaged in shunting three other locomotives, not in steam; SR Class G6 0-6-0T No 30274, Ivatt 2-6-2T No 41248 and Class 3F 0-6-0 No 43216 are backed into the two-road shed, with another 3F, No 43419, standing in the siding alongside. The tender of an unidentified locomotive is seen behind the MPD on the road to the 50ft turntable, whilst in the background a Class 7F 2 8 0 is engaged in moving coal wagons into a siding towards Bridge 152A under which, until 1870, led to the connection with the LSWR Salisbury–Yeovil line. The goods shed, which closed on 5 May 1950, can be seen over the coal wagons. The former Dorset Central station building is hidden from view at the rear of the MPD, the middle siding in front of which, until 1887, connected with the running line at No 1 Junction near Bridge 152 on the right. On the other side of this bridge was Templecombe Lower platform, sandwiched between it and Bridge 153 beyond carrying the LSWR/SR line over the S&D.

On 23 February 1958 the shed code was changed to 82G and from 14 October 1963 to 83G. *Photo: Ivo Peters. Date: 20 July 1957.*

This view taken from near the entrance to the new building shows how the former engine shed has almost been enveloped by the other buildings on site; just a portion of the roof and that of the old stationmaster's house on Combe Throop Lane can be seen over it. *Date: 20 March 1995.*

104
Templecombe shed (2)
183 ST 710227

Going? Templecombe shed plays host to a variety of locomotives, including, in the foreground, 2P 4-4-0 No 40537 with a sister engine, No 40634, up front. Withdrawn from service the same month, No 40537 met its end at Derby Works in September 1962, whilst No 40634 was broken up at Crewe Works a month earlier, having been in storage there since the previous June. The now-preserved 4F No 44422 is seen adjacent to the buildings of the original Dorset Central station, which closed on 17 January 1887 along with No 1 Junction and the small signal box controlling it. BR Class 5 No 73047 is seen just beyond the turntable, whilst S&D Class 7F 2-8-0 No 53804 is pictured in the background, with an unidentified Class 2P ahead of it. No 53804 lasted in service for a further two-and-a-half years before withdrawal, being scrapped at Crewe Works in February 1962. Having been transferred from Bath the previous August, No 73047 was retired at the end of 1964 from 6D Shrewsbury shed and broken up at Cashmore's, Newport, four months later. The running line to Bournemouth is in the foreground and just seen on the far left is the spur to Templecombe Upper. This photograph was taken from Bridge 152 in Combe Throop Lane. *Photo: R.C. Riley. Date: 7 July 1959.*

Going ... Templecombe shed seen in its latter days and only a shadow of its former self: BR 2-6-2T and 2-6-4T tank engines predominate. A solitary BR Class 4 can be seen behind the engine shed. The original Dorset Central station buildings are visible in the middle of the photograph. The running line to Bournemouth is in the foreground. Just apparent on the far left is the spur to Templecombe Upper. *Photo: David Milton. Date: Summer 1965.*

Gone. The extensive factory area can be observed from this photograph: Templecombe shed still stands out defiantly; also of note are the other two surviving railway buildings seen between the tanks in the foreground and former MPD. *Date: 21 March 1995.*

105
Templecombe Lower platform
183 ST 710227

A splendid shot of Drummond T9 4-4-0 No 30721
passing over Bridge 153 on the main SR line with an up
local for Salisbury which also shows how Templecombe
Lower platform was squeezed between the two
bridges. It was basic in the extreme and had no shelter
nor any other passenger comforts provided; access was
via a footpath from Combe Throop Lane bridge from
which this view was obtained. The last train to stop
here was on 3 January 1966, just over three months
before the line's closure.

    Templecombe Lower platform had come into use in
1887 when trains ceased to call at the old station; not
many stopped here, but it was occasionally used for the
exchange of engine crews on services which were not
scheduled to call at the upper station.
Photo: Ivo Peters. Date: 9 July 1955.

The cutting in which the platform was located provides
a rather scruffy garden for the adjacent house. There is
not much left to see, but the platform face still survives,
albeit buried under soil. Although overgrown in parts,
the trackbed is still distinct beyond Bridge 153, which is
now obscured from view. Plans are being made to
extend the nearby 2ft-gauge Gartell Light Railway at
Yenston to a point near here. *Date: 20 March 1995.*

COMMENT: *Despite a hectic schedule, I made a special effort to capture a Waterloo-bound Class 159 unit traversing the bridge, but a low sun thwarted my attempt to secure a more interesting comparison, so this shot snatched on another occasion had to suffice.*

Gartell Light Railway

Situated at Yenston, just south of Templecombe in the lovely Blackmore Vale, this private railway was established a few years ago and is run by three generations of the Gartell family, whose agricultural, plant and machinery business in Common Lane provided the foundation for this 2ft-gauge line. The GLR is run with the help of many friends and enthusiasts, some of whom are professional railwaymen.

Often referred to as 'The Secret Railway', the line extends from a station built behind the company works in Common Lane rising at 1:30 to join the old S&D trackbed, about a hundred yards immediately west of the site at what has become known as Pines Way Junction. It then follows the course of the old S&D railway line to Park Lane Crossing, some three-quarters of a mile south. Halfway between here and Park Lane, there is a crossing point known as Shortlands Loop.

Movements are controlled by two signal boxes built to a very high standard using genuine lever frames and equipment salvaged from various full-sized boxes, including sections from Wyke Crossing between Sherborne and Yeovil Junction on the SR line. The box at Pines Way Junction will eventually have some thirty operational levers. Signals include an impressive array of semaphore types from both GWR and LSWR/SR origins, also colour-light and shunting varieties.

Work has already started on what is to be the northern extension of the light railway and there are plans over the next few years to lay track north to Templecombe. Phase one will involve the reinstatement of a level crossing over Common Lane and the line will temporarily end at a terminus called Tower View, named after Alfred's Tower seen in the distance. Eventually the line will be extended during phase two to finish at Temple Lane on the southern outskirts of Templecombe.

The current motive power is made up of light diesel locomotives, but plans are being made to have steam traction in operation by the time the line has reached Templecombe. A museum, shop, refreshment room and car park are all adjacent to the ticket office in Common Lane.

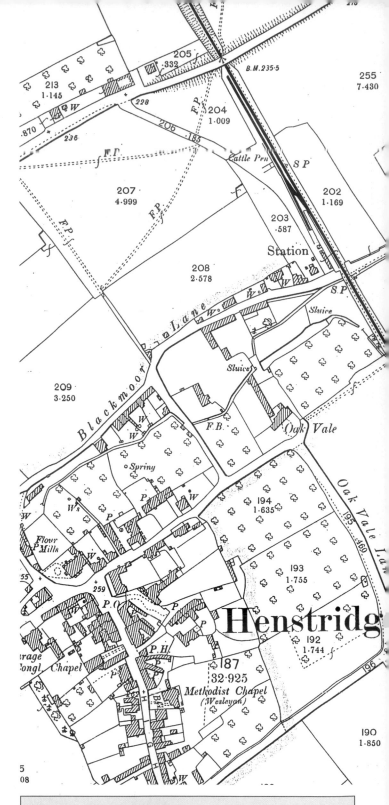

Pines Way Junction and signal box looking south towards Park Lane in the distance. *Date: 20 March 1995.*

Map 25: Henstridge (1903)

Just two miles from Templecombe No 2 Junction on the single track section to Blandford Forum, Henstridge was passed; it was not a block post and had no passing loop.

The smallest station on the S&D's main line, Henstridge opened on 31 May 1863. The buildings were of wooden construction but contained such facilities as ladies' and gentlemen's waiting rooms, booking office and urinal; in addition, there was a goods yard, which had a loading gauge, cattle pen and milk dock; a ground frame controlled access to its one siding. Goods traffic ceased on 5 April 1965.

The lever frame of Pines Way signal box. *Date: 20 March 1995.*

106
Henstridge station
183 ST 726201

The neat and tidy appearance of this station can be seen to good effect: the platform was only some 150ft in length, but had adequate facilities.

Bridge 159 just north of here carries the busy A30 trunk road. It was from this bridge that an American tank transporter crashed onto a passing troop train on 13 March 1944, causing casualties amongst the passengers: at least six soldiers were killed in the first of ten coaches and many more injured. Fortunately no serious injuries, other than shock, were sustained by S&D footplate crews despite the derailment of one of the two locomotives and a member of the station staff, porter William Jackson, being toppled from a signal post up which he had climbed to fill the lamps.
Photo: E. Wilmshurst.
Date: 17 February 1962.

By the time this volume is published, Henstridge station will have been erased from the face of the earth: the last vestiges of the platform were about to be demolished by building contractors. The area to the west of the station has been cleared for development and some forty houses are to be built. The cattle loading dock had already been demolished to make way for a service road, which covers the trackbed off the north end of the platform; however, a short bridle path is hoped to be created from Bridge 159 to a point north of it. To the south, the line formation beyond the remains of Blackmore Lane crossing is in reasonable condition, as is Counties Bridge (No 160), which marked the borders of Somerset and Dorset, some fifty chains distant.
Date: 21 March 1995.

107
Stalbridge station
183 ST 739181

A view looking north of Stalbridge taken on Station Road from behind the crossing gates shows the layout to good advantage. Note the hand-operated crane in the yard, which closed to goods traffic on 5 April 1965; the sidings were taken out of use some three months later on 7 July, but the signal box remained open until closure of the line. *Photo: C.L.Caddy.*
Date: 7 July 1962.

This was once the location of Stalbridge station: the entire area has been enveloped by a large industrial unit of a steel stockholder. Not one artefact could be found to act as a link with the past, except an oil painting dated 1979 by H.Ball a local artist, hanging in the reception area, depicting 2P No 40700 piloting a 'Black Five' through Stalbridge station on the down 'Pines Express'. A slight bump on Station Road marks the position of the level crossing, to the south of which a fair-sized industrial estate has sprung up over the years, providing much-needed local employment, although at least one large unit was empty during this visit.

Between Templecombe and Stalbridge there were no fewer than six manned level crossings where some of the keepers' cottages and original gateposts survive: Common Lane, Park Lane, Plott Lane, Marsh Lane, South Mead and Drew's Lane. *Date: 21 March 1995.*

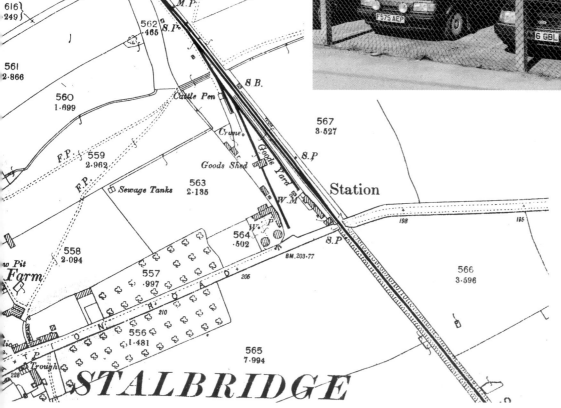

Map 26: Stalbridge (1903)

The station opened on 31 August 1863. The main buildings, of typical Dorset Central design, were on the up platform; an 18-lever signal box abutting the road on the same side controlled the small goods yard to the north of the station, also the level crossing. Stalbridge was the first block post south of Templecombe and had a crossing loop, 1,452ft in length, running through the station; the up line having the straight run past.

108
**Sturminster Newton –
Bridge 171**
194 ST 783143

This was the first of the four flirtations that southbound trains had with the River Stour over the ensuing nine miles. However, unrebuilt SR Pacific 34041 *Wilton* on the 11.40 (SO) Bournemouth–Derby train, rumbles over the girder span and crosses the Stour for the final time on the northward journey. A pedestrian bridge spanning the river provides an ideal vantage point for the photographer. *Photo: Ivo Peters. Date: 22 August 1959.*

COMMENT: *The first photograph conjures up thoughts of halcyon summer days spent lazing by the river with splendid picnics, watching the trains rumble back and forth over the bridge. The truth was more likely to be that one trod in a fresh cowpat; the children were severely bitten by mosquitoes; the wife found a fly had dropped into her tea and nearly choked on it; granny got badly stung by a wasp that had crept into her jam sandwich, whilst grandpa, nonchalantly leaning over the pedestrian bridge and noisily coughing on a Woodbine, expelled his false teeth at great velocity into the river below – and to make matters worse, got terribly sunburnt on his bald pate. C'est la vie!*

They say a picture is worth a thousand words, so here is the same scene today.
Date: 21 March 1995.

The derelict edifice, minus its central span, wears its age and misfortune with quiet dignity, above the water meadows, in the calm of an early spring morning. A similar fate has befallen the viaduct (No 167) across the Stour at Marsh Farm, about halfway between here and Stalbridge to the north; only the three columns remain straddling the river. *Date: 21 March 1995..*

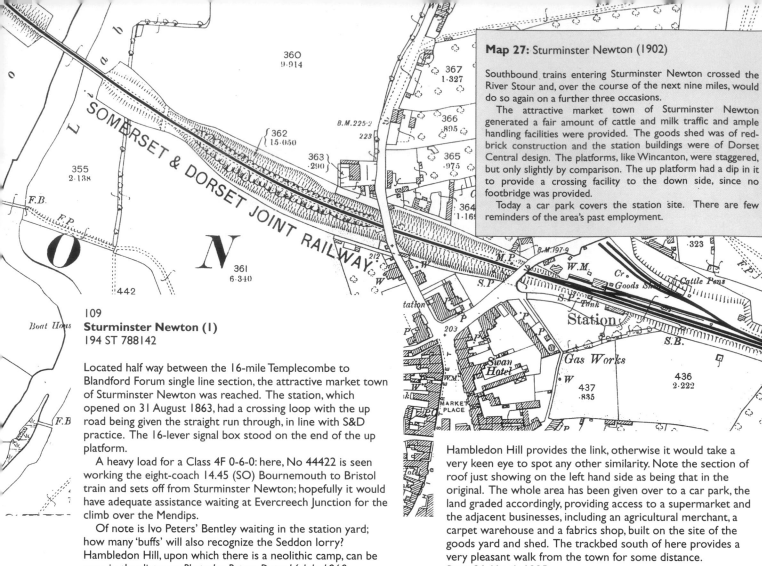

Map 27: Sturminster Newton (1902)

Southbound trains entering Sturminster Newton crossed the River Stour and, over the course of the next nine miles, would do so again on a further three occasions.

The attractive market town of Sturminster Newton generated a fair amount of cattle and milk traffic and ample handling facilities were provided. The goods shed was of red-brick construction and the station buildings were of Dorset Central design. The platforms, like Wincanton, were staggered, but only slightly by comparison. The up platform had a dip in it to provide a crossing facility to the down side, since no footbridge was provided.

Today a car park covers the station site. There are few reminders of the area's past employment.

109
Sturminster Newton (1)
194 ST 788142

Located half way between the 16-mile Templecombe to Blandford Forum single line section, the attractive market town of Sturminster Newton was reached. The station, which opened on 31 August 1863, had a crossing loop with the up road being given the straight run through, in line with S&D practice. The 16-lever signal box stood on the end of the up platform.

A heavy load for a Class 4F 0-6-0: here, No 44422 is seen working the eight-coach 14.45 (SO) Bournemouth to Bristol train and sets off from Sturminster Newton; hopefully it would have adequate assistance waiting at Evercreech Junction for the climb over the Mendips.

Of note is Ivo Peters' Bentley waiting in the station yard; how many 'buffs' will also recognize the Seddon lorry? Hambledon Hill, upon which there is a neolithic camp, can be seen in the distance. *Photo: Ivo Peters. Date: 16 July 1960.*

Hambledon Hill provides the link, otherwise it would take a very keen eye to spot any other similarity. Note the section of roof just showing on the left hand side as being that in the original. The whole area has been given over to a car park, the land graded accordingly, providing access to a supermarket and the adjacent businesses, including an agricultural merchant, a carpet warehouse and a fabrics shop, built on the site of the goods yard and shed. The trackbed south of here provides a very pleasant walk from the town for some distance.
Date: 21 March 1995.

110
Sturminster Newton (2)
194 ST 789141

A good view of the up platform looking north and under the B3091 road bridge (No 173). Note the gas light on the left of the platform and the neat goods shed opposite. The peculiar dip in the up platform, providing access across the track to the down side via a wooden level crossing, is seen just this side of the schoolgirl. One might wonder how many people absentmindedly stepped out of a train on a dark night into this abyss!

The goods yard was located on the down side immediately behind the shed and was quite extensive in so far as it had five sidings, one of which served an adjacent milk factory. In addition, the yard had a cattle dock and pig pens; a 7-ton hand crane facilitated loading other goods from the yard's main siding. The weekly cattle market provided much-needed revenue for the railway and was usually busy in this attractive town. The yard closed on 5 April 1965. *Photo: David Milton. Date: Summer 1961.*

The changes here are dramatic, but the two buildings on the right provide continuity, as does the tree on the far left on the horizon.

The B3091 road bridge (No 173) has been demolished and the road levelled. The land between Bridges 173 and 172 has been infilled and made into a park area. On the north side of Bridge 172, which carries the B3092, the cutting has been filled in almost back to the bridge over the Stour. About a mile south of the town, the viaduct (No 175) over the Stour at Fiddleford Mill has been demolished, but sections of the formation beyond are used as farm tracks, particularly near Child Okeford.
Date: 21 March 1995.

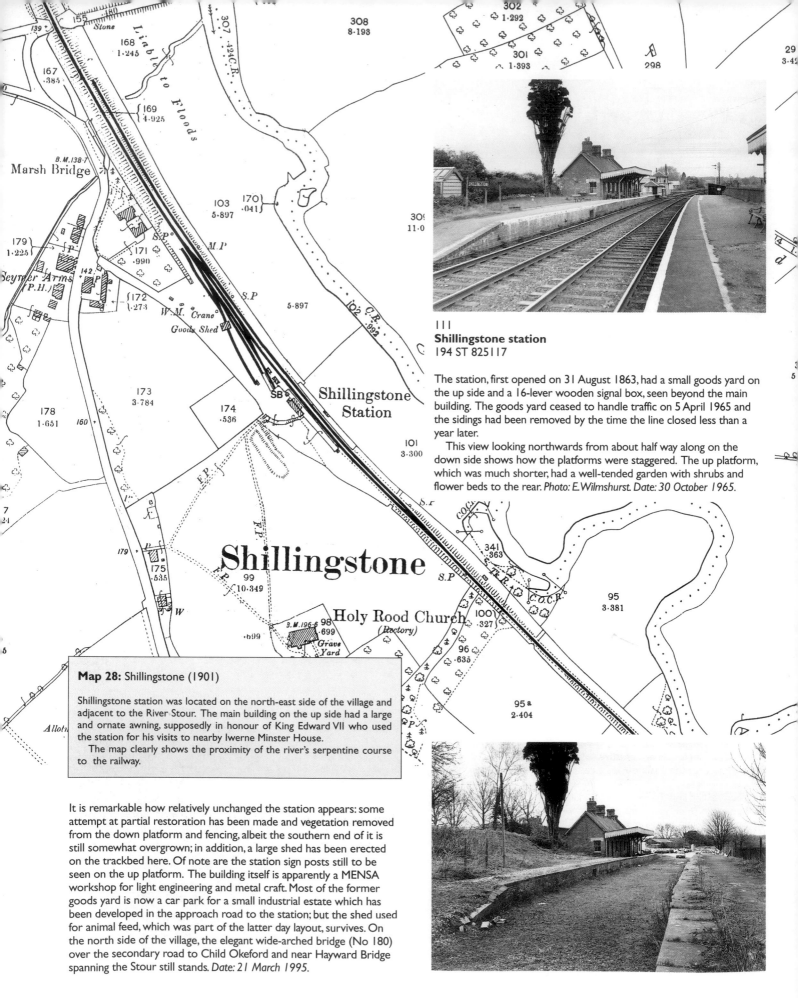

111
Shillingstone station
194 ST 825117

The station, first opened on 31 August 1863, had a small goods yard on the up side and a 16-lever wooden signal box, seen beyond the main building. The goods yard ceased to handle traffic on 5 April 1965 and the sidings had been removed by the time the line closed less than a year later.

This view looking northwards from about half way along on the down side shows how the platforms were staggered. The up platform, which was much shorter, had a well-tended garden with shrubs and flower beds to the rear. *Photo: E. Wilmshurst. Date: 30 October 1965.*

Map 28: Shillingstone (1901)

Shillingstone station was located on the north-east side of the village and adjacent to the River Stour. The main building on the up side had a large and ornate awning, supposedly in honour of King Edward VII who used the station for his visits to nearby Iwerne Minster House.

The map clearly shows the proximity of the river's serpentine course to the railway.

It is remarkable how relatively unchanged the station appears: some attempt at partial restoration has been made and vegetation removed from the down platform and fencing, albeit the southern end of it is still somewhat overgrown; in addition, a large shed has been erected on the trackbed here. Of note are the station sign posts still to be seen on the up platform. The building itself is apparently a MENSA workshop for light engineering and metal craft. Most of the former goods yard is now a car park for a small industrial estate which has been developed in the approach road to the station; but the shed used for animal feed, which was part of the latter day layout, survives. On the north side of the village, the elegant wide-arched bridge (No 180) over the secondary road to Child Okeford and near Hayward Bridge spanning the Stour still stands. *Date: 21 March 1995.*

112
Gain's Cross – Cliff Bridge (No 184)
194 ST 844102

Approximately two miles south of Shillingstone station, the line passed under the three-arch Cliff Bridge situated at Gain's Cross carrying a farm track spanning a steep-sided and deep sand cutting, which, according to Ivo Peters, provided many a home for nesting sand martins in summer. The line courted the River Stour all the way to Blandford, passing through magnificent country; the chalk downs and Hod Hill to the east provided interesting features, together with the abundantly wooded hills of Blandford Forest on the south-western side of the line.

S&D Class 7F 2-8-0 No 53810 heading north up the long straight from Stourpaine, is about to pass under Cliff Bridge with the 11.12 (SO) Bournemouth–Sheffield.
Photo: Ivo Peters. Date: 22 July 1961.

The distant views to the attractive village of Stourpaine with the chalk downs as a backdrop give an idea of the beautiful setting. The cutting has proved a convenient dumping ground for spoil removed from the Blandford by-pass completed in the mid-1980s and, besides being utilised as a farm track, now forms a pleasant sloping field which is used for grazing. The northern parapet of Cliff Bridge is all that is to be found of the structure, since landfill has enveloped it on both sides.

Just 34 chains south of this point, the viaduct (No 185) over the River Stour has been demolished, but Bridge 183, some 32 chains to the north of here, survives.
Date: 21 March 1995.

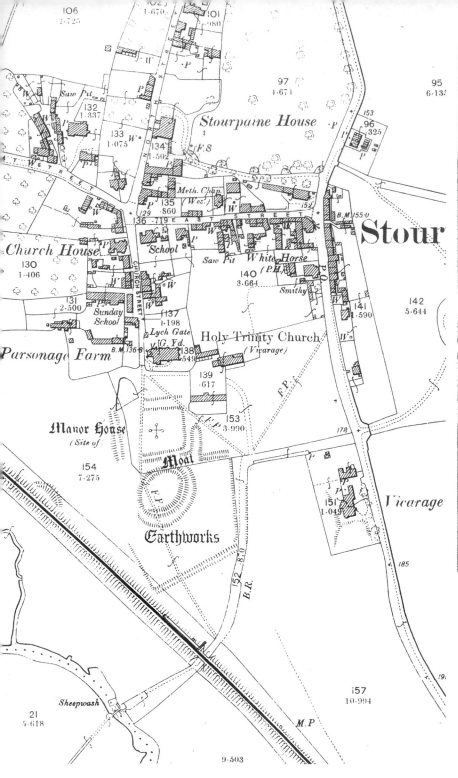

113

Stourpaine & Durweston Halt
194 ST 860091

A general view of the simple halt taken from the trackside also shows Holy Trinity church in Stourpaine village in the background.

Half a mile to the north of the station there was a crossing loop, controlled by a small signal box, which broke up the 5½ mile block section from Shillingstone to Blandford; subsequently this was removed and the box closed on 18 December 1951. *Photo: C.L.Caddy. Date: 7 July 1962.*

Recent felling of some trees and removal of undergrowth along this section of the trackbed has made it much easier to view the halt from Bridge 187 adjacent to it. The halt is still in reasonable condition, despite superficial vandalism; however, some of the slabs from the ramp at the far end of the platform have been removed, one of which has been dumped in the foreground near the steps.

Much of this section of the S&D's formation is used as a farm track; but beyond where the line rose slightly from the Stour valley and once passed under the A350 road (Bridge 188), just a few chains south of here, it becomes very indistinct: the formation has largely been absorbed into farm land, particularly the banked section near Nutford Farm alongside the main Shaftesbury to Blandford road. On the east side of the bypass at Milldown it is again distinct, although overgrown with trees. *Date: 21 March 1995.*

Map 29: Stourpaine (1901 with 1928 additions)

This halt was another latecomer to the S&D scene and opened on 9 July 1928, but was closed after only 28 years of operation. Set between the two villages of Stourpaine and Durweston, adjacent to the River Stour, it was built to a typical SR-style in prefabricated concrete; its shelter was constructed later and stood on precarious-looking concrete stilts over the embankment.

The map shows the site of the old manor house, moat and earthworks, part of which still can be discerned today within a meadow.

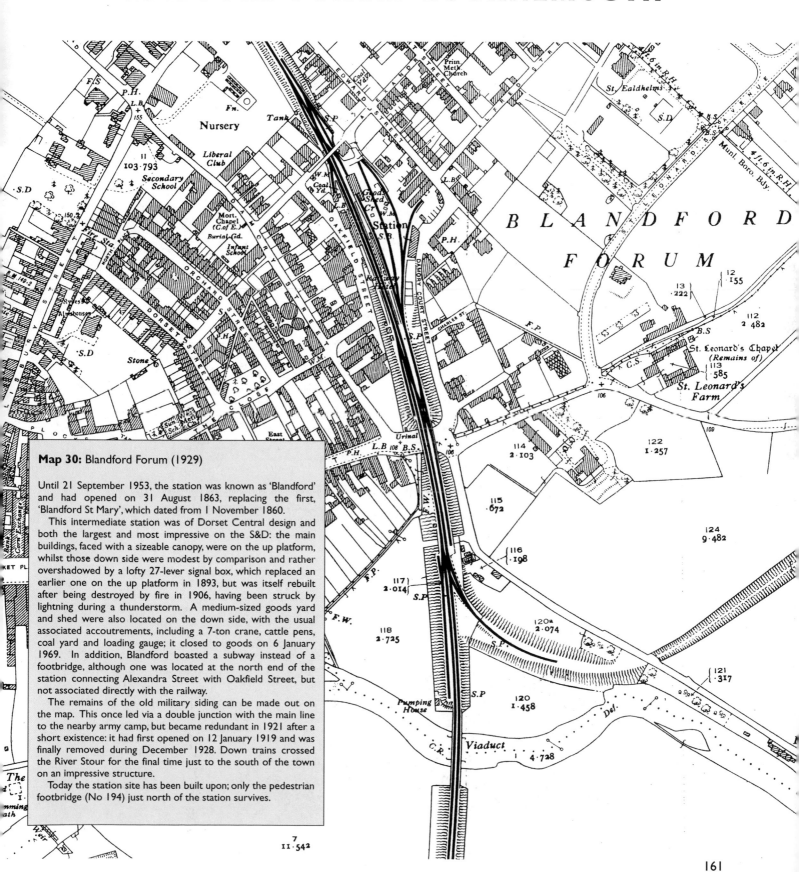

Map 30: Blandford Forum (1929)

Until 21 September 1953, the station was known as 'Blandford' and had opened on 31 August 1863, replacing the first, 'Blandford St Mary', which dated from 1 November 1860.

This intermediate station was of Dorset Central design and both the largest and most impressive on the S&D: the main buildings, faced with a sizeable canopy, were on the up platform, whilst those down side were modest by comparison and rather overshadowed by a lofty 27-lever signal box, which replaced an earlier one on the up platform in 1893, but was itself rebuilt after being destroyed by fire in 1906, having been struck by lightning during a thunderstorm. A medium-sized goods yard and shed were also located on the down side, with the usual associated accoutrements, including a 7-ton crane, cattle pens, coal yard and loading gauge; it closed to goods on 6 January 1969. In addition, Blandford boasted a subway instead of a footbridge, although one was located at the north end of the station connecting Alexandra Street with Oakfield Street, but not associated directly with the railway.

The remains of the old military siding can be made out on the map. This once led via a double junction with the main line to the nearby army camp, but became redundant in 1921 after a short existence: it had first opened on 12 January 1919 and was finally removed during December 1928. Down trains crossed the River Stour for the final time just to the south of the town on an impressive structure.

Today the station site has been built upon; only the pedestrian footbridge (No 194) just north of the station survives.

114
Blandford Forum
194 ST 888067

BR Class 5 4-6-0 No 73047, with an excursion from Bristol to Bournemouth, drifts down the 1:80 gradient from the summit at Milldown and under the Salisbury road bridge (No 193). The train has just regained double track before passing through the station; it will remain thus for the next eight miles to Corfe Mullen, where it reverts to a single section to Broadstone Junction, the end of S&D metals.

Of note in this shot is the tall LSWR up starting signal, which could be clearly seen from the other side of the footbridge and to the south of the station. Note the seldom-used loading dock on the right, served by a short siding. The reservoir tank for the water cranes on each platform is on the extreme left.
Photo: Ivo Peters. Date: 5 August 1963.

The base of the water tank is still visible on the left, as is the building behind the trees. The trackbed has been made into a linear park, along which a good walk to the northern outskirts of the town is provided, almost to the point where the Blandford bypass severs the S&D's formation.
Date: 21 March 1995.

The footbridge (Bridge 194) has been preserved and still remains with one steam/smoke deflector in the middle of its span; directly underneath, a short piece of track with a rail sectioned buffer provides a tentative link with the past. *Date: 23 May 1985 (revisited 21 March 1995).*

115
Blandford Forum station
194 ST 888067

A truly atmospheric shot of Blandford Forum with Class 9F 2-10-0 No 92204 entering the station with the up 'Pines', whilst Class 4F 0-6-0 No 44102 passes through in the opposite direction with the 06.35 Evercreech–Poole goods. This view from the footbridge off the north end of the up platform clearly shows the extensive layout of the largest station on the S&D system. The slightly shorter down platform makes way for the goods shed. The tall 27-lever signal box located just beyond commands an excellent view both north and south. The jib of the 7-ton crane in the goods yard is just poking above the shed. The station was provided with a subway (No 195) and not a footbridge.
Photo: G.A.Richardson. Date: August 1960.

Unbelievably, this was Blandford station! The whole site is now dominated by a variety of modern housing, both council and privately owned; the goods yard area has been converted into a car park. At the time of this visit, the footbridge abutments were being repointed and the iron span repainted by the council. The work was scheduled to last a month.

Two tangible links with the past can just be discerned in this photograph: the tree on the horizon to the left of the picture (previously seen between the goods shed and signal box) and the chimneys of a hotel over the roof of the house in the foreground. Immediately to the south of here a section of the abutment of Bridge 196, once spanning East Street, is still to be found, beyond which Bridge 197 has been demolished and a Kwik Save supermarket now covers the site. *Date: 21 March 1995.*

116
Blandford Forum – Bridge 198
194/195 ST 890062

The last southbound crossing of the Stour was made just after leaving Blandford station. Seen here is BR 9F 2-10-0 No 92206, with the 08.16 (SO) Bournemouth West–Liverpool Lime Street, traversing the lattice girder bridge just on the southern outskirts of the town, which was very similar in design to the one at Sturminster Newton. This photograph was taken from the formation of the old military siding.
Photo: Ivo Peters. Date: 16 July 1960.

The last vestiges of the bridge grimly cling on to a useless existence. The arches on the southern bank have been removed, together with the embankments and Bridge 199, for use in constructing the Blandford bypass. The old line formation is now just a chalk scar extending for some chains, then disappears under a new out-of-town Tesco store developed at the junction of the bypass and the A350 Poole road, on the other side of which there is no trace of the S&D across adjacent fields for a short distance southwards towards Charlton Marshall. With the absence of trees, a clearer view is obtained of Hall & Woodhouse's brewery, the chimney of which can just be spotted in the former view.
Date: 22 March 1995.

> **COMMENT:** *In order to stand where Ivo Peters once obtained his view, selective trimming had to be undertaken to gain this vista of the bridge and many brambles and a variety of thorn bushes had to be cut back: my well-worn barbour jacket was an absolute necessity in this prickly environment. On emerging from the bushes and onto the footpath, I came face to face with an elderly lady walking her dog. Fearing that she must have been startled on seeing a large man suddenly emerge from the bushes armed with a sickle and long pruners, reassuringly, I told her that I had only been trying to photograph the viaduct; whether she believed me or not is another matter entirely!*

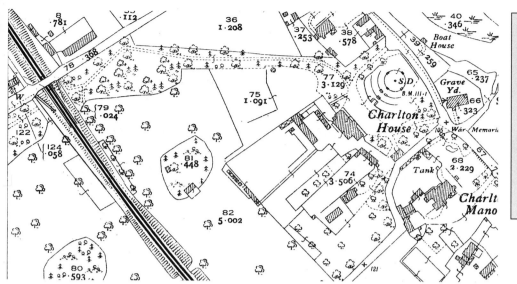

Map 31: Charlton Marshall (1929)

The halt was short lived, like Stourpaine & Durweston, opening only four days previously on 5 July 1928, it closed on the same date: 17 September 1956. Facilities were very rudimentary and no shelter was provided for waiting passengers. Steps leading from the road bridge provided access to the platforms, which were very short and could accommodate little more than a locomotive and single coach.

Although it was printed in 1929, the map did not show the diminutive halt set in a short cutting to the west of the village and Charlton House and it had to be added.

117
Charlton Marshall Halt
195 ST 898040

This section of track provided an opportunity for some fast running, having an official speed limit of 70mph which was often exceeded if everything was going well. Here BR Class 5 4-6-0 No 73068, with the 12.23 down local from Templecombe to Bournemouth West, dips under the bridge (No 203) at 1:100 to pass Charlton Marshall Halt at speed. Footplate crews found this halt difficult to see when driving a train on a dark night, because of the poor lighting on the platforms. The Class 5 must have been on one of its final runs, for it was withdrawn during December and spent the next three months in storage, before being cut up for scrap at Cashmore's, Newport, in April 1966. *Photo: J.W.T.House/C.L.Caddy collection. Date: December 1965.*

The halt's platforms remain in good shape and the steps to both the up and down sides are used by walkers to gain access to the old trackbed, which has recently been partially cleared of trees and undergrowth for much of its length between Blandford and beyond Spetisbury. This has been undertaken by countryside rangers employed by Dorset County Council, partly in response to a scheme to create a cycleway along the length of the S&D's formation between Blandford and Wimborne to form part of the Stour Way. A feasibility study, due to be commissioned in mid-1995, will determine if it is a viable proposition. It is likely that Sustrans, a charity which designs and builds cycleways and paths forming a national network, will be asked to undertake this.
Date: 21 March 1995.

Spettisbury

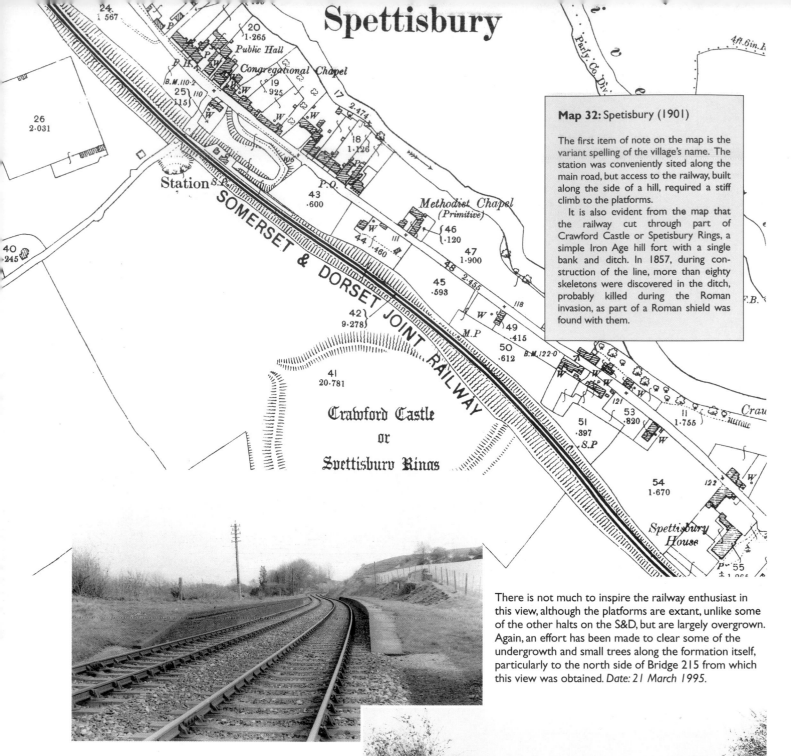

SOMERSET & DORSET JOINT RAILWAY

Crawford Castle
or
Spettisbury Rings

Map 32: Spetisbury (1901)

The first item of note on the map is the variant spelling of the village's name. The station was conveniently sited along the main road, but access to the railway, built along the side of a hill, required a stiff climb to the platforms.

It is also evident from the map that the railway cut through part of Crawford Castle or Spetisbury Rings, a simple Iron Age hill fort with a single bank and ditch. In 1857, during construction of the line, more than eighty skeletons were discovered in the ditch, probably killed during the Roman invasion, as part of a Roman shield was found with them.

There is not much to inspire the railway enthusiast in this view, although the platforms are extant, unlike some of the other halts on the S&D, but are largely overgrown. Again, an effort has been made to clear some of the undergrowth and small trees along the formation itself, particularly to the north side of Bridge 215 from which this view was obtained. *Date: 21 March 1995.*

118
Spetisbury Halt
195 ST 908029

Opened as a station on 1 November 1860 and later downgraded to a halt, this photograph shows the remaining vestiges of Spetisbury, which had closed on 17 September 1956 along with its two northerly neighbours. A signal box, which formerly divided the block section between Blandford and Bailey Gate, had closed four years earlier in 1952. Only the down platform had been provided with passenger facilities: a wooden building contained the ticket office, waiting rooms and lavatories. Neither goods handling facilities nor sidings were provided here. Spetisbury was unstaffed from 13 August 1934. *Photo: C.L.Caddy. Date: 24 April 1965.*

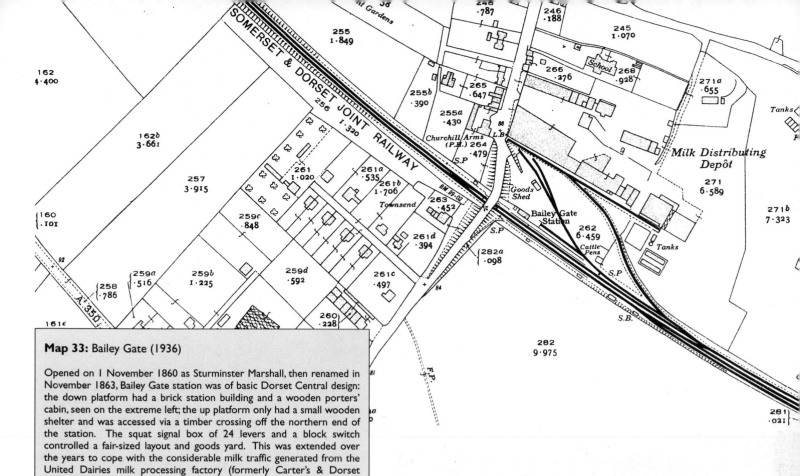

119

Bailey Gate station
195 SY 949995

In this view of Bailey Gate station, which was obtained from Bridge 220, barrels of whey are seen to be stored in part of the milk factory in the background. Although milk traffic continued to be handled for another few years, general goods traffic ceased on 5 April 1965, but the station remained open until closure of the line.

Down trains were able to attain high speeds through here on the falling 1:100 gradient and gently curving stretch of line. Similarly, up trains, following a fast descent of Corfe Mullen Bank, were also able to achieve a good speed. *Photo: David Milton. Date: Summer 1961.*

The platforms remained at Bailey Gate (spelt Bailie locally) for well over two decades following closure, but were demolished a few years ago along with Bridge 220, now replaced by a roundabout. The site of the station has been landscaped and forms part of an industrial estate converted from the old milk factory, which appears rather untidy in this view. At least two buildings in the background can be identified with those seen in the 1961 photograph. A large housing development, accessed by 'Railway Drive', is currently under construction to the north-west of the roundabout and between the site of Bridge 219, some twenty-seven chains distant, obliterating the formation. *Date: 21 March 1995.*

COMMENT: *In the absence of the bridge, this view was obtained by standing on a pair of steps in the middle of a traffic island with the camera held aloft on poles to simulate the correct height. Workers leaving the estate at 5pm on this fine evening must have wondered at the strange sight I presented!*

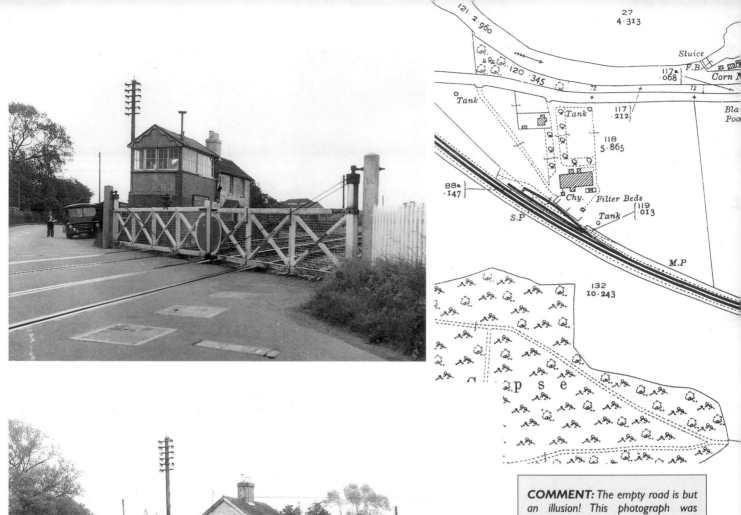

120
Bailey Gate Crossing
195 SY 969986

Bailey Gate Crossing, over the Wimborne–Dorchester (A31) road, was located just over a mile and a quarter from Bailey Gate station. The box, which ceased to be a block post on 5 April 1923, also controlled Admiralty Siding, a two-road affair, on the down side of the line between here and Corfe Mullen; these were removed prior to 1955. Shortly after grouping, plans were drawn up in 1925 to eliminate both the crossings at Corfe Mullen and Bailey Gate by diverting a minor road at the former, and with a bridge being built over the A31 here, but never implemented. The ground frame here was taken out of use on 7 May 1968, when the remaining portion of line from Broadstone to Blandford, used for milk traffic from Bailey Gate, was converted to a siding, until that too eventually closed on 6 January 1969.

A Post Office telephone engineer cleans himself up whilst parked next to the tall signal box controlling the crossing on the A31 Dorchester to Wimborne road. It was a signal and telegraph engineer who bore witness to the occasion when an unfortunate Templecombe driver working the 06.55 Bath to Bournemouth train smashed through the crossing gates, reducing them to matchwood. A passing motorist, forced to stop whilst the debris was cleared, asked the engineer what was the cause. The answer was given in true 'Old Bill' style: "Termites!" *Photo: David Milton. Date: Spring 1961.*

No gates remain here, but the brick base of the signal box has survived along with the former crossing keeper's cottage. The track formation provides car parking space. *Date: 4 June 1985 (revisited 21 March 1995).*

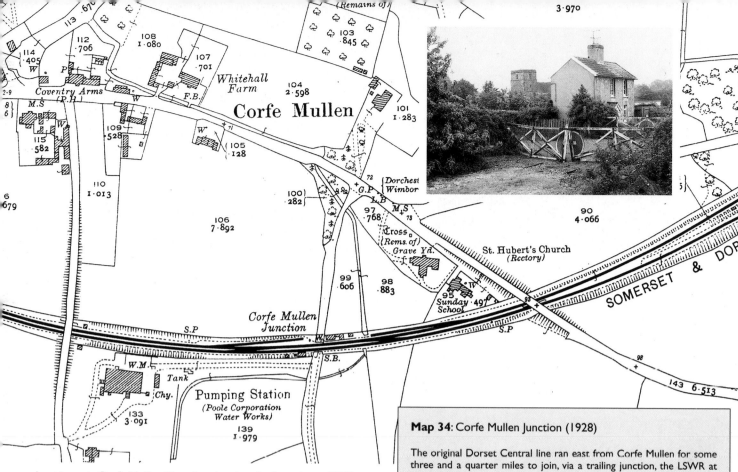

Inset in map: Corfe Mullen Crossing showing the last piece of S&D track to remain *in situ*. This picture was taken from the site of the signal box that used to control it. Having remained empty for many years, the keeper's cottage is now inhabited.

121
Corfe Mullen Junction and Crossing
195 SY 978983

BR Class 9F No 92204, with the 08.40 (SO) Bournemouth–Bradford, speeds towards Corfe Mullen Junction near the end of the three mile section from Broadstone, having had a good run down the 1:80 falling gradient.

In 1933 the old route to Wimborne was truncated, but a mile of the track was retained to serve Carter's Siding, which eventually closed on 19 September 1959, although it was used for wagon storage for a further ten years. *Photo: Ivo Peters. Date: 16 July 1960.*

Map 34: Corfe Mullen Junction (1928)

The original Dorset Central line ran east from Corfe Mullen for some three and a quarter miles to join, via a trailing junction, the LSWR at Wimborne; this meant S&D trains had to reverse before proceeding to Bournemouth. However, in 1884/5 a new line of just under three miles was built from Corfe Mullen direct to Broadstone, where it again joined the LSWR. At Bailey Gate a junction and its signal box controlled the two parallel tracks, which were operated as single lines, before diverging just east of Corfe Mullen Crossing.

In 1905 a 24-lever signal box and a junction were built at Corfe Mullen, straddling the level crossing, two short sidings were also constructed here. Apart from the line to Wimborne, which eventually became a siding, the box controlled the double section from Bailey Gate and the single 'cut off' line to Broadstone. Prior to 1905, the two crossings and signals had been controlled by gate boxes at each location.

The map shows Admiralty siding to the west of the junction and also illustrates how the Wimborne and Broadstone lines diverged to the east of it.

The trackbed is kept grazed by a large rabbit population, although this wider view taken from alongside Bridge 223 on the B3074 road had to be obtained by some selective nibbling of the hedge! *Date: 22 March 1995.*

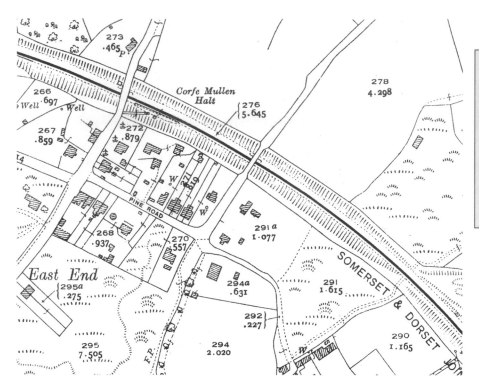

Map 35: Corfe Mullen Halt (1934)

Due to local pressure, first applied in 1884, a halt was eventually built in 1928 and opened on 28 July that year. It was sited almost at the summit of the 1:80 climb from the junction in a deep cutting on the north side of the village and was rudimentary to say the least: no shelter was built and only one gas lamp provided illumination on the short platform. Access was gained via steps from Bridge 235 on Wimborne Road. The halt was short-lived and closed on 19 September 1956.

122
Corfe Mullen Halt
195 SY 995984

This view taken nearly eleven years after closure depicts how basic the halt was and only one of the posts remains from the nameboard.
Photo: C.L.Caddy. Date: 24 April 1965.

The cutting in which the halt was sited was filled in during the mid-1980s and now forms part of the drive and garden of 112 Wimborne Road. The cutting on the north side of the road has also been filled in and developed.

The parapets of Bridge 236 in Lambs Green Lane survive just to the south side of the site, beyond which the wide sand cutting through which the Wimborne cut-off ran, is quite distinct and 29 chains distant the handsome triple-arched Bridge 238 still stands. *Date: 22 March 1995.*

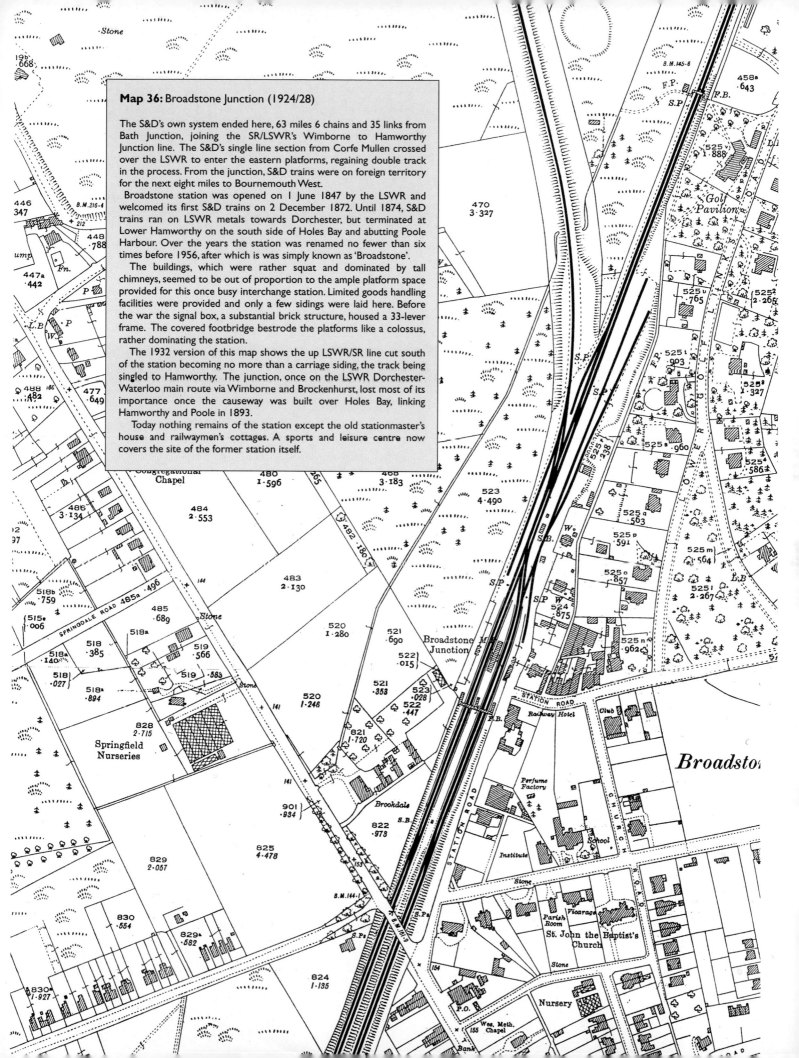

Map 36: Broadstone Junction (1924/28)

The S&D's own system ended here, 63 miles 6 chains and 35 links from Bath Junction, joining the SR/LSWR's Wimborne to Hamworthy Junction line. The S&D's single line section from Corfe Mullen crossed over the LSWR to enter the eastern platforms, regaining double track in the process. From the junction, S&D trains were on foreign territory for the next eight miles to Bournemouth West.

Broadstone station was opened on 1 June 1847 by the LSWR and welcomed its first S&D trains on 2 December 1872. Until 1874, S&D trains ran on LSWR metals towards Dorchester, but terminated at Lower Hamworthy on the south side of Holes Bay and abutting Poole Harbour. Over the years the station was renamed no fewer than six times before 1956, after which is was simply known as 'Broadstone'.

The buildings, which were rather squat and dominated by tall chimneys, seemed to be out of proportion to the ample platform space provided for this once busy interchange station. Limited goods handling facilities were provided and only a few sidings were laid here. Before the war the signal box, a substantial brick structure, housed a 33-lever frame. The covered footbridge bestrode the platforms like a colossus, rather dominating the station.

The 1932 version of this map shows the up LSWR/SR line cut south of the station becoming no more than a carriage siding, the track being singled to Hamworthy. The junction, once on the LSWR Dorchester-Waterloo main route via Wimborne and Brockenhurst, lost most of its importance once the causeway was built over Holes Bay, linking Hamworthy and Poole in 1893.

Today nothing remains of the station except the old stationmaster's house and railwaymen's cottages. A sports and leisure centre now covers the site of the former station itself.

123
Broadstone Junction
195 SY 005963

Although not strictly an 'S&D' working, Class 4 2-6-0 No 76006, from 71C Dorchester shed, approaches Broadstone Junction on the LSWR/SR line via Wimborne with a train from Salisbury for Bournemouth West. Rising from the junction at 1:97, the S&D's line can just be seen curving away to the left towards the golf course crossing and Corfe Mullen, nearly three miles away. Of note are the tall LSWR-designed home signals on both lines: the one on the right often provided a suitable photographic perch for Ivo Peters to gain a better view of the junction. The two sidings constituting the main goods yard, used by local coal merchants, are seen to good effect.

No 76006 was eventually allocated to Bournemouth MPD and occasionally ran over the S&D line; it saw out the end of steam on the Southern Region in July 1967. *Photo: Ivo Peters. Date: 3 August 1954.*

This area was enveloped by housing in the mid-1980s, but the road in the foreground now also provides access to the nearby club house of Broadstone Golf Club, long established. The old S&D single track, now a footpath, disappears to the left and continues for several hundred yards before petering out. When visiting here in 1985, the occasional signal wire pulley was still to be found at the side of the line formation.

Today there is nothing left to see of Broadstone Junction or station, but fortunately some vestiges have been saved: the station building was removed and re-erected at Medstead & Four Marks on the Watercress Line. *Date: 22 March 1995.*

Broadstone station
195 SY 004958

A wonderful panoramic shot of Broadstone, full of interesting detail, taken from the road bridge (No 79) which skewed across the line just south of the station. One of Bath's Class 5 4-6-0s, No 73028, with an excursion for Bournemouth, carefully negotiates the station and drops down the 1:75 gradient heading towards Creekmoor Halt and Holes Bay Junction, just over three miles distant. The Broadstone (formerly Railway) Hotel is seen beyond the double-decker bus.

By this date the line to Hamworthy Junction was singled and seldom used; the up side on the left of the picture was truncated a few chains south of the bridge, constituting no more than a siding. It is quite noticeable how the footbridge dominated the station. The junction with the S&D can just be made out in the background beyond the up platform on the extreme left.
Photo: J.W.T.House/C.L.Caddy collection. Date: Summer 1958.

This comparison was taken from near the middle of a large roundabout: the only recognizable features today are The Broadstone Hotel, a few shops and other buildings on Station Road. Broadstone Sports and Leisure Centre dominates the scene, with a car park in the foreground; a footpath has been created alongside and extends in either direction, including via a subway under the roundabout for a short distance southwards towards Upton. There is virtually no trace of either line formation or of Creekmoor Halt towards Holes Bay, which has almost entirely disappeared under housing and industrial estates. *Date: 22 March 1995.*

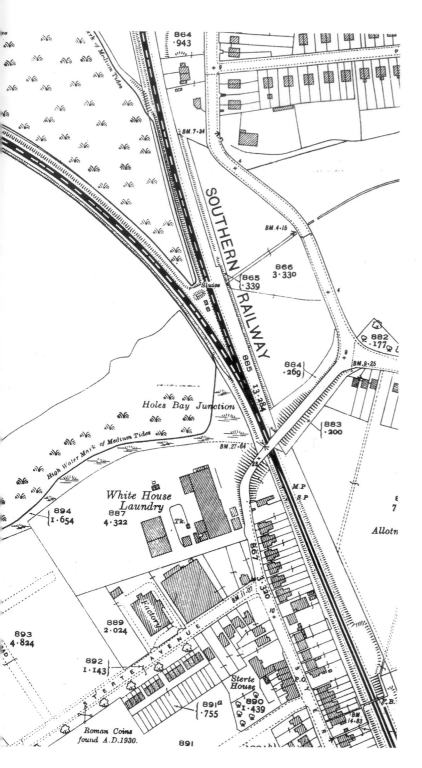

Map 37: Holes Bay Junction (1936)

S&D trains drawing near to Poole merged with the Southern's Weymouth–Waterloo main line at Holes Bay Junction.

There has been considerable land reclamation since publication of this map and extensive industrial development in the area, especially at Holes Bay. Factories and industrial units now cover the site of the old railway line from Broadstone.

125
Holes Bay Junction
195 SY 011919

S&D Class 7F 2-8-0 No 53808 with the 07.43 (SO) Birmingham–Bournemouth train joins the Southern main line from Weymouth to Waterloo at Holes Bay, which skirted the bay on a causeway, part of which is just visible on the left. *Photo: Ivo Peters. Date: 7 August 1954.*

Again, the dramatic changes are evident in this shot: the extent of industrial development can be judged from this photograph. Land reclamation for this purpose in the area has been extensive; the junction long since removed. However, close examination will reveal the odd 1930's house in the backgound providing some continuity.

An unidentified Class 442 unit forms a Weymouth-bound train and heads around the bend passing the site of the junction in the process; not quite as interesting as a haughty 7F 2-8-0 working an S&D train, one might think! *Date: 22 March 1995.*

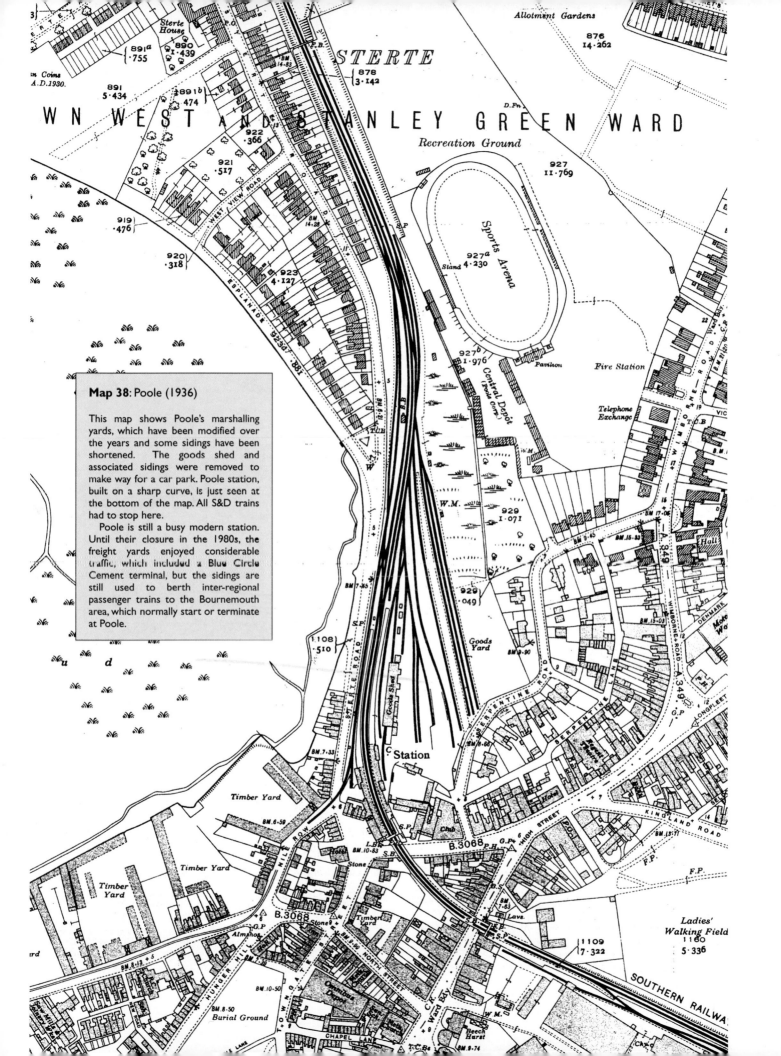

Map 38: Poole (1936)

This map shows Poole's marshalling yards, which have been modified over the years and some sidings have been shortened. The goods shed and associated sidings were removed to make way for a car park. Poole station, built on a sharp curve, is just seen at the bottom of the map. All S&D trains had to stop here.

Poole is still a busy modern station. Until their closure in the 1980s, the freight yards enjoyed considerable traffic, which included a Blue Circle Cement terminal, but the sidings are still used to berth inter-regional passenger trains to the Bournemouth area, which normally start or terminate at Poole.

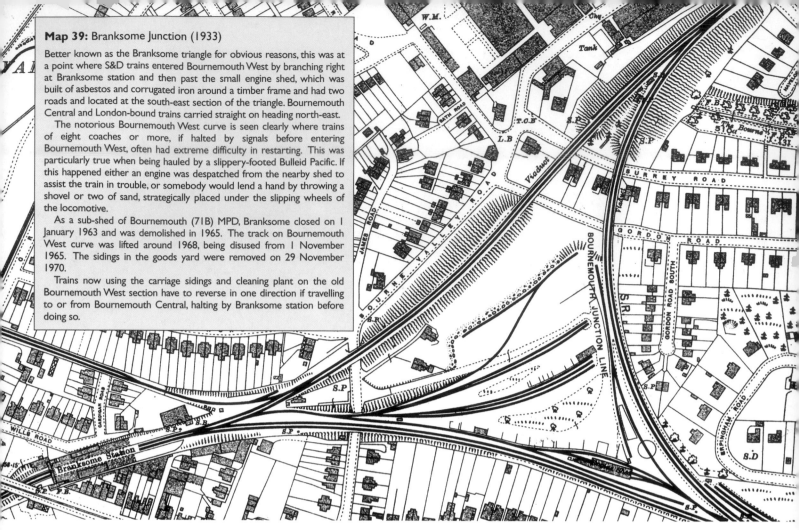

Map 39: Branksome Junction (1933)

Better known as the Branksome triangle for obvious reasons, this was at a point where S&D trains entered Bournemouth West by branching right at Branksome station and then past the small engine shed, which was built of asbestos and corrugated iron around a timber frame and had two roads and located at the south-east section of the triangle. Bournemouth Central and London-bound trains carried straight on heading north-east.

The notorious Bournemouth West curve is seen clearly where trains of eight coaches or more, if halted by signals before entering Bournemouth West, often had extreme difficulty in restarting. This was particularly true when being hauled by a slippery-footed Bulleid Pacific. If this happened either an engine was despatched from the nearby shed to assist the train in trouble, or somebody would lend a hand by throwing a shovel or two of sand, strategically placed under the slipping wheels of the locomotive.

As a sub-shed of Bournemouth (71B) MPD, Branksome closed on 1 January 1963 and was demolished in 1965. The track on Bournemouth West curve was lifted around 1968, being disused from 1 November 1965. The sidings in the goods yard were removed on 29 November 1970.

Trains now using the carriage sidings and cleaning plant on the old Bournemouth West section have to reverse in one direction if travelling to or from Bournemouth Central, halting by Branksome station before doing so.

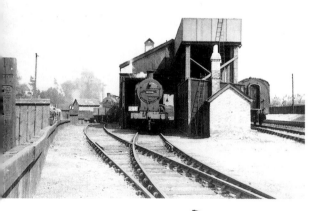

126
Branksome Shed
195 SY 062919

This pre-war study of the small Branksome shed taken from the west end shows 4F 0-6-0 No 3898 standing in No 2 shed road. The small engineers' mess room is seen directly underneath the water tank. On the right are the running lines to Bournemouth West station, approximately one-and-a-quarter miles to the east. The shed closed on 1 January 1963. *Photo: R.C.Riley. Date: 2 July 1938.*

Apart from the trees in the background, which are recognisable, this study could have been taken anywhere. The site of the engine shed is now occupied by a number of companies including a scaffolding business and a mini-skip/salvage firm. There are a few reminders of previous days: the viaduct on the curve still stands and is a listed structure. This site is scheduled for housing development over the next few years and all the tenants currently running their businesses from here will have to vacate their premises by 1998 or thereabouts. *Date: 22 March 1995.*

COMMENT: On 23 May 1985 I was privileged to have the company of both Donald Beale and Peter Smith, two ex-Branksome men, who were revisiting the site for the first time since they left railway employment. For a while I left them to wander around the site wrapped up in their memories and later photographed them together against once familiar backdrops, including the now defunct viaduct of the Bournemouth West curve.

I listened with tears of laughter pouring down my cheeks to some of Peter Smith's anecdotes emanating from the enginemen's mess room at Branksome; one I must share: on a fine summer Sunday morning whilst standing at the trackside adjacent to Bournemouth West Junction signal box awaiting the arrival of a Bulleid Pacific from Bournemouth Central shed with which to work the 09.45 to Bristol, driver Bert Brewer and Peter Smith were hailed by the box's harassed occupant, known to local railwaymen as 'Yorkie'.

"What a shift I'm having," he yelled down in despairing tones, "there's flippin' trains everywhere this morning – I haven't stopped since I came on duty!" Whereupon Bert, one of the many characters that the S&D produced and who sometimes did not get things quite right, shouted back: "You'm like the Scarlet Pimple then, mate – you sees 'em here, you sees 'em there, you sees the buggers everywhere!"

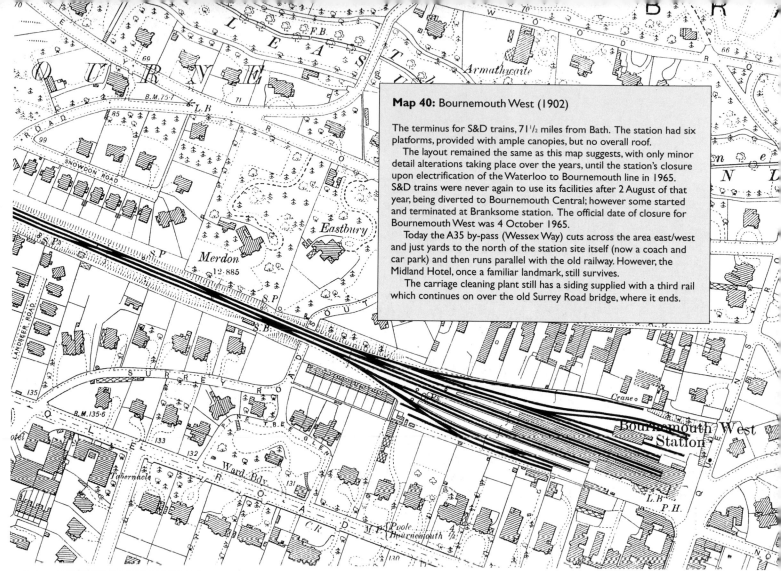

The celebrated duo: Donald Beale and Peter Smith revisit the site of Bournemouth West with the author and stand in front of the Midland Hotel to have their picture taken. *Date: 23 May 1985.*

127 *(Overleaf)*
Bournemouth West station
195 SY 074915

A superb study of Bournemouth West, which shows the layout to excellent advantage. As soon as it has the road, Class 4F 0-6-0 No 44561 is about to depart from the centre island platform with the 15.35 up mail to Bristol Temple Meads: it will face a reasonably stiff climb for the first quarter of a mile at 1:90, which will be a precursor for a much greater test to come over the Mendips, but the train will be given priority over all other traffic on the S&D single line sections to Bath.

A fine array of LSWR signals are positioned off the end of each of the island platforms, whilst every face has a water crane provided. The moderate-sized goods yard is on the left; traffic ceased to be handled here on 4 October 1965, the same day as the station itself closed. The Midland Hotel stands behind the station in the centre background. *Photo: Ivo Peters. Date: 10 August 1954.*

As evening shadows start to steal across the site, the same view today shows a completely different scene: the busy A35 slices across the area of the former goods yard, leaving only the Midland Hotel to provide a familiar backdrop over the coach and car park which now usurps the station, long since demolished.

Just out of camera sight to the immediate left on the other side of the A35 (Wessex Way), is the headshunt for the carriage shed and cleaning plant and provides the last railway link with the area. *Date: 22 March 1995.*

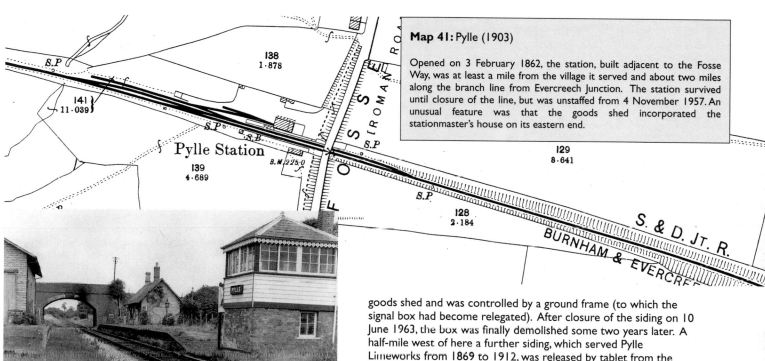

Map 41: Pylle (1903)

Opened on 3 February 1862, the station, built adjacent to the Fosse Way, was at least a mile from the village it served and about two miles along the branch line from Evercreech Junction. The station survived until closure of the line, but was unstaffed from 4 November 1957. An unusual feature was that the goods shed incorporated the stationmaster's house on its eastern end.

goods shed and was controlled by a ground frame (to which the signal box had become relegated). After closure of the siding on 10 June 1963, the box was finally demolished some two years later. A half-mile west of here a further siding, which served Pylle Limeworks from 1869 to 1912, was released by tablet from the station. *Photo: Lens of Sutton. Date: 1961.*

Sometime after the line's closure the goods shed became a meat packing plant for a period. It was subsequently put up for sale, but lay empty until purchased in the late 1980s. As this picture suggests, by the amount of building materials in the foreground, the goods shed was in the process of being converted into a 7-bedroom house. Over the last few years the station building itself has been turned into a dwelling with an extension built onto it. Some portions of the up platform remain, but the road bridge (No 243) carrying the A37 Fosse Way has been demolished, beyond which there is little sign of the line formation back towards Evercreech Junction, but at Elbow Corner Crossing the keeper's cottage and gates survive. West of here the trackbed is still quite distinct in parts, particularly through Pylle Woods, and the keeper's cottage at Cockmill Crossing still stands, although it was derelict when visited in 1985. *Date: 19 March 1995.*

128
Pylle station
183 ST 618389

This view of the station also shows the 17-lever signal box, which had closed in 1929. The passing loop was removed at the same time, thus the down platform and milk loading dock became disused. Although the crossover off the end of the platform was removed in May 1960, a siding remained to the attractive stone-built

The former goods shed and stationmaster's house.
Date: 19 March 1995.

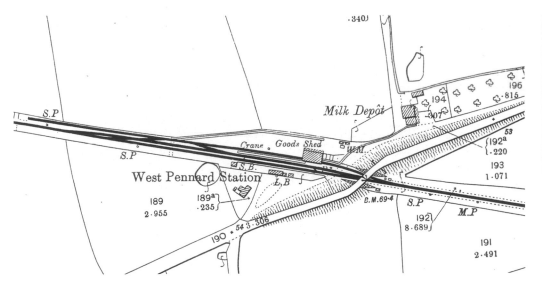

Map 42: West Pennard (1904)

The station opened on 3 February 1862 and like others on the branch was some distance from the village it served, being about two miles away. The attractive main building constructed in stone had the usual facilities of a booking office and a waiting room; it was well proportioned and compact. The large stone-built goods shed and 7-ton hand crane were served by a lengthy double-ended siding. The yard closed to goods on 10 June 1963 and the 26-lever signal box on 26 August 1964.

129
West Pennard station
182/183 ST 568395

West Pennard was the first block post and crossing place after Evercreech Junction, since the one at Pylle was taken out of use in 1929. Having descended for the previous four miles, at West Pennard the line started its journey across the Somerset Levels and ran dead straight for a further four miles to the bridge under the A39 near Glastonbury (No 264).

This photograph taken from the A361 road bridge (No 257), shows Class 3F 0-6-0 No 43216 departing from West Pennard with a Highbridge–Evercreech local. The locomotive, then based at Templecombe (82G) shed, only had a further three months in service before being scrapped at Derby Works in September 1962.
Photo: Derek Cross. Date: 29 June 1962.

The buildings remain in remarkable condition and like Pylle, the site was up for sale for many years before being purchased in 1987, but now a transport company, R.C.Withers, runs its business from here and the owners live in the former stationmaster's house, whilst the station building has been converted into a home for senior members of the family. The main A361 road was realigned many years ago and the railway bridge (No 257) removed.

Much of the line formation immediately to the east of the station has been obliterated and turned back into farm land, however it becomes quite distinct nearer Steanbow Crossing, where the keeper's cottage still stands. To the west, the trackbed is still evident in places, although much of it has been swallowed up by agriculture; there is no trace of Pennard Lane Crossing or the cottage, which has been demolished. At the end of the four-mile straight, Bridge 264 at Glastonbury survived until demolition in September 1994 during construction of the relief road, using the line formation from there to a point near the former station in the town. *Date: 8 March 1995.*

COMMENT: *When I visited here in 1985, the booking hall and office still had a crumbling BR closure notice poignantly adorning a wall. The fireplaces remained, as did the lavatories in the waiting room and on the platform. The booking office even had all its shelves and cupboards intact, as if it were only vacated the day before.*

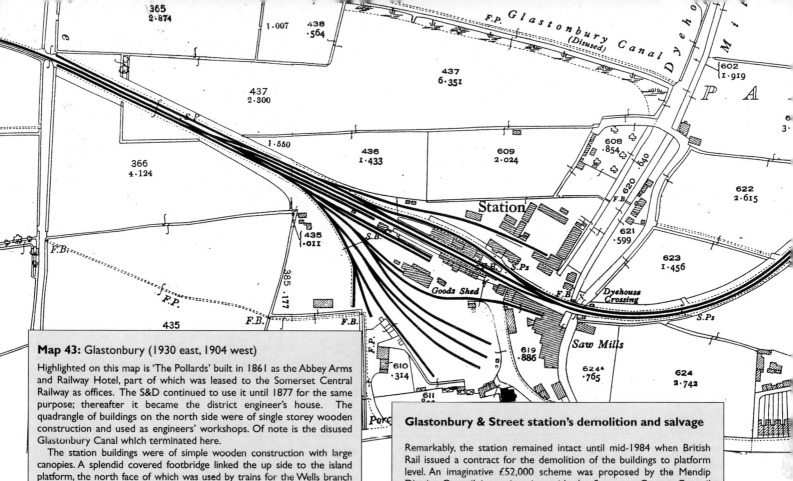

Map 43: Glastonbury (1930 east, 1904 west)

Highlighted on this map is 'The Pollards' built in 1861 as the Abbey Arms and Railway Hotel, part of which was leased to the Somerset Central Railway as offices. The S&D continued to use it until 1877 for the same purpose; thereafter it became the district engineer's house. The quadrangle of buildings on the north side were of single storey wooden construction and used as engineers' workshops. Of note is the disused Glastonbury Canal which terminated here.

The station buildings were of simple wooden construction with large canopies. A splendid covered footbridge linked the up side to the island platform, the north face of which was used by trains for the Wells branch until its closure in 1951. The line for the Wells branch ran parallel around the 9½-chain radius curve with the one to Evercreech Junction, as if it were double track, before parting after a mile or so to the north-east. This was once the location of Wells Branch Junction where trains diverged from the original single line. A signal box controlled the junction, but with its removal, a second track was laid from Glastonbury.

The goods yard was spacious and provided with two cranes (1-ton and 7-ton hand operated types), shed and cattle loading docks. It was the scene of considerable activity during its life. The substantial 29-lever signal box was strategically placed off the west end of the up platform.

The station remained intact until it was dismantled in 1984; the island platform canopy was subsequently re-erected in Glastonbury's open air market under the auspices of the Manpower Services Commission.

Today the sawmills and timber yard operate as part of J.Bradford & Sons Ltd, a large building supplies group, but still trade as Snow's Timber; 'The Pollards' is used by the company as an office building.

Glastonbury & Street station's demolition and salvage

Remarkably, the station remained intact until mid-1984 when British Rail issued a contract for the demolition of the buildings to platform level. An imaginative £52,000 scheme was proposed by the Mendip District Council in conjunction with the Somerset County Council Probation Service Community Programme and the Manpower Service Commission to dismantle the island platform canopy and re-erect it in a car park at Glastonbury town centre, also the site of an open air market. The PSCP provided the management and labour, whilst the MSC, MDC and a conservation society paid the wages.

The buildings were gradually dismantled and all salvageable materials were stored in the goods shed prior to transportation and re-erection. A small building just east of the goods shed was partly refurbished for use as a mess room by the PSCP labour force. The major work of dismantling had to be completed by the autumn of 1984 to take advantage of the weather before the onset of winter, when conditions would become difficult.

After a period of uncertainty brought about by the year's contract being due to expire and delays caused by British Rail selling all the metal (including the goods shed) remaining on the site, the PSCP had to move all salvaged materials to a new site near the town centre. However, by May 1985 the re-erection work on the car park site was under way and the footings had been dug for the supporting timber pillars which were renewed. The Somerset & Dorset Railway Trust were consulted regarding the correct colour scheme and as a result Glastonbury has been able to retain part of its railway heritage, which is now used as a covered market.

A photograph showing the dereliction following the removal of the salvageable materials from the site, leaving just the platforms which survived a little longer before being demolished.
Date: 31 May 1985.

Glastonbury – Dyehouse Lane Crossing and Bridge 266
182/183 ST 491389

A Whit Monday excursion from Weston-super-Mare to Bournemouth gets under way from Glastonbury, hauled by 4F 0-6-0 No 44417, and is about to pass over Bridge 266 and Dyehouse Lane Crossing. The disused portion of the bridge (spanning a mill stream running parallel to the road) used to carry the Wells branch line before it was dismantled, following closure in 1951. The ornate footbridge of Glastonbury station is just visible over the train and the hopper is that of an adjacent sawmill.

Although this and some other crossings on the Highbridge branch were controlled by station staff (here a gatekeeper's hut was provided for shelter on the east side), there were no fewer than nine others with keeper's cottages at intermediate locations, many in isolated rural areas; these were: Elbow Corner, Cockmill, Steanbow, Pennard Lane, Cemetery Lane, Aqueduct, Sharpham, Catcott and Huntspill. The cottages were mostly without electricity or mains water; the latter was delivered in churns by train.
Photo: David Milton. Date: 1961.

Today the former level crossing is fenced off, but the bridge over the stream is relatively unchanged and its girders are still *in situ,* although they are obscured in this view. As is evident, the gateposts still stand on the west side of the road, but those opposite have been removed: the lane is now linked into the new Glastonbury relief road which uses the S&D's formation from this location, absorbing both the Paradise and Cemetery Lane crossings, to the site of the now-demolished Bridge 264 on Wells road (A361), where a large roundabout has been constructed. Northload Bridge (No 265), 32 chains from Dyehouse Lane, carrying the B3151 over the S&D formation has also succumbed; it was removed in favour of a roundabout.
Date: 1 March 1995.

The new relief road under construction, looking east from Dyehouse Lane Crossing.
Date: 1 March 1995.

131
Glastonbury & Street station (1)
182/183 ST 491389

A view taken from the access road to the engineers' offices and workshops near Dyehouse Lane Crossing shows clearly the generous proportions of the station: the buildings were of wooden construction with fine canopies linked at the eastern end by an elegant footbridge with a latticed lower section and covered top. The north face of the island down platform (this had a refreshment room opened in 1899 run by the Abbey Temperance Hotel Company, but it soon went bankrupt!) on the right was used by Wells branch line trains until its closure in 1951. The main booking hall and waiting rooms were on the up platform opposite. Of note

is the tall repeating down starting signal, which aided visibility from beyond the footbridge; its lowest arm, used for shunting movements, was marked with an 'S'.

The building on the immediate left formed part of John Snow's sawmills, whilst the one next to it was railway property within the station complex and used as a parcels' office. *Photo: C.L.Caddy. Date: 29 August 1964.*

There is little to signify the station ever existed: the area in the foreground, owned by J.C.Thomas & Sons, scrap metal processors of Glastonbury, will eventually be used for open storage, but currently is a contractor's site for the new relief road scheduled to open in May 1995. The buildings previously on the left were demolished a few years ago. *Date: 1 March 1995.*

132
Glastonbury & Street station (2)
182 ST 491389

Ivatt 2-6-2T No 41296 stands at the station with the 14.20 from Highbridge to Templecombe. A closer view of the covered footbridge (No 267) shows its latticed lower half did not afford much protection against wind-driven rain for those crossing to and from the island platform on the right. A stack of parcels awaits dispatch on the up platform: C & J.Clark Ltd, the shoe manufacturers, sent a large quantity of their goods by rail and remained a regular customer of the S&D line until closure.

No 41296, a Templecombe-based engine, worked the line until March 1966 and subsequently was stored on shed before being scrapped at Cohen's, Morriston, Swansea, in July 1966.
Photo: R.M.Casserley. Date: 29 March 1965.

There really is not much to say about a civil engineering contractor's site: there is nothing which one can relate to the previous scene after the remaining portions of the platforms were demolished a few years ago. Once the relief road has been completed and the contractor, Messrs Birse, has left, it is likely to be used for the storage of caravans and ISO containers.
Date: 1 March 1995.

133
Glastonbury & Street station (3)
182 ST 491389

Class 3F 0-6-0 No 43218 sets off from the station with a down local from Highbridge to Templecombe. Glastonbury Tor, probably Somerset's most celebrated landmark, surmounted by the derelict tower of St Michael's chapel, dominates the background.

Of interest is the notice on the shed showing 'Southern' influence. The line in the background curved sharply for 9½ chains and had a 5mph speed restriction. It then skirted Glastonbury round the town's northern side before heading east towards Evercreech. The Wells branch ran parallel to it for about a mile; the lines then diverged north of the town. *Photo: R.E. Toop. Date: 13 June 1959.*

When the shed in the foreground was demolished in 1984 many goods labels were found between the timber cladding of the walls and must have dated from a considerable period before the line's closure. Small trees have all but obscured the view to Glastonbury Tor, which still acts as a focal point. *Date: 1 March 1995.*

134

Glastonbury & Street station (4)
182 ST 490390

A panorama taken from the signal box affords an excellent view of the station and surroundings: the engineers' workshops can be seen behind the island canopy on the left and Glastonbury Tor is clearly visible in the background, as is the magnificent tower of St John the Baptist parish church in the town's High Street. At 134ft it was

second only in height to St Mary's, Taunton.
Photo: R.E. Toop. Date: 13 June 1959.

This comparison was taken from a fence dividing the contractor's site from the scrap yard of Messrs J.C. Thomas & Sons. The former engineers' offices, now private dwellings, are seen on the left and were mostly obscured by the now-preserved island canopy in the 1959 view. *Date: 1 March 1995.*

135
**Glastonbury & Street station –
goods yard and signal box**
182 ST 490390

The attractive 29-lever wooden signal box also controlled the goods yard, which was large, well laid out, usually busy and remained so until closure of the line on 7 March 1966. Seen here is Class 22XX 0-6-0 No 2218 indulging in some shunting before proceeding with an east-bound goods.

The Collett 0-6-0 did not have long to remain in service, for it was withdrawn a month later at Templecombe shed, where it was stored until February 1965; it was scrapped at Cashmore's, Newport, during the following April.
Photo: Ivo Peters.
Date: 8 October 1964.

A total contrast: behind this fence is the compound of Messrs Thomas's scrap yard, but there is nothing which relates to the previous view, save for the tops of a few trees just seen in the background which have grown considerably since 1964, making it impossible to identify them individually.

The company moved here in 1985 and was responsible for demolishing the last remains of the station platforms. The column and pulley wheel of the one-ton crane had stood forlornly amongst the dereliction along with the old cattle pens and these were also removed at the same time and an access road was built. Before the entire station and goods yard site was sold by British Rail to Messrs Thomas, the trackbed at the western end towards Middle Drove was used by John Snow's timber yard for many years for the burning of waste materials from the saw mill operations.
Date: 1 March 1995.

The iron bridge (No 268) at Aqueduct Crossing still spans the River Brue at 182 ST 480392. The former crossing keeper's cottage stands on the west side of the lane and is a private dwelling, as is the one at Sharpham, 38 chains west of here, where the gateposts also remain. *Date: 1 March 1995.*

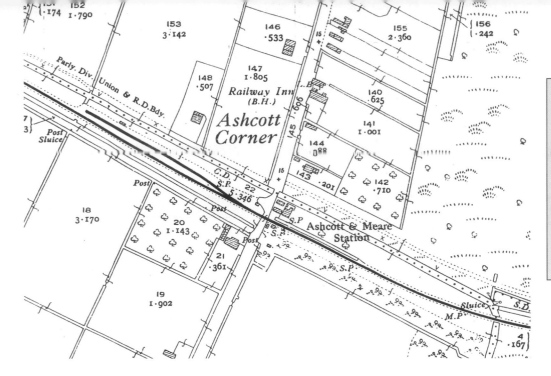

Map 44: Ashcott Corner (1904)

The station was located at Ashcott Corner, on the south bank of the old canal and South Drain; it was an inconvenient two miles from the villages of Ashcott to the south and Meare a mile to the north. It opened in July 1856 and was known as Ashcott & Meare until renamed in 1876, although the signs continued to signify both villages it served until well into the twentieth-century.

136
Ashcott (& Meare) station
182 ST 449397

This simple concrete platform replaced an earlier wooden structure in the 1920s, but had no facilities on it: the booking office and waiting room were annexed to Station House adjacent to the Ashcott–Meare road.

The small goods yard consisting of a single siding and a loading gauge, controlled by a 10-lever ground frame, was on the west side of the station and the road. The siding closed on 13 July 1964. Some three-quarters of a mile east of the station, alongside the former Glastonbury Canal, the Petfu siding, opened in 1920, served an adjacent peat works. *Photo: David Milton. Date: June 1960.*

There is nothing much to see of the former station from this aspect; the remaining portions of the platform supports are hidden by undergrowth, save for the nameboard posts, which still can be seen. Archie Attwell, the latter-day Ashcott porter who still lives here with his wife, had this bungalow built following the demolition of Station House which was suffering from subsidence, probably due to the Sedgemoor's South Drain that ran east/west directly behind the building.

Although all the ballast has been removed, the course of the railway is still well defined in both directions and used as a vehicle track in this nature conservation area; much of it is owned by the NRA. To the east it is passable to Sharpham Crossing and 10 chains from Ashcott Corner, Bridge 269 still straddles a drain from Ashcott Heath. There is little evidence of either Alexander's siding or the former Eclipse Peat Company's level crossing 50 chains west of here, where a 2ft-gauge railway crossed the S&D. This was the site of a collision on 19 August 1949 which resulted in Johnson 0-6-0 No 3260 (S&D No 76) ending up in South Drain. It was eventually cut up for scrap where it lay. *Date: 17 February 1995.*

The station nameboard posts stand out defiantly from the undergrowth.
Date: 17 February 1995.

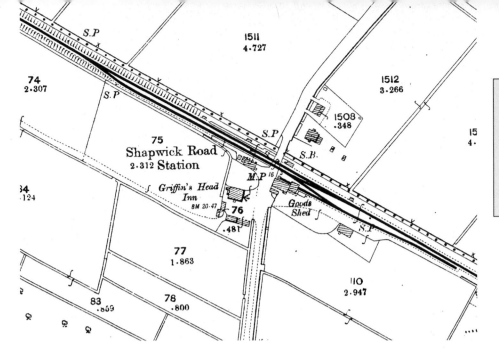

Map 45: Shapwick (1904)

Like Ashcott, the station (named as Shapwick Road on this map) was remotely situated in the heart of the Somerset Levels 2¼ miles north of the village it served. Shapwick was a block post with a lengthy crossing loop and had two sidings on the up side of the line to the east of the station.

137
Shapwick station (1)
182 ST 423412

A low-level view of the station looking towards Glastonbury shows the layout well. The wooden 17-lever signal box stood adjacent to the crossing which it also controlled and was used for that purpose until the closure of the line in 1966. The up platform had a simple wooden building, which replaced an earlier one which burnt down on 25 September 1900. It had two waiting rooms and a booking office, whilst the down side had a small shelter which was subsequently demolished when the station was rebuilt by the SR substituting the earth and timber platforms with concrete ones.

Peat traffic was a major source of revenue here in the first quarter of this century, but road traffic gradually eroded this. The goods yard, seen beyond the crossing gates in this worm's-eye view, closed on 10 June 1963; also noticeable is the distance between the two tracks, which emphasises the line's broad gauge heritage. *Photo: David Milton. Date: 10 June 1960.*

Absolutely nothing remains. South Drain seen on the left has been widened, the bridge has been replaced and in turn displaced the site of the signal box.
Date: 25 February 1995.

138
Shapwick station (2)
182 ST 423412

A view from the other side of the tracks: Class 3F 0-6-0 No 43436 stands at Shapwick with an up local for Highbridge. The semi-detached stationmaster and signalman's house can be seen in the background beyond the down platform, which still retained its oil lights if not its building. Of note are the neat row of fire buckets off the end of the platform ramp.
Photo: J.W.T.House/C.L.Caddy collection. Date: August 1958.

The former stationmaster and signalman's house has long since been demolished. The trackbed towards Catcott Crossing and Edington Junction becomes indistinct west of here and many stretches have been obliterated.

South Drain is a well stocked river and popular for coarse fishing during the season. English Nature (or the Nature Conservancy Council of England) are responsible for large tracts of land on Shapwick Heath, which is a haven for an infinite variety of wildlife. Over the last few years peat extraction has been severely curtailed on the moors and in some areas has ceased altogether; in certain cases the land has been allowed to flood creating ideal habitats for wildfowl and many other water birds.
Date: 25 February 1995.

The only vestige that does give a hint of the former rôle of the area is the gate of the goods yard on the east of the road, opposite which, just out of camera sight, is a large stockpile of peat. Near here are the discovered remains of a neolithic walkway.
Date: 25 February 1995.

139
Edington Junction (1)
182 ST 392428

This view of Edington Junction looking towards Glastonbury shows the generous proportions of this remote station prior to removal of the loop and down platform. The wooden station buildings and the large island canopy can be seen clearly in this photograph, beyond which was the small goods yard; the siding's buffer can just be discerned on the extreme right. Of interest is the shunting signal seen just over the down platform's shelter. *Photo: Will Locke collection. Date: Summer 1951.*

A substantial portion of the island platform survives, although it has been reduced in length by a hundred feet or so. The owners of Station House, who purchased it in 1976/7, have extensively modernised the building over the last few years. They have also cut back much of the undergrowth which once surrounded the island platform and have created a garden on the trackbed along part of the remaining section. The goods yard gate survived until fairly recently, but has since been replaced by the NRA, who own the site. The cottage on the right seems relatively unchanged by the passage of time.

The keeper's cottage at Catcott Crossing 40 chains east of here has been extensively refurbished over the past few years; however, the line formation in between has been totally rubbed from the face of the earth, giving no indication that a railway was ever constructed here alongside the north bank of the old Glastonbury Canal (South Drain).
Date: 25 February 1995.

Map 46: Edington Junction (1904)

Edington Road station opened in 1856 to serve the villages of Edington and Burtle, some two-and-a-half miles apart. Like other stations on the Somerset Levels, it was rather remote, but achieved higher status by becoming Edington Junction in 1890 upon the opening of the Bridgwater branch. The station was renamed Edington Burtle on 8 June 1953 after the closure of the latter.

The layout was fairly comprehensive: the up platform became an island with the south face providing access for Bridgwater branch trains. The station building, of wooden construction, was at the eastern end of the up platform, which also had a large canopy extending to half its length. A charming 39-lever wooden signal box situated off the west end controlled the junction and small goods yard. The down platform was provided with a wooden shelter and staff rooms.

After the Bridgwater branch had closed to passengers on 1 December 1952, it lingered on for goods traffic until October 1954, when it was shut completely. The station's down platform fell into disrepair and in February 1956 it was removed along with the crossing loop and all sidings, except one serving the small goods shed. The signal box was then closed and the remaining siding was controlled by a ground frame; goods ceased to be handled from here on 13 July 1964.

Most of the former station and goods yard are now owned by the NRA. The Railway Hotel has been renamed the Tom Mogg Inn after one of the station's latter-day signalmen/porters. The sign shows him holding the SCR hand bell, which was rung at the level crossing to warn of an approaching train in earlier times.

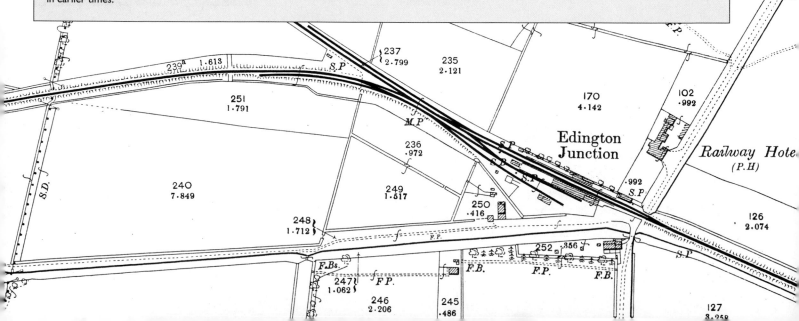

Edington Junction (2)
182 ST 392428

Pictured here is the most attractive 39-lever wooden signal box situated off the west end of the island platform. The box controlled the branch for Bridgwater, seen curving to the left in the distance, also the adjacent goods yard and crossover. The cattle pens are just visible on the extreme left. The oil light on the platform and trolley underneath with a number of milk churns complete the scene.

The lines of the Burnham and Bridgwater branches ran parallel from Edington before diverging some six chains west of the island platform. This was on occasion the scene of friendly rivalry: a Bridgwater branch train, having waited for the arrival of an Evercreech–Highbridge connection, was able to race it away from the station, resulting in spectacular performances from both engines as their crews vied for the lead over the few chains before going their separate way – the steam version of Santa Pod raceway! *Photo: Will Locke collection. Date: Summer 1951.*

This portion of the island platform has all but succumbed to brambles, whilst the remains of the down platform, now an untidy pile of rubble, has become completely overgrown. Although they look old, most of the agricultural buildings were built no more than ten years ago. The line formation to the west of the former junction is still quite distinct in parts, but much of it has disappeared. Chilton Drove crossing keeper's cottage on the Bridgwater branch survives today, but there is no trace of the one at Stone End Crossing a little further towards New Close Drove and Cossington. *Date: 25 February 1995.*

141
Huntspill Crossing
182 ST 372444

One of the idiosyncrasies of the branch line was that water had to be delivered to some crossing keepers' cottages in the remote areas of the moor! This crossing, mid-point between Edington and Bason Bridge, was an example and seen here are the crew of Collett 0-6-0 No 3206, with an up goods, making such a stop to unload the small churns of water for the level crossing keeper's cottage which was located beyond the far side of the tender. *Photo: R.E. Toop. Date: 16 June 1962.*

A few vestiges remain of the level crossing; however, the posts are a familiar pointer and some discarded iron bracing off one of the gates can be seen next to the kissing gate. The tile-faced crossing keeper's cottage, always very damp because of the high water table, has long since been demolished.

This photograph shows the remote area to advantage with the distant Mendip Hills in the background. *Date: 5 March 1985 (revisited 17 February 1995).*

BASON BRIDGE–BURNHAM-ON-SEA

142
Bason Bridge – milk factory
182 ST 348457

In 1909 Wilts United Dairies established a milk factory at Bason Bridge, which provided substantial traffic for the Somerset & Dorset line. Pre-nationalisation of the railways the milk traffic for London was routed via Templecombe and afterwards mostly via Highbridge and the Western Region. Although general goods ceased to be handled on 10 June 1963, the milk traffic lasted until 2 October 1972, some years after closure of the branch. The construction of the M5 motorway 1½ miles to the west of Bason Bridge around this time almost certainly precipitated the end of milk traffic by rail; but road transport was on the increase and therefore to continue the link, involving expensive construction of a new rail bridge and bank formation to elevate the line over the M5, was not practical.

With the River Brue in the foreground, Class 4F 0-6-0 No 44272 leaves the Bason Bridge factory with a milk train. The siding was controlled by the east ground frame, the hut of which is seen perched precariously over the river bank. *Photo: R.E. Toop. Date: 18 May 1963.*

The milk factory expanded greatly over the years; however, United Dairies (Dairy Crest) closed it in 1987. Today the buildings form the Brue Business Park and a variety of companies has located here, including Agriproducts, which specialises in spray-drying food products for use in flavourings etc. Other companies include a maker of firefighters' helmets, aluminium window manufacturers, a plastics salvage company and a dental chair manufacturer. *Date: 1 May 1985 (revisited 18 February 1995).*

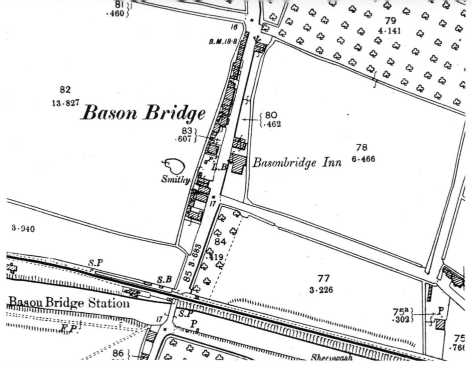

Map 47: Bason Bridge (1904)

This map was printed a few years before the milk factory was established here and the area it was to occupy is shown as a green field site. The single-platform station had opened many years earlier in July 1856. At one time it had no fewer than six staff: the stationmaster, two clerks, two porter/shunters and a junior porter. Its simple buildings were sited on the end nearest the road, but these rather cramped the amount of standing room on the platform in front of them. Bason Bridge survived until closure of the line.

143
Bason Bridge station
182 ST 345458

A nice view of the station with its neat and tidy wooden buildings; the stationmaster's house is in the background on the left. The crossing gates over the B3141 road were controlled from the west ground frame opposite the eastern end of the platform ramp; its shadow is visible in this photograph. The level crossing here was one of a total of 14 manned crossings over the 21 miles to Evercreech Junction. *Photo: David Milton. Date: 10 June 1960.*

The platform survives, even though it is entirely overgrown with brambles and cannot be seen. The former stationmaster's house still stands in the background and is a private dwelling. The line formation is largely overgrown from this point westwards, although until a few years ago a path along it from here made it more apparent than is seen to be the case in this photograph.
Date: 2 March 1995.

195

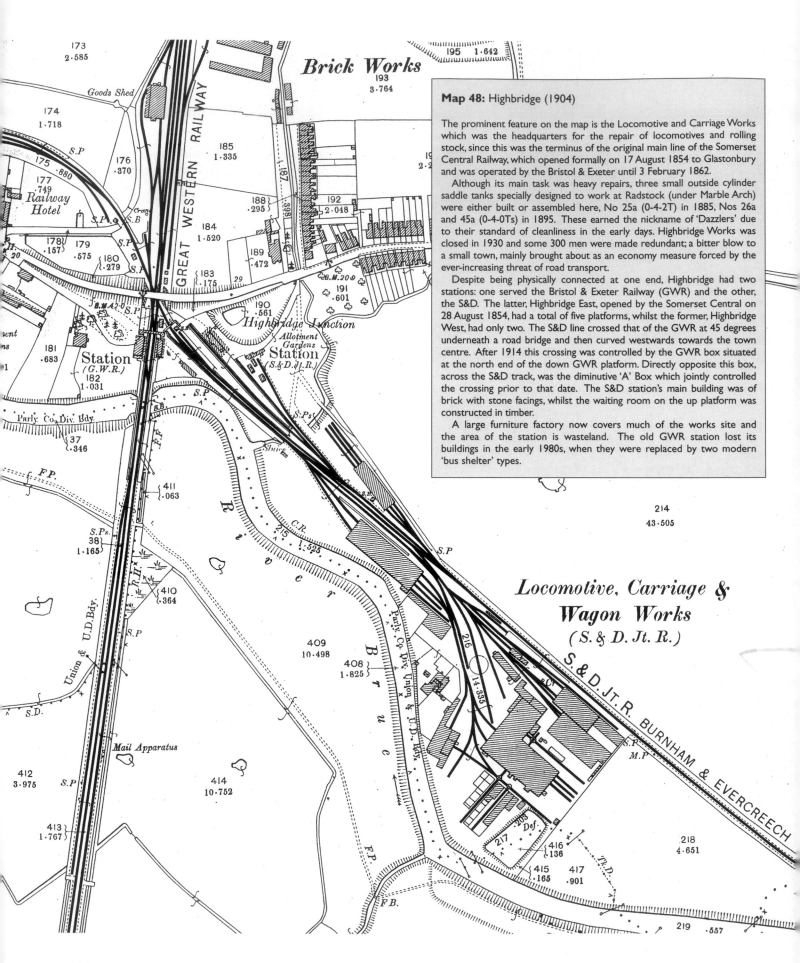

Map 48: Highbridge (1904)

The prominent feature on the map is the Locomotive and Carriage Works which was the headquarters for the repair of locomotives and rolling stock, since this was the terminus of the original main line of the Somerset Central Railway, which opened formally on 17 August 1854 to Glastonbury and was operated by the Bristol & Exeter until 3 February 1862.

Although its main task was heavy repairs, three small outside cylinder saddle tanks specially designed to work at Radstock (under Marble Arch) were either built or assembled here, No 25a (0-4-2T) in 1885, Nos 26a and 45a (0-4-0Ts) in 1895. These earned the nickname of 'Dazzlers' due to their standard of cleanliness in the early days. Highbridge Works was closed in 1930 and some 300 men were made redundant; a bitter blow to a small town, mainly brought about as an economy measure forced by the ever-increasing threat of road transport.

Despite being physically connected at one end, Highbridge had two stations: one served the Bristol & Exeter Railway (GWR) and the other, the S&D. The latter, Highbridge East, opened by the Somerset Central on 28 August 1854, had a total of five platforms, whilst the former, Highbridge West, had only two. The S&D line crossed that of the GWR at 45 degrees underneath a road bridge and then curved westwards towards the town centre. After 1914 this crossing was controlled by the GWR box situated at the north end of the down GWR platform. Directly opposite this box, across the S&D track, was the diminutive 'A' Box which jointly controlled the crossing prior to that date. The S&D station's main building was of brick with stone facings, whilst the waiting room on the up platform was constructed in timber.

A large furniture factory now covers much of the works site and the area of the station is wasteland. The old GWR station lost its buildings in the early 1980s, when they were replaced by two modern 'bus shelter' types.

144
Highbridge Works
182 ST 324469

A view looking east of Highbridge Works taken from the steps of the 25-lever Highbridge East 'C' or 'Loco' box, as it was called until 1948. The signal box controlled the southern end of the station and access to the works and shed. In the background an unidentified locomotive is standing alongside the water tower, beyond which is the former paint shop with the running shed seen to the left of it. Although there is plenty of rolling stock in evidence, the works had largely become disused since its closure in 1930. Beyond the trucks in the centre of the picture is the road leading to the 49ft 9in turntable. The tallest building seen in the background once housed the erecting shop, boiler shop and foundry. The base of the carriage and wagon erecting shop is on the immediate right; this had burned down in the 1950s. The lines on the left once led to the carriage shed which had been demolished by this date. *Photo: E. Wilmshurst. Date: 16 June 1962.*

There is nothing to be seen in this photograph to which one can relate in the 1962 view and over the last few years this huge factory has been built covering much of the site of the former works. Along with another long-established company in the town, Caxton Furniture (Woodberry Bros & Haines Ltd) employs many craftsmen with joinery skills, thus maintaining a tradition for which Highbridge has become synonymous, particularly since the railway founded its works here in the middle of the last century. The foreground is a trailer park for the factory, which covers many thousands of square feet and is almost certainly the largest industrial building in the area, although it may not be obvious from this perspective.
Date: 23 March 1995.

145
Highbridge East station (1)
182 ST 323469

Signs of activity at Highbridge, but the station was not always so busy in its latter days, with long periods of inactivity in between trains. Here the 13.15 from Evercreech Junction has just arrived on the up platform (No 5) and disgorges its passengers, whilst Ivatt 2-6-2T No 41249 prepares to depart with the 14.20 to Evercreech from the bay separating platforms 2 and 3.

The main station building, behind the locomotive in the bay was an attractive structure built in brick and stone. A war memorial was set into its westerly end to commemorate those in the railway's employ who gave their lives in the service of the country. Following the closure of the Burnham branch in 1951, the terminal platforms at Highbridge saw greater use and the station signs had 'for Burnham-on-Sea' added to them. Goods ceased to be handled here from 2 November 1964.

Highbridge 'A' box, seen in front of the concrete footbridge (No 281) which linked all the platforms and the GWR station, was closed in 1914; it had served as a staff mess room for many years. *Photo: Derek Cross.*
Date: October 1965.

The black bridge (No 281A) carrying the B3139 over the Western Region main line stands the test of time whilst all about has been torn asunder, apart from a remaining portion of the concrete footbridge which dates from 1933 and still links the two platforms of the former GWR station. A wizened tree on the extreme right can be identified with one seen over the van standing alongside Platform 1 in the 1965 photograph.

Up until the mid-1980s, the S&D's concrete up platform could be discerned, but now has been buried under rubble covered with top soil to a depth of more than three feet, which covers the entire station site.
Date: 26 February 1995.

Class 3F 0-6-0 No 43194 stands in the bay between platforms 2 and 3 with a train for Evercreech.

Then based at Templecombe (82G) shed, No 43194 was withdrawn from service in December 1960 and scrapped at Crewe Works three months later.
Photo: C.L.Caddy. Date: c1958.

146
Highbridge East station (2)
182 ST 322470

A familiar scene: Collett 0-6-0 No 3218 arrives on time at Platform 5 with the 13.15 from Evercreech, whilst another ex-GWR 0-6-0 of the class awaits to depart with the 14.20.

Since April 1960 no fewer than fifteen of these handsome ex-GWR light mixed-traffic locomotives had been allocated at one time or another to 83G Templecombe MPD. By the beginning of 1965 only Nos 3200 (withdrawn in January), 3201 and 3218 remained, until the latter two were taken out of service the following May. During the same month the now-preserved No 3205 was transferred to the S&D from 83D Laira shed, only to be withdrawn at the same time as the others.

This excellent view taken from the footbridge gives an idea of the extensive layout of the station and its five platforms, which had no canopies: the brick station building provided the only shelter on this vast expanse. Seen in the background are the sheds and old works closed in 1930. The line in the immediate foreground crossed the GWR main line to Highbridge Wharf and Burnham-on-Sea.
Photo: C.L.Caddy. Date: 9 January 1965.

With the background dominated by Caxton Furniture's factory, this barren piece of land is all there is to see.

During the construction of the M5 motorway which required many thousands of tons of ballast for the settlement of the flatlands across which it was being built, a new spur was connected from the down Western main line to a reception terminal adjacent to the old works site off the end of the former S&D up platform. This also involved erecting a temporary 'Armco' culvert just to the east of the original bridge (No 281A) under which the new spur passed connecting to the Bason Bridge line which was slewed northwards.

Class 37 diesels worked in pairs hauling fly ash mainly from the coal-fired power stations in South Wales; some three-quarters of a million tons were handled here between 27 April and 21 August 1971. Trains climbed a newly-built embankment to discharge their loads over a screen and a run round loop was built enabling them to be hauled back out. The last rails were lifted in the early 1980s; the temporary bridge having been removed some time before and the road was made good again. *Date: 26 February 1995.*

147
Highbridge crossover (1)
182 ST 322470

This aspect taken from near the wooden waiting room on Platform 5 gives a good impression of what the narrow passage trains were afforded leading to the crossover. The former 'A' box nestles closely to the rather incongruous concrete footbridge, which replaced an iron one erected in 1896, behind which West box that also controlled S&D trains traversing the Bristol main line can just be spotted. Highbridge East 'B' box is seen in the background.

Judging from the direction sign on the footbridge, there was a reluctance to ignore individual railway boundaries and reference is still made to distinguish GWR trains from those on the S&D line! *Photo: LRGP/Real Photographs. Date: c1951.*

A chain-link fence marks the station boundary now and this parcel of land is owned by Caxton Furniture, but the remaining portion of the footbridge is on railway property. *Date: 26 February 1995.*

COMMENT: *This comparison had to be taken from the prone position with the camera almost resting on the ground due to the amount of spoil that has been spread here, raising the level considerably. After a long wet spell, I had to lie on a sodden patch of earth, which did not do much for my morale – or anything else – on this Sunday morning!*

148
Highbridge crossover (2)
182 ST 322471

A worm's-eye view looking over the crossover back towards Highbridge East station. The elegant wedge-shaped Highbridge West box can be judged well in this study: not only did it control the flat crossover and the main line, but also movements in the GWR yard as well. The attractive Brunel-designed building on the GWR down platform contrasts greatly with the simple wooden affair on the S&D's Platform 5 visible in the background behind the box. Bridge 281A carrying the B3139 to Wedmore and Wells dominates the foreground and the white patch on it was a screen for the backing signal in the GWR yard. *Photo: E. Wilmshurst. Date: 21 July 1962.*

Closed on 20 March 1972, the signal box was dismantled soon after, as was the ex-GWR goods yard and S&D crossing which it controlled. The facing crossover points served a goods loop just south of Highbridge station on the up side of the main line. All the buildings on the former GWR station were also demolished in the 1970s and have been replaced with two miserable bus-type shelters. In April 1995 a joint project was announced between British Rail, Sedgemoor District Council and a developer, to enhance the station approach and develop an adjoining parcel of land, on part of which residential properties will be built and a small public park created.

A Class 143 Pacer unit draws into the station with the 15.05 Bristol Temple Meads to Taunton service. Although partially obscured by the footbridge, Bridge 281A has not changed much, except the smoke deflectors have been removed. *Date: 23 March 1995.*

149
Highbridge East 'B' signal box
182 ST 322471

A photograph that is a real feast for the eyes and like many railway scenes of yesteryear it has splendid variety: the small 12-lever East 'B' box controlled the entrance to the S&D goods yard (further to the left out of sight) and the crossing adjacent to it. Beyond the signals in a siding are a couple of engineers' wagons with oil drums placed in one of them. East 'B' box closed on 16 May 1965 along with East 'A' after the line to the wharf and Burnham had been taken up, following which a direct connection was then made via the GWR yard between the S&D branch and the Bristol main line; this link was used for milk traffic until that ceased in October 1972. The corrugated iron hut in the foreground was apparently used as an oil store.
Photo: David Milton.
Date: July 1960.

This photograph had to be taken from the pedestrian bridge erected on the north side of the B3139 road bridge spanning the GWR main line, so was slightly forward of the position adopted by David Milton.

The GWR goods yard and its shed have gone, but Cowells, a stockholder specialising in pipes, valves and fittings, have turned the site into a depot. There is nothing of particular interest to catch the eye in this scene except for the intolerable amount of rubbish which has blown against the railway boundary fence. There is nothing left of the S&D formation: a Kwik Save supermarket and a car park have been built on the site of the goods shed and yard. Entrance to both is gained from Market Street.
Date: 26 February 1995.

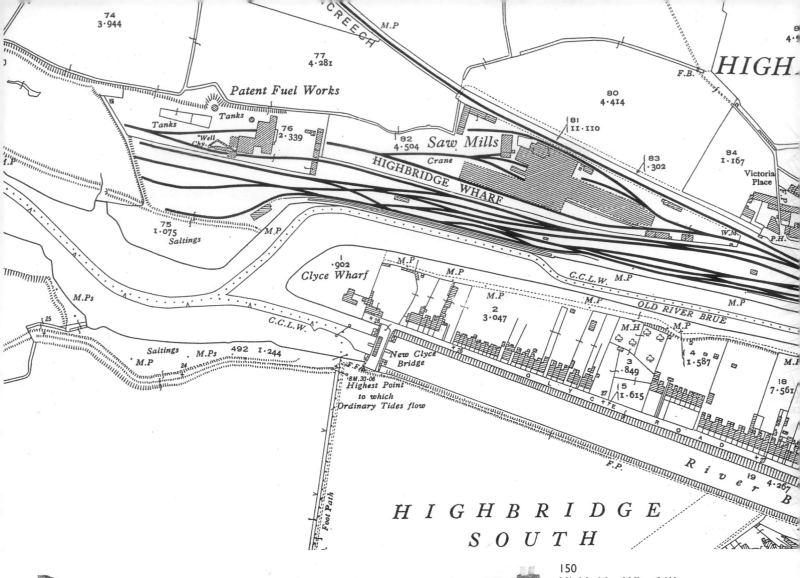

HIGHBRIDGE SOUTH

150
Highbridge Wharf (1)
182 ST 320472

The attractive 19-lever Highbridge East 'A' signal box with its delightful balustrade controlled the crossing over the busy A38 in the foreground, also the wharf line and Burnham branch seen swinging to the right. The roofs of holiday-makers' cars are seen crossing over the railway line: Highbridge was a notorious bottleneck for holiday traffic in the days before the M5 motorway.

Again this picture taken from a footbridge (No 283) is full of variety. Obviously the old man leaning on the crossing gate thought there was plenty to look at; he was a retired merchant seaman called Charlie Redwood, who worked on the last sailing ship to berth at the wharf. Judging by the signalman walking back down the line to his box, he had most probably been along the wharf to have a chat with the shunter seen standing in the distance. The pub on the left proudly displays the black horse symbol of Starkey's Ales; this was a well-known West Country brewery, now absorbed by the giant Whitbread group. The Regal cinema is on the extreme right of the picture.
Photo: David Milton. Date: July 1960.

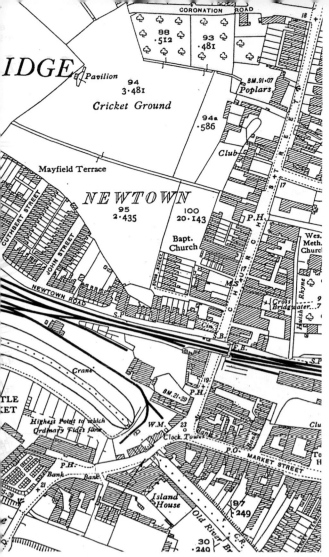

Map 49: Highbridge Wharf (1930)

Highbridge Wharf was situated about a half-mile west of Highbridge station. Access was gained by a crossing over the main road (A38) controlled by the delightful Highbridge 'C' box, renamed Highbridge East 'A' in BR days.

For almost a century the wharf presented a busy scene: coal, timber and rails were some of the cargoes handled. Local dairy and agricultural products were also shipped from here in considerable quantities. The S&D owned a fleet of its own ships, finally disposing of the two remaining vessels in 1933/4 upon the winding up of their marine interests, but the wharf continued to be used by commercial shipping until around 1950. The wharf was finally closed on 2 November 1964.

Glastonbury Canal, access to which was through the gates of a sea lock at the eastern end of the wharf, terminated near here. Today all the wharves have finally been filled in and a housing development covers part of it, although most of it forms part of a compound for a boatyard.

The former saw mills and storage sheds of Sheppard Bros/John Bland & Co were latterly used by Jewsons, the well-known builders' merchants, until they relocated to Bridgwater around 1990.

Another comparison taken a mere ten years later shows how things can change very quickly. The supermarket from which the 1985 photograph was taken closed and was rented out as a museum, which in turn has shut leaving the building empty. The area in the background once occupied by the railway has been developed for housing and the former Regal cinema, latterly a night club, has been demolished over the last few years and flats are to be built on the site. *Date: 2 March 1995.*

The butcher's boy has grown a little older! He has got DIY commitments, no doubt to fix that long overdue shelf for the wife. The egg advert may be prophetic if he fails to get the job done on time! This photograph was taken from a supermarket's upstairs window (kindly held open by the manager) and is full of coincidences. It is quite uncanny how many people can be seen who are in approximately the same position as some twenty-five years earlier. The pub on the left is a guest house and the A38 road is much quieter these days as the volume of traffic has gone onto the M5. Note Jewsons yard in the distance. *Date: 20 April 1985 (revisited 2 March 1995).*

151
Highbridge Wharf (2)
182 ST 314473

The 195-ton *Radstock* was owned by the S&D and joined the fleet in 1925 to replace the *Alpha* which, in 1920, had been sucked into the mud at No 2 berth, failing to rise on the tide. Unfortunately she was carrying 130 tons of flour at the time!

Radstock is having its cargo of coal unloaded into a hotch-potch of LMS trucks at the wharf side. The S&D wound up their shipping interests in 1933 and subsequently the *Radstock* was sold in 1934. *Photo: British Rail (Railprint). Date: late 1920s.*

This rather desolate scene was where the *Radstock* and her sister vessels once plied their trade, although it is difficult to imagine it today; even new housing has started to encroach on the former wharf's area. The compound in the foreground forms part of Brue Yachts' boatyard. The last vestiges of the wharf were still to be seen until 1985 when the remaining portion was filled in. The derelict sheds still stand, but are due for demolition fairly shortly, as there are plans to develop housing on the site of the former saw mills and timber yard, where Jewsons had a premises until 1990. *Date: 2 March 1995.*

152 *(Opposite)*
Burnham-on-Sea station (1)
182 ST 305488

An atmospheric study of Burnham station taken on a sleepy summer's afternoon shows Class 3F 0-6-0 No 43427 standing at the platform, having arrived earlier with a stopping train from Evercreech. Occasional excursions were run in the summer months after the cessation of regular services on 29 October 1951 until 8 September 1962, when all through trains on the S&D system ended. The locomotive was withdrawn from Templecombe shed in July 1961 and scrapped at Crewe Works a month later.

This study was taken from the excursion platform which was 225yd in length and built at a later date. The overall roof and the west side wall made the station building seem rather dark, but provided good protection from the off-shore sea breezes. Of note is the tiny four-lever signal box, which closed before 1960, located at the eastern end of the 95yd original platform. The crossover was operated by levers between the tracks, but released from the box. The Queen's Hotel is behind the station roof and stands on the sea front promenade; the scout hut is on the extreme left.

The late John Betjeman's film of a trip from Evercreech terminated here and he was finally seen skipping across Burnham sands in front of the hotel, issuing dire warnings to Dr Beeching against closure of the line! *Photo: R.E. Toop. Date: 22 August 1959.*

The Queen's Hotel and the large building in the background provide the clues, as does the scout hut. A relief road has been built following the course of the S&D's trackbed from the outskirts of the town, thus saving considerable time getting to the sea front from outlying areas. The diminutive signal box has been preserved by the Somerset & Dorset Railway Trust and now resides on the West Somerset Railway at Washford. *Date: 24 February 1995.*

BURNHAM

Map 50: Burnham-on-Sea (1903)

The station opened on 3 May 1858 after the 1¾-mile extension from Highbridge was completed. As befitting a terminus, it was supplied with a train shed, having an overall roof under which it had the usual facilities, also a small goods yard nearby complete with a small signal box. The roof afforded some protection from the off-shore gales blowing across the nearby Bristol Channel.

A 1:23 incline took the line out onto a pier extending some way into the estuary of the River Parrett. The pier was used by shipping for a limited time, trucks being hauled up and down the gradient by wire ropes.

Alongside the station building can be seen the lifeboat station which had its own siding down which the lifeboat could be launched off the end of the pier. The lifeboat was removed in 1930 and eventually the building was taken over by the local scouts as their hut. The railway station closed on 29 October 1951, although holiday excursions continued until 8 September 1962.

Today the station site forms part of a new road, which has also absorbed much of the trackbed leading from the wharves, but the lifeboat house survives as a Scout hut. The pier is now used to launch pleasure craft. The Queen's Hotel still occupies its rightful position on the promenade. The nearby Somerset & Dorset Hotel is now resplendent in a new coat of paint with smart signs commemorating the railway of the same name.

153
Burnham-on-Sea station (2)
182 ST 304487

Class 3F 0-6-0 No 43194 pokes out from Burnham's overall roof after having arrived with a summer excursion. The road to the left of the fence in front of the station building was and still is used as a coach and bus stop, which provided competition to the railway, ultimately leading to its demise, also hastened by the burgeoning use of the motor car by visitors to this popular seaside resort.

The scout hut on the right, once the old lifeboat station, was taken over by the organisation in 1937. A group of nuns, probably from the nearby La Retraite convent, are seen standing near the crossing gates indulging in a bit of train spotting – quite a change of habit, maybe! *Photo: R.M.Casserley. Date: 16 July 1958.*

The scout hut is still in evidence and continues to be used for the purpose. Somerfield's have built a supermarket here, part of which can be seen on the extreme right. Quite a few buildings can be recognised on the left and also in the background, but one would never guess this spot was once a railway terminus. *Date: 26 February 1995.*

The Somerset & Dorset public house adjacent to the station site sports some magnificently painted signs: this one in High Street depicts Class 7F No 86, whilst on the Abingdon Street side, a Johnson 4-4-0 is represented.
Date: 24 February 1995.

BRIDGWATER AND WELLS BRANCHES

Bridgwater Branch

154
Cossington Bank and Board's siding
182 ST 363408

The climb of the Polden Hills, on a rising gradient of 1:72 for about a mile, would on occasions be the downfall of an Edington–Bridgwater train, particularly a heavy goods, which could not quite make it to the summit at Cossington; it then had to reverse down towards the junction in order to have another attempt at it with a flying start!

This is one of a series of publicity photographs taken of Class 2P 4-4-0 S&D No 70, still in Prussian blue livery, climbing Cossington Bank whilst undergoing a trial on the Bridgwater branch. However Class 2Ps were seldom seen on the line, so this event apparently came to nothing. The cutting to Board's siding, just visible on the right of the picture, served a quarry which provided the branch with good revenue until 1933 when it closed. Glastonbury Tor is seen on the horizon. *Photo: British Rail (Railprint). Date: 10 September 1924.*

Up until the late 1970s the former quarry had been used as a council refuse tip, but is now landscaped and forms a pasture for grazing cattle. After closure of the tip, there was a problem with foul water leaching from it into the nearby water courses. To overcome this, a pipeline was laid along the course of the railway towards Bridgwater in order that the contaminated water could be pumped to a treatment plant before dispersal.

The Mendip Hills and Glastonbury Tor seen in the distance across the levels pinpoint the location. The formation back towards Edington Junction is still well defined and some overbridges survive, including Nos 299 and 300. The latter, in Landshire Lane, has been used unofficially to dump rubbish into the shallow cutting on its eastern side. *Date: 31 May 1985 (revisited 17 February 1995).*

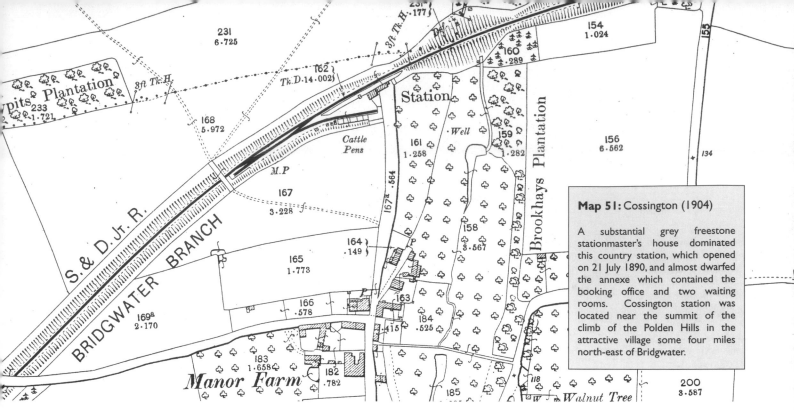

Map 51: Cossington (1904)

A substantial grey freestone stationmaster's house dominated this country station, which opened on 21 July 1890, and almost dwarfed the annexe which contained the booking office and two waiting rooms. Cossington station was located near the summit of the climb of the Polden Hills in the attractive village some four miles north-east of Bridgwater.

155
Cossington station (1)
182 ST 358408

A hurriedly snapped view of Cossington taken from the 13.40 Bridgwater–Edington mixed train, hauled by Johnson 0-4-4T No 58072, as it sets off from the station. Of note is the gradient post on the end of the platform: the line dropped at 1:72 for almost a mile towards the junction with only a short level stretch of a few chains in between; the line rose at 1:300 through the station towards Bridgwater. The occupation bridge (No 303) in the background spanned a cutting on the west side of the station.

One quaint note in the Somerset & Dorset working timetables stated: 'All engines working passenger trains not running funnel first must stop at Cossington, whether marked to do so or not'. The station closed to passenger traffic on 1 December 1952 and to goods on 4 October 1954. *Photo: H.C. Casserley. Date: 5 September 1952.*

Although practical, the extension to the former booking office is not entirely in keeping with either the design or the original materials used for the building. Around 1989/90 three executive-style houses were erected on the site of the goods yard and trackbed on the western side of the station, but although it cannot be seen from this aspect, Bridge 303 is still used as a right of way and carries a public footpath to Woolavington.

With the leachate pipe having been laid along it some years ago, the trackbed is still well defined in the deep cutting south-west of the village, although it has become rather overgrown in recent years and is liable to flooding at the end nearest the old station. *Date: 1 March 1995.*

156
Cossington station (2)
182 ST 357408

Nine months before the line's closure to passengers, Class 3F 0-6-0 No 43216, working tender-first on the 10.38 Bridgwater–Edington Junction, pauses at Cossington and waits whilst its photograph is taken. The staff and locomotive crew look on with amusement. It was often the case that a crew would wait for a regular passenger to arrive and even on occasions the train would be reversed in order to pick someone up who got to the station a few moments too late!

From the embankment on the north side of the line a better view is had of the impressive stationmaster's house. The ground frame on the platform controlled a siding which served cattle pens and an end loading dock. Cattle traffic was substantial at one time with animals being freighted to the markets at Highbridge and Bridgwater. *Photo: Douglas Allen collection. Date: 1 March 1952.*

Now converted into two private dwellings the station looks very much the same, although the platform supports a variety of sheds. The ground frame hut was saved and has gone to the East Somerset Railway at Cranmore. Although Bridge 301 in Bell Lane just to the east survives, the deep cutting between it and the station has been filled in for many years.

In 1983 the residents of the village won a major battle to prevent a stretch between Brent Road (Bridge 304), which once marked the summit of the climb of the Poldens, and the A39 (Bridge 305) being infilled with industrial waste. *Date: 10 June 1985 (revisited 1 March 1995).*

> **COMMENT:** *A family connection with the former station enabled me to obtain permission to fell a few small trees on the embankment in order to take this photograph. Imagine my surprise when I stood in the same spot some ten years later and was hardly able to see the building for the new growth that has sprouted since!*

From the approach road Cossington station looks much as it did when built 105 years previously. *Date: 1 March 1995.*

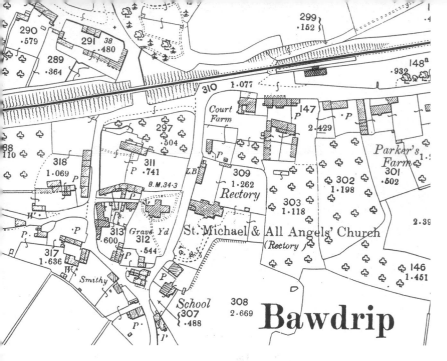

157
Bawdrip Halt
182 ST 342397

Having returned by train from Bridgwater, two shoppers – their heads fashionably crowned with hats of the period – are seen alighting at Bawdrip Halt. In the background behind the shelter is the village hall, which has often been mistaken for the booking hall and main building; in fact it was never attached to the halt in any way. Bawdrip closed for passengers on 1 December 1952; there were no facilities for handling goods here.
Photo: LRGP/Real Photographs. Date: c1932.

A comparison taken in drizzly conditions does not help to make this scruffy piece of land any more attractive; only the village hall remains and is in reasonable shape. In the 1980s, however, the formation back from here to the A39 road bridge (No 305) was cleared by a local landowner for use as a gallop. The trackbed beyond the trees in the foreground now forms a garden for a bungalow (appropriately named *Essandee*) built on the formation between here and Bridge 306, which still straddles the village road. The steel girder bridge across King's Sedgemoor Drain at 182 ST 336396 has long since been demolished. *Date: 23 February 1995.*

158
Bawdrip – Bridge 308 (A39)
182 ST 328394

An idyllic country railway scene: Johnson 0-4-4T No 58073 fitted with condensing apparatus, a legacy from working through the Metropolitan tunnels in the London area, is about to pass under the A39 road bridge (No 308) with an Edington Junction to Bridgwater goods. Note the fireman's relaxed stance in riding the footplate – almost certainly it matched the speed of the train!

By this date the line was solely used for goods traffic, which judging by the short train was slight and would hardly have been economic in today's harsh market conditions. *Photo: Ivo Peters. Date: 12 August 1953.*

Perhaps the dramatic sky aids what otherwise might have been a singularly boring view! Despite appearing to the contrary, the amount of traffic using the A39 Bridgwater–Glastonbury road today is colossal.

The sunlit tower of St Michael's church in Bawdrip village is highlighted in the background. It is difficult to identify this scene with the 1953 view, but the pylons and old elm trees, which have since been cut down, give an indication that this is the same location. The main A39 road was straightened after the removal of the bridge in the 1960s, but the line formation can still be seen behind the hedgerow on the left and is often used for cattle. The formation towards Horsey level crossing (182 ST 321390) is quite well defined, but the M5 motorway bisects it, a few chains west of which a machine shop for British Cellophane was built many years ago on the trackbed itself. *Date: 21 May 1985 (revisited 1 March 1995).*

159

Bridgwater – Bristol Road (A38)
182 ST 307384

One would suspect many people remember staring at this bridge for hours on end, for this road into Bridgwater used to be the main holiday route to the Westcountry from the Midlands and the North. In the 1950s and 1960s the resulting jams caused by traffic trying to get through the town were horrendous.

On the last day of passenger services, Johnson 0-4-4T No 58073 hurries along with the 15.55 Bridgwater North–Edington train and crosses over the A38 road bridge. The embankment continued over the WR main line 18 chains distant and dropped at 1:72 to take the S&D branch towards Horsey Crossing three-quarters of a mile beyond.

The beer advertisement is now a relic of the past as is the brick and tile industry in Bridgwater proffered by John Board & Co. whose sign is seen on the right. *Photo: Douglas Allen. Date: 29 November 1952.*

The bridge has long since disappeared; the embankment towards Bridgwater (North) on the west side of the A38 was removed many years ago to make way for industrial development, including the B&Q DIY Supercentre in the background. However, the embankment on the east side and the pillbox remained here until the early 1980s. The traffic on the A38 through the town is still busy, with Wylds Road Trading Estate generating even more, as can be judged here. *Date: 23 February 1995.*

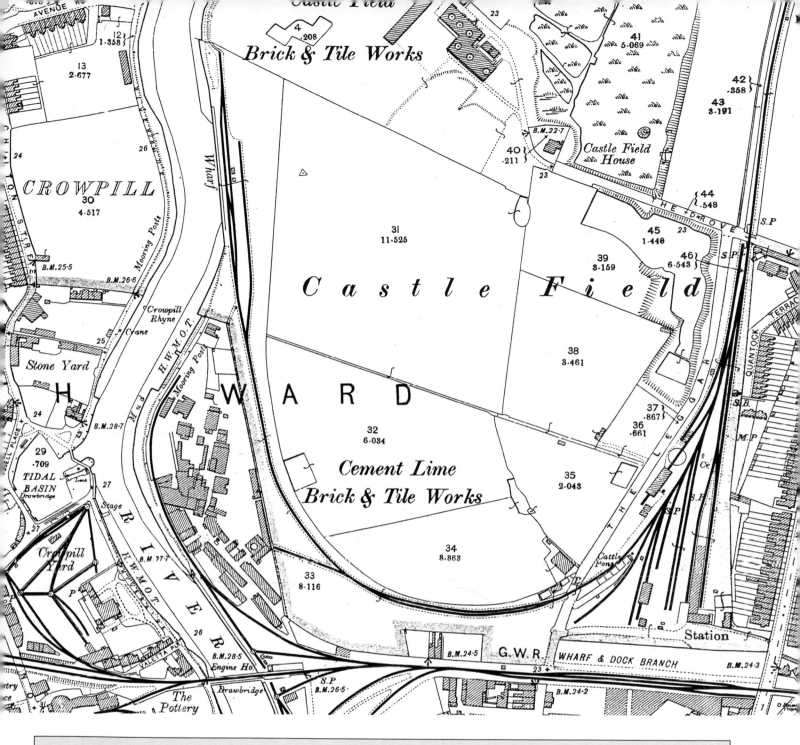

Map 53: Bridgwater North (1904)

As the map suggests, Bridgwater had a thriving brick and tile industry, which used local marl deposits; sadly it is no longer the case today, with the last works closing in the 1960s.

The line from Bridgwater to Edington was opened on 21 July 1890, being built by an independent company, the Bridgwater Railway, and was never legally owned by the S&D. The station building was of local brick and had the appearance of an LSWR design. It stood at right angles to the two-bay island platform, upon which an awning was built covering half its length. The suffix 'North' was added to the station's name on 26 September 1949.

The goods yard, complete with shed, had ample facilities to handle many commodities including bricks, tiles and livestock. When the branch to Edington was finally closed in 1954 a new spur was added from the S&D yard to connect it to the GWR docks branch. The goods yard remained in use until 7 July 1962 and the docks branch finally closed on 2 January 1967.

A fairly large single-road engine shed of brick construction was also built, together with a 50ft turntable in front of its entrance. The shed, although extended in 1898 to accommodate two locomotives, was not used to stable engines overnight after 1928 and was subsequently leased to the Co-operative Society as a store.

Up until 1942 there was a 48 chain extension which swung through 180 degrees to provide wharfage facilities on the bank of the River Parrett. The map also shows the GWR docks branch which crossed the river via the Telescopic (or Black) Bridge gaining access to Bridgwater Docks. This was a drawbridge, the design of which was ingenious and unusual: when operated, it allowed the passage of ships up river. In the early 1980s it was converted to carry road traffic, but with the advent of a new river crossing built adjacent to it a few years later, the bridge was pedestrianised.

160
Bridgwater North – signal box and The Drove level crossing
182 ST 304376

A well-known photograph taken from the end of Bridgwater North's platform looking towards the 17-lever signal box, just beyond which is the level crossing over The Drove; the gates were operated by hand. Originally, the signal box was on the east side of the line adjacent to Quantock Terrace, the houses of which are seen on the right. A few chains north of the crossing a siding diverged westwards to serve a cement works.

   Johnson 0-4-4T No 58072 emerges from the goods yard with some trucks during shunting operations to make up its mixed train, which is scheduled to depart from the island platform for Edington Junction at 13.40. *Photo: H.C.Casserley. Date: 5 September 1952.*

This is the north-west corner of Sainsbury's store which all but blots out the view of Quantock Terrace, the roof of the end house can just be spotted through the bushes on the extreme right. The store itself covers much of the former goods yard and sidings. A staff car park to the rear (north side) takes Sainsbury's property to abut the access road to Quantock Terrace. *Date: 25 February 1995.*

161
Bridgwater North station (1)
182 ST 304376

This was another one of a sequence of photographs taken by Henry Casserley on the occasion of his last visit to the Bridgwater branch and shows No 58072 preparing to leave the island platform with the 13.40 to Edington Junction. The two coaches will be coupled to the line of trucks the locomotive has previously shunted into the other platform road; a brake van is already attached to the rear of the wagons to lend assistance down Cossington Bank on the steep descent towards the junction at Edington.

   The roof of St John's in Church Street can be made out in the background on the right. In between the station and the church are the wooden sheds of a timber yard alongside the Clink; the GWR docks branch ran on the far side of these buildings.
Photo: H.C.Casserley. Date: 5 September 1952.

If it were not for the portion of the roof of St John's church, there would be no identifiable link with the 1952 view. This is the eastern end of Sainsbury's car park looking south. *Date: 25 February 1995.*

162
Bridgwater North station (2)
182 ST 303375

An unidentified Class 3F 0-6-0 waits at Bridgwater North to take its train to Edington Junction. By the position of the shadows on the roofs of adjacent houses, this is likely to be either the 13.40 or the 15.55 service. Although the turntable remained operable until the line's closure, push-pull workings were instigated in 1928.

The station building ran at right angles to the buffer stops. The canopy, which can be seen to good advantage, covers half the island platform's length. The stationmaster's house is visible between the awning and the station sign. *Photo: LRGP/Real Photographs.*
Date: Summer 1951.

For many years the station site was used by BRS as a transport depot. The goods shed survived intact until July 1985 when it burnt down; the station building itself was demolished in August 1984 and the engine shed in December 1985. After BRS had vacated the site, it then lay derelict for a number of years until sold to J.Sainsbury, who built a supermarket here which opened in 1989.

This is the view from the same spot today: all one can see is the bread counter of the supermarket! *Date: 23 February 1995.*

COMMENT: *I have done some strange things in my time, but this must rate as one of the oddest! The incredulous looks from shoppers as I aimed my camera at the well-stocked shelves was a sight to behold.*

163
Bridgwater North station (3)
182 ST 303374

The design of Bridgwater North station frontage had LSWR influence: constructed in local red brick with round-headed windows to set it off, it was a most attractive and well-proportioned building. Being fairly commodious, it housed a booking office and hall, two waiting rooms and lavatories. The station was a hive of activity on market days and it was not uncommon to see the odd bedstead or sack of potatoes, which had been bought by one of the engine crews, travelling home on the back of the tender!
Photo: LRGP/Real Photographs.
Date: 1935.

This sad view was taken during demolition of the building: already the tiles have been removed from the roof and it was totally demolished less than a week later.

The former stationmaster's house, visible on the right, was renovated in the mid-1980s, only to burn down mysteriously around 1988 and was demolished when Sainsbury's started construction work on the site. *Date: 4 August 1984 (revisited 23 February 1995).*

An up-to-date comparison from approximately the same place, showing Sainsbury's car park and little else; certainly no reminders are left of the station, goods yard and any artefact once associated with the railway. On the right are the terraced houses in Bristol Road; the chimney on the extreme left poking above their roofs in the background belongs to the factory of Courtaulds Films Cellophane.
Date: 23 February 1995.

Wells Branch

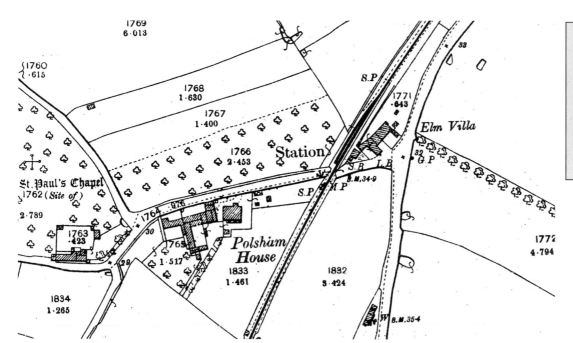

Map 54: Polsham (1904)

The station, which was the only intermediate one on the branch, was situated midway between Glastonbury and Wells. It opened in December 1861, mainly serving a small farming community, as there was no sizeable village except Coley a mile away.

164
Polsham station
182/183 ST 517428

Photographs of Polsham station are rare, as this rather poor example would suggest; nevertheless, it shows the layout quite well. The platform was 200ft long and had a simple building providing basic facilities. A ground frame on the platform (seen in the foreground) controlled the crossing and a single siding. The main building seen in this photograph dated from 1894, but in the 1920s, a large stationmaster's house was added to the platform's western end (nearest the camera). A new ground frame hut was sited a few feet nearer the platform ramp; in addition another rodding tunnel was constructed to serve it and the old one was blocked up.

In addition to the passenger services (in 1906, 11 in each direction and reduced to four by 1950), at one time a goods train called every day to service the station. Polsham closed both to passengers and goods on 29 October 1951.
Photo: LRGP/Real Photographs. Date: 1912.

The station is now an attractive private dwelling and sports various LSWR railway artefacts – but the signal is definitely Great Western! The platform lavatory is still in place, complete with coin-operated lock. The owner's son has constructed a light gauge railway in the garden, which he intends to extend along part of the platform.

Although it has been totally obliterated in places, from the site of Wells Branch Junction the formation is still quite well defined in parts as are the four intermediate crossings: Crab Tree Drove, Chasey's Drove, Upper Crannel Drove and Lower Crannel Drove. *Date: 1 March 1995.*

165
Coxley
182/183 ST 528438

This rare photograph shows 0-4-4T No 1346 with a Glastonbury–Wells push-pull train approaching Coxley and is about to pass under Bridge 289. This branch was little used in its latter days and one might have been the only passenger on one of the four trains a day to run in either direction.
Photo: H.C. Casserley.
Date: 22 July 1937.

This land has had over forty years to heal and provides little clue to its railway heritage. The shed on the right can be identified as can the river bridge on the left. The pillboxes in the background formed part of GHQ Stop Line Green, a second world war defence line which extended from Burnham-on-Sea to The Wash. Since these were built between 1940-2, they did not feature in the original photograph.

Much of the formation between Polsham and Coxley to Wells is fairly indistinct and can only be defined in places by a surviving railway boundary fence. *Date: 7 May 1985 (revisited 1 March 1995).*

166
Wells Priory Road station (1)
182/183 ST 544453

A panoramic view of Wells Priory Road, taken some years after closure to passengers, showing the layout of the goods shed and attendant yard. The station building, seen middle right, lost its overall roof soon after passenger services ceased on 29 October 1951. The S&D engine shed sited at the western edge of the complex was used until 27 October 1951; it was finally demolished in December 1955. The attractive stone signal box on the left controlled the goods yard and crossing. The GWR line ran in front of this and on past Priory Road station platform towards Wells East and Witham. *Photo: David Milton.* *Date: 13 June 1960.*

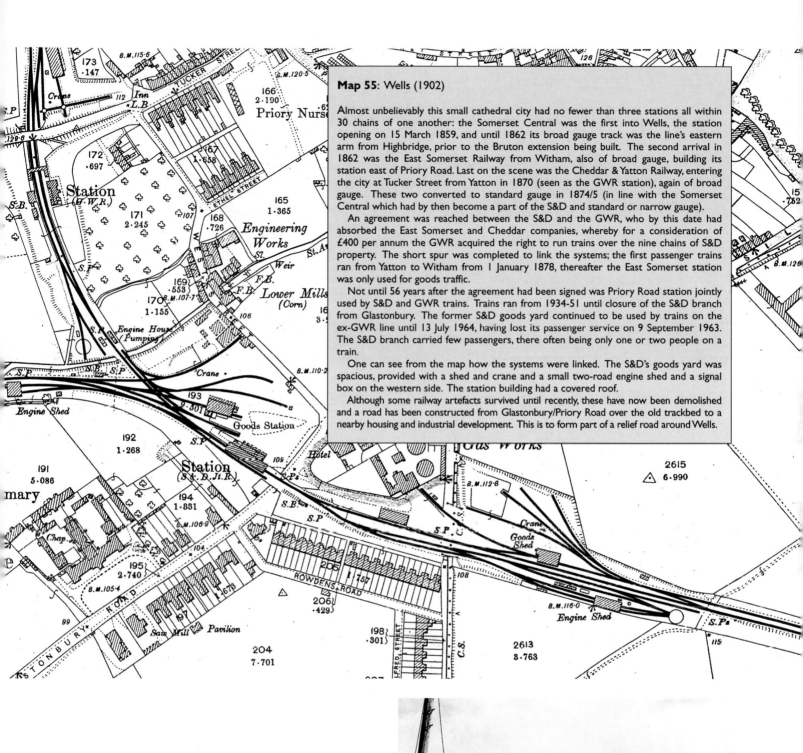

Map 55: Wells (1902)

Almost unbelievably this small cathedral city had no fewer than three stations all within 30 chains of one another: the Somerset Central was the first into Wells, the station opening on 15 March 1859, and until 1862 its broad gauge track was the line's eastern arm from Highbridge, prior to the Bruton extension being built. The second arrival in 1862 was the East Somerset Railway from Witham, also of broad gauge, building its station east of Priory Road. Last on the scene was the Cheddar & Yatton Railway, entering the city at Tucker Street from Yatton in 1870 (seen as the GWR station), again of broad gauge. These two converted to standard gauge in 1874/5 (in line with the Somerset Central which had by then become a part of the S&D and standard or narrow gauge).

An agreement was reached between the S&D and the GWR, who by this date had absorbed the East Somerset and Cheddar companies, whereby for a consideration of £400 per annum the GWR acquired the right to run trains over the nine chains of S&D property. The short spur was completed to link the systems; the first passenger trains ran from Yatton to Witham from 1 January 1878, thereafter the East Somerset station was only used for goods traffic.

Not until 56 years after the agreement had been signed was Priory Road station jointly used by S&D and GWR trains. Trains ran from 1934-51 until closure of the S&D branch from Glastonbury. The former S&D goods yard continued to be used by trains on the ex-GWR line until 13 July 1964, having lost its passenger service on 9 September 1963. The S&D branch carried few passengers, there often being only one or two people on a train.

One can see from the map how the systems were linked. The S&D's goods yard was spacious, provided with a shed and crane and a small two-road engine shed and a signal box on the western side. The station building had a covered roof.

Although some railway artefacts survived until recently, these have now been demolished and a road has been constructed from Glastonbury/Priory Road over the old trackbed to a nearby housing and industrial development. This is to form part of a relief road around Wells.

The yard in the foreground is owned by Tincknells, agricultural engineers, who are also agents for John Deere tractors. The ramp is not of railway heritage but was built for the loading/unloading of flatbed lorries with agricultural equipment and is to be resited in the near future. Of note are the telegraph poles, albeit the one on the left has developed a distinct list, and also the former stationmaster's house in the background which provide some tangible links with the past. The stone-built goods shed was dismantled in 1988 for re-erection on the East Somerset Railway at Cranmore and the wooden office once attached to it has been preserved by the S&DRT at Washford on the West Somerset Railway. *Date: 1 March 1995.*

167
Wells Priory Road station (2)
182/183 ST 545453

A fine study of the station area which admirably shows the covered roof of the former terminus; the goods shed is just seen to the left and the stationmaster's house is clearly visible in between. Also of note are the rather unusual set of signals, which were known to some as 'The Gallows', presumably as they resembled a gibbet! Beyond the level crossing over the main A39 road is East Somerset signal box and the GWR line to the former Wells East station and Witham. In October 1883 the suffix 'Priory Road' was added to the S&D station, which had just been known as 'Wells' until then.
  One possible reason for the demise of the S&D's Wells branch was increased competition from buses, as they offered a service from town centre to town centre locally, which the railway unfortunately could not, with the stations being on the outskirts of both this city and Glastonbury. *Photo: LRGP/Real Photographs. Date: 1934.*

The scene today: with its windows smashed and left ajar, the stationmaster's house still survives in this view – but only just, as it was demolished a few days later to make way for a roundabout to be constructed as part of the Wells relief road scheme. The access road in the foreground will be widened roughly in line with the bollards on the left. The unit on the left is that of Goodlands, the builders' merchants, who opened their premises here in January 1990, having built it on the site of the goods shed. *Date: 1 March 1995.*

FEATURED STEAM LOCOMOTIVES

Withdrawal dates and fate

Class/Number/Name	Shed*	With-drawn	Scrapped/Preserved	Date
S&D (Highbridge) 0-4-0ST				
26a	22C	12/29	Highbridge	12/30
GWR Collett Class 22XX/32XX 0-6-0				
2218	83G	11/64	J.Cashmore, Newport	4/65
3206	83G	12/63	Messrs Bird, Risca	5/64
3218	83G	5/65	Messrs Bird, Bynea	8/65
LSWR/SR Adams Class G6 0-6-0T				
30274	71B	10/60	Eastleigh Works	11/60
LSWR/SR Drummond Class T9 4-4-0				
30721	72B	1/58	Eastleigh Works	1/58
SR Maunsell U1 2-6-0				
31906	75C	12/62	Eastleigh Works	11/63
SR Bulleid West Country/Battle of Britain class 4-6-2				
34006 *Bude*	70E	3/67	Cashmore, Newport	9/67
34041 *Wilton*	70D	1/66	J.Cashmore, Newport	3/66–5/66
34042 *Dorchester*	70D	10/65	J.Buttigieg, Newport	4/66–9/66
34043 *Combe Martin*	71B	6/63	Eastleigh Works	6/63
34046 *Braunton*	70F	10/65	**Preserved: Brighton Works project (ex-Barry)**	
34057 *Biggin Hill*	70E	5/67	J.Cashmore, Newport	12/67
34093 *Saunton*	70D	1/67	J.Cashmore, Newport	3/68
34095 *Brentor*	70D	7/67	J.Cashmore, Newport	4/68
34107 *Blandford Forum*	83D	9/64	Messrs Bird, Morriston, Swansea	12/64–2/65
34108 *Wincanton*	70E	6/67	J.Buttigieg, Newport	8/68–10/68
SR Bulleid Merchant Navy class 4-6-2				
35011 *General Steam Navigation*	70F	2/66	**Preserved: Brighton Works project (ex-Barry)**	
LMS/Johnson/Fowler Class 2P 4-4-0				
40322 (S&DJR No 70)	5C	3/53	Derby Works (?)	-/53
40505	22C	10/53	Derby Works (?)	-/53
40537	82G	9/62	Derby Works	9/62
40563	82G	5/62	Crewe Works	7/62
40564	82G	2/62	Crewe Works	2/62
40568	21B	11/59	Derby Works	12/59
40569	82G	11/61	Crewe Works	12/61
40634	82G	5/62	Crewe Works	8/62
40696	82F	6/62	Crewe Works	8/62
40697	82F	2/62	Crewe Works	3/62
40700	82F	9/62	Derby Works	12/62
LMS Ivatt Class 2 2-6-2T				
41216	83G	3/66	G.Cohen, Morriston, Swansea	7/66
41248	3F	11/64	D.Woodham, Barry	3/65
41249	83G	3/66	G.Cohen, Morriston, Swansea	7/66
41296	83G	3/66	G.Cohen, Morriston, Swansea	7/66
LMS Johnson Class 3F 0-6-0				
43194	82G	12/60	Crewe Works	3/61
43216	82G	9/62	Derby Works	9/62
43218	82G	5/60	Derby Works	7/60
43419	82G	9/58	Messrs McLellan, Langloan	7/59
43427	82G	7/61	Crewe Works	8/61
43436	24B	6/62	Central Wagon Co, Ince, Wigan	11/62
LMS Fowler Class 4F 0-6-0				
3898	15D	7/57	Derby Works	7/57
44102	82F	9/64	Messrs Bird, Risca	1/65–4/65
44272	82G	6/63	Derby Works	9/63
44417	82G	10/62	Derby Works	5/63
44422 (4422)	85B	6/65	**Preserved: Cheddleton Railway Centre**	
44557	12A	9/62	Derby Works	9/62
44559	82F	11/62	Derby Works	5/63
44560	85B	9/65	Messrs Bird, Long Marston	12/65
44561	82F	4/62	Derby Works	5/62
LMS Stanier Class 5MT 4-6-0				
44666	8A	2/67	A.Draper, Hull	9/67
44667	10A	8/67	J.McWilliam, Shettleston	2/68
44775	12A	10/67	J.McWilliam, Shettleston	3/68
44804	9E	3/68	A.Draper, Hull	6/68
44888	10D	8/68	J.Cashmore, Great Bridge	5/69
LMS Fowler Class 3F 0-6-0T				
47557	82F	2/64	Swindon Works	4/64
LMS Stanier Class 8F 2-8-0				
48737	82F	5/65	J.Cashmore, Newport	8/65
S&D Fowler Class 7F 2-8-0				
53800	82F	7/59	Derby Works	10/59
53801	82F	7/61	Crewe Works	9/61
53802	82F	3/60	Doncaster Works	4/60
53803	82F	2/62	Crewe Works	2/62
53804	82F	2/62	Crewe Works	2/62
53805	82F	3/61	Crewe Works	4/61
53806	82F	1/64	J.Cashmore, Newport	7/64
53807	82F	10/64	J.Cashmore, Newport	1/65–4/65
53808 (S&DJR No 88)	82F	3/64	**Preserved: S&D Railway Trust (WSR), Washford**	
53809	82F	6/64	**Preserved: Midland Railway Centre, Butterley**	
53810	82F	12/63	J.Cashmore, Newport	2/64
LMS Johnson Class 1P 0-4-4T				
1346	71J	11/47	Not known	47–48
58072	71J	10/56	Bristol Barrow Road (?)	56–57
58073	71J	1/56	Bristol Barrow Road (?)	56–57
BR Standard Class 5 4-6-0				
73001	82F	12/65	J.Cashmore, Newport	5/66

Class/Number/Name	Shed*	Withdrawn	Scrapped/Preserved	Date
73028	9K	12/66	J.Cashmore, Newport	4/67
73047	6D	12/64	J.Cashmore, Newport	4/65
73049	81F	3/65	Messrs Bird, Risca	6/65
73050 *City of Peterborough*†	9H	6/68	**Preserved: Nene Valley Railway, Wansford**	
73051	82F	8/65	J.Cashmore, Newport	11/65
73052	82F	12/64	J.Buttigieg, Newport	4/65
73068	82F	12/65	J.Cashmore, Newport	4/66
73164	81F	12/64	Friswells Ltd, 2D Banbury	4/65

BR Standard Class 4 4-6-0

Class/Number/Name	Shed*	Withdrawn	Scrapped/Preserved	Date
75007	83E	4/65	Messrs Bird, Bynea	8/65
75009	10A	8/68	Messrs Campbell, Aidrie	11/68
75023	5D	1/66	Thomas Ward, Beighton, Sheffield	4/66
75027	10A	8/68	**Preserved: Bluebell Railway, Sheffield Park**	
75071	5D	8/67	Messrs Bird, Long Marston	2/68
75072	83G	12/65	Thomas Ward, Ringwood, Hants	4/66
75073	83G	12/65	Thomas Ward, Ringwood, Hants	4/66

BR Standard Class 4 2-6-0

Class/Number/Name	Shed*	Withdrawn	Scrapped/Preserved	Date
76006	70F	7/67	Messrs Bird, Morriston, Swansea	11/67
76007	70F	7/67	Messrs Bird, Risca	11/67
76015	70F	10/65	G.Cohen, Morriston, Swansea	1/66
76018	70C	10/66	J.Cashmore, Newport	6/67
76019	70D	2/66	G.Cohen, Morriston, Swansea	6/66
76025	70F	10/65	J.Cashmore, Newport	2/66

PRESERVED LOCOMOTIVES NOT FEATURED
(once allocated to S&D sheds)

GWR Collett Class 32XX 0-6-0
3205   West Somerset Railway, Minehead

Class/Number/Name	Shed*	Withdrawn	Scrapped/Preserved	Date
BR Standard Class 3 2-6-2T				
82004	82F	10/65	Messrs Bird, Bridgend	5/66–7/66
BR Standard Class 4 2-6-4T				
80043	83G	3/66	J.Cashmore, Newport	7/66
80059	82F	11/65	J.Buttigieg, Newport	3/66
80067	82E	6/65	D.Woodham, Barry	9/65
80138	70F	10/66	J.Cashmore, Newport	2/67
80147	70F	6/65	Messrs Bird, Morriston, Swansea	1/66

BR Standard Class 9F 2-10-0

Class/Number/Name	Shed*	Withdrawn	Scrapped/Preserved	Date
92000	85B	7/65	Messrs Bird, Long Marston	11/65
92001	56A	1/67	Cox & Danks, Wadsley Bridge	5/67
92204	10A	3/68	J.Cashmore, Newport	7/68
92205	50A	8/65	Thomas Ward, Beighton, Sheffield	12/65
92206	56A	4/67	A.Draper, Hull	11/67
92210	86B	11/64	J.Buttigieg, Newport	3/65
92212	10A	1/68	**Preserved: Great Central Railway, Loughborough**	
92214	86E	8/65	**Preserved: Midland Railway Centre, Butterley**	
92220 *Evening Star*	88A	3/65	**Preserved: National Railway Collection, York**	
92238	86E	9/65	J.Cashmore, Newport	12/65
92245	81C	12/64	**Preserved: Vale of Glamorgan Railway, Cardiff**	

* Last allocated shed
† Named in private ownership

LMS Ivatt Class 2 2-6-2T
4124   Keighley & Worth Valley Railway, Haworth

BR Standard Class 9F 2-10-0
92203 *Black Prince* East Somerset Railway, Cranmore

MOTIVE POWER DEPOTS

Code/shed		Closed/to steam*
5C	Stafford	19/7/65*
5D	Stoke	6/8/67*
6D	Shrewsbury	6/3/67*
8A	Edge Hill	6/5/68*
9E	Trafford Park	4/3/68*
9H	Patricroft	1/7/68*
9K	Bolton	1/7/68*
10A	Carnforth	5/8/68
10D	Lostock Hall	5/8/68
12A	Carlisle (Kingmoor)	1/1/68
15D	Bedford	-/9/63*
21B	Bournville	14/2/60
22C	Bath Green Park/Radstock‡	(see 82F)
24B	Rose Grove	5/8/68
50A	York	1/7/67*
56A	Wakefield	1/8/67
70C	Guildford	9/7/67
70D	Eastleigh	9/7/67*
70E	Salisbury (31/12/62-)	9/7/67*
70F	Bournemouth (9/9/63-)	9/7/67
71B	Bournemouth	(see 70F)
71J	Highbridge	7/3/66
72B	Salisbury	(see 70E)
75C	Norwood Junction	6/1/64*
81C	Southall	-/12/65*
81F	Oxford	3/1/66*
82E	Bristol (Barrow Road)	20/11/65
82F	Bath Green Park (71G-23/2/58)	7/3/66
82G	Templecombe (71H-23/2/58)	(see 83G)
83D	Laira	-/4/64*
83D	Exmouth Junction	7/2/66
83E	Yeovil	-/6/65
83F	Truro	-/3/62*
83G	Templecombe (14/10/63-)	7/3/66
85B	Gloucester (Horton Road)	3/1/66*
86E	Severn Tunnel Junction	4/10/65*
88A	Cardiff East Dock	2/8/65

‡ Sub-shed

ACKNOWLEDGEMENTS

It is always difficult to single out individuals for special mention, but I feel that it is most appropriate in the case of Julian Peters, who not only kindly consented to write the foreword for this book, but also delved into his father's photographic collection once again to help me ferret out prints used in the first edition of the book. In addition to which Julian spent many hours looking through his father's notebooks to enable me to caption and include many unpublished prints from the Ivo Peters' Collection, which had been in my possession for a number of years. I must acknowledge the fact that it was the late Ivo Peters whose superb volumes on the S&D inspired me to produce the first 'then and now' book; indeed had I not been so enthused by his work, I am sure my writing career would have come to nought.

I would particularly like to thank the following, some of whom are old friends, fellow authors and photographers, who have kindly allowed me to reproduce material from their photographic collections – often going to a lot of trouble in having them specially printed. They include David Milton, Ron Toop, David Cross, Will Locke, Richard Casserley, Tony Wadley, Tony Richardson, Colin Caddy, Dick Riley, Angela O'Shea, Douglas Allen, Edwin Wilmshurst and Lens of Sutton.

A special mention must go to Mike Arlett, an acknowledged expert on the S&D and author of several fine books, for the unfailing help he has given me in supplying all sorts of pieces of information when I have come unstuck. Thanks must go to Derek Mercer whose printing skills have been well utilised in interpreting my photographs so accurately; and also to Dave Rankin who proof read the manuscript in double-quick time! Valuable assistance has been rendered by Mike Palmer, Peter Hands and Frank Hornby who have provided much detailed information on featured locomotives.

I am also indebted to those companies and individuals encountered during my forays on the former line, who allowed me to photograph from their land or properties, some of which were former stations, like Masbury where Mr Wilfrid Couling, an ex-S&D relief stationmaster, and his wife live. Thanks go to them for another guided tour ten years after the first!

Finally I would like to pay a special tribute to my long-suffering wife, Jenny, who typed up a large portion of the original manuscript and spent many a long hour into the night – and in the early morning – reading the first drafts as they came hot off the printer and for the endless patience shown in helping me in the selection of the odd pair of photographs, when indecision ruled!

The Somerset & Dorset Railway Trust

The Trust started as the S&D Railway Circle in 1966 with the prime aim of collecting and circulating information about the S&DJR. From 1969 to 1973 the Trust leased Radstock North engine shed and yard, which housed a working railway museum. Upon expiry of the lease in 1975, the Trust moved to Washford on the West Somerset Railway, reopening that station in 1977.

Restoration work is undertaken by volunteers at Washford, where a large shed has been constructed in the yard. One of the main projects in the early days was the partial rebuilding of the Trust's own locomotive, S&D Class 7F 2-8-0 No 53808 (S&D No 88) built in 1925 by Robert Stephenson & Co Ltd to a Fowler design. After the locomotive's restoration was completed by the West Somerset Railway at Minehead, it returned to steam in 1987 and is now regularly used hauling trains on the line, particularly in the summer months.

A full-size replica of Midford signal box lever frame has been re-created at Washford and the Trust's museum has many other S&D relics of interest. The museum is open when trains are running on the West Somerset Railway, particularly at weekends. Staffed on a voluntary basis by members, it is well worth a visit.

The Trust has about eight hundred members and regional meetings are held on a regular basis around the country. A well-produced bi-monthly magazine called the *Pines Express* is published for its membership. The annual AGM is held in April at Edington Village Hall, near Bridgwater, Somerset. A model railway exhibition is held around the New Year at the same hall, put on by members of the Trust's modelling fraternity.

The Somerset & Dorset Railway Trust Secretary is: *M.J. Palmer, The Haven, Chandlers Lane, Edington, Bridgwater, TA7 9JY.*

INDEX

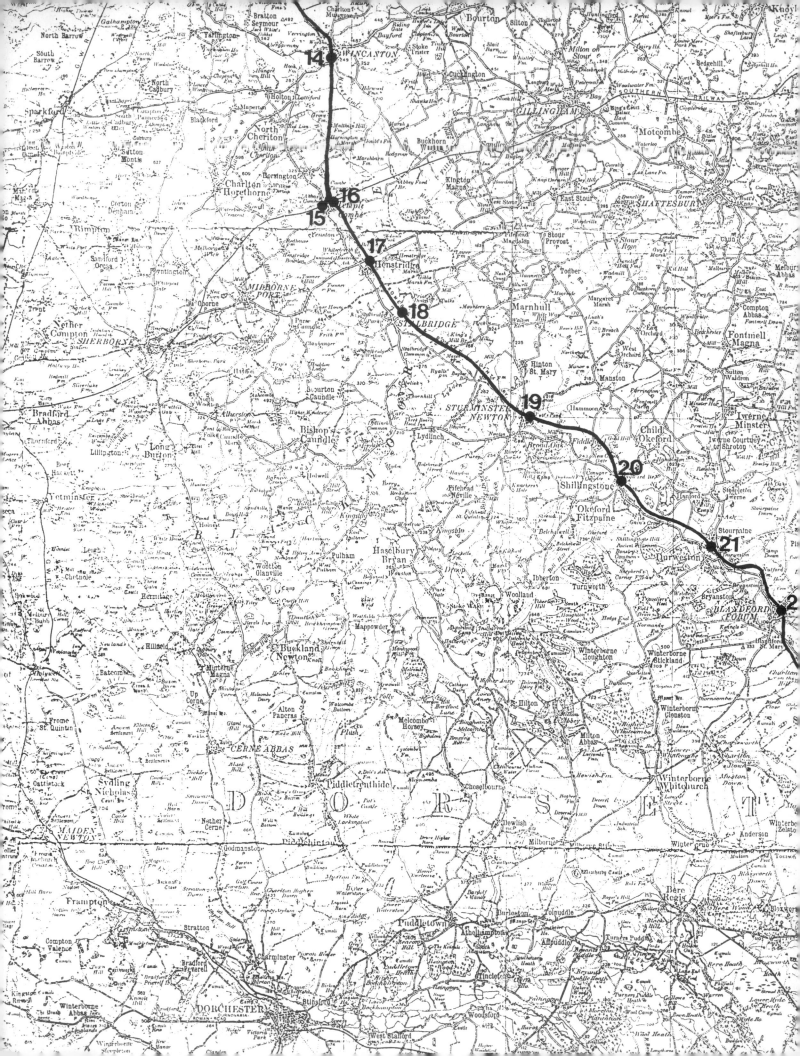